French Music i

MW01536538

French Music in Britain 1830–1914 investigates the presence, reception and influence of French art music in Britain between 1830 (roughly the arrival of 'grand opera' and *opéra comique* in London) and the outbreak of the First World War. Five chronologically ordered chapters investigate key questions such as:

- Where and to whom was French music performed in Britain in the nineteenth century?
- How was this music received, especially by journal and newspaper critics and other arbiters of taste?
- What characteristics and qualities did British audiences associate with French music?
- Was the presence and reception of French music in any way influenced by Franco-British political relations, or other aspects of cultural transfer and exchange?
- Were British composers influenced by their French contemporaries to any extent and, if so, in what ways?

Placed within the wider social and cultural context of Britain's most ambiguous and beguiling international relationship, this volume demonstrates how French music became an increasingly significant part of the British musician's repertory and influenced many composers. This is an important resource for musicologists specialising in Nineteenth-Century Music, Music History and European Music. It is also relevant for scholars and researchers of French Studies and Cultural Studies.

Paul Rodmell is a Senior Lecturer in the Department of Music at the University of Birmingham, UK. His research focuses on British musical culture of the nineteenth and early twentieth centuries; he is the author of monographs on *Charles Villiers Stanford* and *Opera in the British Isles, 1875–1918*.

Music in Nineteenth-Century Britain

Series Editor: Bennett Zon, Durham University, UK

So much of our 'common' knowledge of music in nineteenth-century Britain is bound up with received ideas. This series disputes their validity through research critically reassessing our perceptions of the period. Volumes in the series cover wide-ranging areas such as composers and composition; conductors, management and entrepreneurship; performers and performing; music criticism and the press; concert venues and promoters; church music and music theology; repertoire, genre, analysis and theory; instruments and technology; music education and pedagogy; publishing, printing and book selling; reception, historiography and biography; women and music; masculinity and music; gender and sexuality; domestic music-making; empire, orientalism and exoticism; and music in literature, poetry, theatre and dance.

The Musical Life of Nineteenth-Century Belfast
Roy Johnston with Declan Plummer

Music in *The Girl's Own Paper*: An Annotated Catalogue, 1880–1910
Judith Barger

Figures of the Imagination
Roger Hansford

Arthur Sullivan
Benedict Taylor

Richard D'Oyly Carte
Paul Seeley

Music and World-Building in the Colonial City: Newcastle, NSW, and its Townships, 1860–1880
Helen English

For more information about this series, please visit: www.routledge.com/music/series/MNCB

French Music in Britain 1830–1914

Paul Rodmell

Routledge
Taylor & Francis Group

LONDON AND NEW YORK

First published 2021
by Routledge
2 Park Square, Milton Park, Abingdon, Oxon OX14 4RN

and by Routledge
52 Vanderbilt Avenue, New York, NY 10017

Routledge is an imprint of the Taylor & Francis Group, an informa business

British Library Cataloguing-in-Publication Data
A catalogue record for this book is available from the British Library

Library of Congress Cataloging-in-Publication Data
A catalog record has been requested for this book

ISBN: 978-0-367-21939-0 (hbk)
ISBN: 978-0-429-26886-1 (ebk)

Typeset in Times New Roman
by Newgen Publishing UK

To my father

Contents

Illustrations

Figures

All illustrations are from the author's personal collection unless otherwise stated.

Table

Abbreviations

References in Chapters 1 to 5 in the format **nnnn**-n (e.g. **1850**-1) indicate entries in the Appendix.

Journals and newspapers

Published in London unless otherwise stated

AYR	*All the Year Round*
BB	*Bow Bells*
BDP	*Birmingham Daily Post* (Birmingham)
CM	*Court Magazine*
DN	*Daily News*
FJ	*Freeman's Journal* (Dublin)
FR	*Fortnightly Review*
HW	*Household Words*
ILN	*Illustrated London News*
ISDN	*Illustrated Sporting and Dramatic News*
LGa	*Literary Gazette*
LGu	*Literary Guardian*
MC	*Morning Chronicle*
MG	*Manchester Guardian* (Manchester)
MGz	*Musical Gazette*
MH	*Musical Herald*
MMR	*Monthly Musical Record*
MN	*Musical News*
MOMTR	*Musical Opinion & Music Trade Review*
MoM	*Magazine of Music*
MP	*Morning Post*
MS	*Musical Standard*
MT	*Musical Times*
MW	*Musical World*
PMG	*Pall Mall Gazette*
SN	*Saunders's Newsletter* (Dublin)

SR	*Saturday Review*
TO	*Theatrical Observer*
VSW	*Violin and String World* (supplement to *MS*)

Libraries and archives

BL	British Library, London
LoB	Library of Birmingham
NLW	National Library of Wales, Aberystwyth

Acknowledgements

As always, I would like to thank my friends, family and colleagues for their enduring support; also, the University of Birmingham for its provision of research resources and granting me a year of study leave in addition to normal research time. The British Library became almost a second home and remains a fundamental resource for researchers such as me, via not only its physical presence but also the increasing digitisation of its collections. While my friends' patience and encouragement has been essential, I must thank above all Heidi Bishop and the other music staff at Routledge, whose forbearance in the face of many revised deadlines has been both astonishing and life-saving.

Paul Rodmell
Birmingham
February 2020

Introduction

I believe in the French, the makers of all fashions.

I acknowledge their superiority in conversation, and their supremacy in dancing.

I believe in their fanaticism for what is new, not in their enthusiasm for what is great, and I expect neither consistency in their plans nor constancy in their sentiments.

I believe in the King, the weakest and most injured of all mortals, and in the Queen, as equal to him in sufferings and surpassing him in understanding; and in the Dauphin, whose kingdom will never come.

I believe equally in the folly of the Princes, the baseness of their counsellors, and the cruelty and madness of their enemies.

I expect neither the resurrection of order, nor the regeneration of morals, and I look neither for the coming of liberty, nor the permanence of their constitution. Amen.[1]

It is perhaps the most complex of Britain's international relationships. The temporal length, twists and turns, and persistence of certain (often mythologised) perceptions, balanced by regular interrogation and reappraisal, make Britain's relationship with France its most ambiguous and beguiling. It remains central to understanding British history and identity and features regularly in day-to-day life. Mary Berry's frivolous parody of the Apostles' Creed, written in 1792, encapsulates many aspects of the Georgian gentry's view but, while her references to monarchy and Revolution are solely contemporaneous, those to fashion, dancing, conversation and morality are broadly representative of long-standing cultured and popular British attitudes.

Franco-British relations have been of intense interest for the British – and especially the English – for centuries, ranging from rigorous academic scrutiny to popular journalism and street conversations. In modern academic research, politics and diplomacy have attracted greatest interest, but intercultural connections, especially post-1600, have also drawn attention in recent decades (see Bibliography); literature, philosophy, fine art, cuisine, fashion, poetry, theatre and drama, ballet, furniture, decorative and applied arts, conduct and etiquette have all been examined. Although not all scholars explicitly employ theoretical frameworks, the concepts of cultural transfer and exchange form the underlying foundations; of particular interest to anglophone scholars has been the transfer, reception and assimilation of the 'typically French' into British life. As Mary Berry stated, the French were thought, particularly by 'leaders of fashion', to be cultural pioneers, whose taste and manners should be emulated by those of good breeding, whose actions were in turn imitated by the aspirational middle classes in a cultural version of economic 'trickle-down theory'.

This study's aim is initially straightforward: it is to investigate the presence and reception of French art music in Britain between 1830 (the approximate arrival of 'grand opera' in London) and the outbreak of the Great War. In so doing, I pose research questions aimed at extending scholarship on nineteenth-century British musical culture. The simplest justification is to fill a lacuna in current research: while many aspects of Franco-British cultural relations and nineteenth-century British musical culture have attracted attention in the last 30 years, British engagement with French music has mainly been considered only in passing. When French music *is* mentioned, it is typically as a foil, juxtaposed with German music in concerts and domestic settings, or Italian opera. In short, the most interesting thing about French art music in Victorian and Edwardian Britain is its retrospective marginalisation, all the more remarkable given the prominence of French culture in other aspects of British life.

It is not my intention to reject the long-held understanding that Victorian Britain's primary interlocutor in the consumption of art music was German-speaking central Europe,[2] or to dispute the role of Italian opera. Rather, I argue that French music formed a significant part of British musical culture, and that commentators' sustained focus on the Italian/German axis has led to an unwarranted neglect of French music. To understand nineteenth-century British musical culture fully, we must relocate the standpoint from which we view it.

To take two examples, neither H R Haweis, in his popular *Music and Morals* (1870), nor Robert Stradling and Meirion Hughes, in their revisionist study *The English Musical Renaissance 1840–1940: Constructing a National Music* (1993, revised 2001), say much about French music. For Haweis, the concept of 'national schools' was a secondary issue, covered in just five pages, and the supremacy of German music since the late Baroque incontestable: 'it is a truer expression, and a more disciplined expression, of the emotions'.[3] Placing Beethoven at his pyramid's apex, Haweis continued,

> To follow a movement of Beethoven is, in the first place, a bracing exercise of the intellect ... In the masterful grip of the great composer we are conducted through a cycle of naturally progressive feeling, which always ends by leaving the mind recreated, balanced, and ennobled by the exercise.[4]

Non-German composers such as Auber and Verdi might have particular merits, but Haweis's overall view was that Italian music was 'essentially voluptuous', French music 'frivolous and sentimental', while German music was 'moral, many-sided and philosophical'.[5] While deeming French music one of Europe's three principal traditions, it is summarily dismissed.

Stradling and Hughes eschew nineteenth-century national stereotypes and explicit value judgements regarding the 'worth' of music of different nations. The significance they attach to German music's position in Britain is, nevertheless, essentially similar to Haweis's. German composers are referenced frequently, and British musicians' engagement with and veneration of German music is a major theme; indeed, Stradling and Hughes are inclined to disregard both French *and* Italian music, the latter being implicitly considered a luxury performed to rich, predominantly non-musical elites at Covent Garden, of little consequence beyond its immediate environs. The essential relationship, in their view, is Germano-British, focused on a line of composers mainly familiar to Haweis, from Handel to Brahms and Wagner.

Such views, and especially that of Haweis, should be seen in the context of what William Weber has referred to as the 'great transformation of taste',[6] that is, the ongoing process of what is now generally referred to as the formation of a canon of 'great' musical works. A variety of terms has been applied to music deemed to be canonic, including 'masterpiece', 'monument', and 'classic', etc.; it is not my intention to debate the relative merits of these terms but, clearly, the reception of French music in nineteenth-century Britain was continually affected by the process of canon formation and must be seen in this context. Weber has helpfully proposed three types of canon insofar as art music is concerned, i.e. the pedagogical, philosophical and performed, and it is the last of these upon which this study focuses. The extent to which French music's success in Britain was affected by the desire to assemble and consolidate a corpus of monumental works varied by genre. Weber suggests that, as far as the performed canon is concerned, British arbiters of taste were some of the first in Europe to start evaluating compositions in this manner, roughly from the mid-eighteenth century onwards. Primarily, though, this process affected instrumental music, especially genres such as the symphony and string quartet. Regarding oratorios, despite an undoubted yearning for a corpus of great works to form, arguably, by 1914, works which were widely accepted by British observers to fit into this category could still be counted on the fingers of one or two hands. In opera, meanwhile, the process was acutely affected by commercial realities and social function, and any sense of a work's being great did not prevent it from being discarded from the repertories of British opera companies if something more financially profitable became available. To many nineteenth-century observers, the concept of a canon of *opéras comiques* or, still more, *opéras bouffes* would have seemed mildly ludicrous, given that these were never considered genres of 'high art'. As, before 1870, the French music known in Britain was predominantly theatrical, it is unsurprising that French composers were not placed alongside Beethoven or Mendelssohn as 'greats' (with the highly debatable exception of Meyerbeer); even by 1914, when a much wider variety of French music was known in Britain, no French composer, living or dead, enjoyed 'canonic' status, and none had gained a renown equal to that of their most esteemed German contemporaries.

My aim, then, is not to destabilise the narrative of Britain's primary musical relationships in the nineteenth century being with Germany and Italy, as enthusiastic British engagement with these repertories *was* fundamental in this period, but to widen and refine it. The intention is to show how French music was disseminated and received in Britain, contextualising British musical culture more comprehensively. To this end, I pose research questions, engaging with various theories and methodologies. Research questions divide into two sets, the first focusing on cultural context and empirical data. What French music was performed? Where? Who were its audiences? What and who facilitated it? From these, a second, more interesting, set of queries arises. How was this music received, especially by journalists, critics and other arbiters of taste? What characteristics and qualities did British audiences associate with French music? Were these assessments reasoned or reflexive? Were they fixed, or changeable? How was French music viewed in comparison to that of other European nations, especially music from Germany and Italy? How was the British perception of French music affected by concepts of 'taste' and 'quality'? Was the consumption and reception of French music affected by political relations, or other aspects of cultural transfer and exchange?

Even with a topic apparently so specific, parameters are needed to maintain manageability. Firstly, I focus on French music in Britain, that is, a one-way process of cultural transfer, rather than bi-directional exchange. Although a project examining British music in France would be valuable, flows of 'traffic' are sufficiently separate to be studied successfully in isolation, rather than one being the concomitant of the other.

Secondly, I focus on art music and professional performances. Popular musics and amateur musicians are important, but their inclusion would make this study unwieldy and impractical: they are projects in themselves. Nevertheless, Britain's art music culture was not insular, with performers, critics and audiences all regularly experiencing both 'art' and 'popular' music: professional musicians, for example, worked in many contexts and roles, and might perform at one of London's main opera houses, a concert of highbrow art music, a middlebrow promenade concert and teach diverse amateurs within weeks if not days. Music was encountered in pleasure gardens, theatres, resorts, churches and other venues, through to itinerant performers singing ballads and popular songs on street corners. Domestic music-making also requires acknowledgement. Beneath the richest, who had long had access to keyboard instruments and scores, domestic music-making was transformed by the piano's ever-increasing affordability and desirability; its importance, especially for those with irregular access to concerts and theatres, is undoubted. The rapid expansion of music publishing disseminated scores to a much broader audience than metropolitan concertgoers,[7] complemented by increasing musical literacy. These possibilities notwithstanding, however, the professional performance of art music remained central: the imprimatur of high-profile performers and good reviews, although neither indispensable nor a guarantee, greatly aided a new work's acceptance. Although popular music is generally excluded, I do consider *opéras bouffes* and operettas on the basis that there are sufficient affinities between their composers and those of *opéra comique* and even 'French grand opera' to make commentary on British 'light' opera culture more logical than not.

A third parameter is a definition of 'French music'. In literal terms, it is defined here as works originating in France and presented in Britain as being French. Meyerbeer and Offenbach are therefore included but the Parisian works of composers such as Verdi, Donizetti and Rossini, which were presented as Italian, are not.

Taken more broadly, this parameter requires a brief examination of definitions and perceptions of national styles, then and now. It is impractical here to discuss theories of nationality, explored extensively elsewhere, and I assume readers have a working knowledge of nineteenth-century and more recent thought on the formation of national identities and characteristics. While nineteenth-century writers often referred to 'national styles' of art music, their characterisations were typically vague or focus on superficial external qualities. Few outside the music profession had the technical knowledge or vocabulary to discuss such a complex subject, and few demanded to read such a discussion in print. Consequently, characterisations tended to recur, especially regarding the 'three principal schools' of European composition, mythologising them without substantiation; such discourses are far removed from the lexicon of national characteristics used today. As Matthew Riley and Anthony Smith have argued,

> [T]here had long been concepts of 'national styles' in [art] music, reflected especially in music theorists' distinctions between French, German and Italian styles. But these styles were associated with the traditions and tastes of the courts and urban publics, not the music of rural or other lower-class peoples. The styles were sometimes not even defined by internal features: the German style, for instance, was thought to be a mixture of the others.[8]

In the eighteenth and early nineteenth centuries, such characteristics were not thought to be biologically inherent but adoptable at will. 'Folk music' was not yet viewed as a national possession and international appropriation was widespread. English cultured elites started to enjoy arrangements of Scottish 'folk music' in the 1720s (the 'Scots Drawing Room Style'), wherein the source material possessed an appealing 'exotic Otherness' or 'local colour' suitably tailored for its audience: 'tunes were harmonized, endowed with features of the fashionable, pan-European "galant style" and published for middle-class consumption'.[9] As a more scholarly view of folk music emanated from writers such as Rousseau and Herder, more rigorously conceived song compendia were published, for example the 'Lvov-Pratsch Collection' of Russian folksongs in 1790 (though still with *style galant* accompaniments), and Edward Bunting's *The Ancient Music of Ireland*, the first volume of which appeared in 1796. Ongoing interest in 'folk music' is also evidenced by the continuing publication of 'sanitized' collections, as defined by Riley and Smith, such as *Moore's Irish Melodies* (ten volumes, 1808–34). Technical analyses of European folk traditions lagged behind: in English, such appraisals only appeared after 1850.[10]

In art music, incorporation of 'folksong' to represent a composer's authentic inherited national identity – as opposed to the social elite's learned internationalism or exotic 'local colour' – appeared widely only from the mid-nineteenth century and neither French nor British composers became especially interested in this trend until still later. In England, more energy was expended on agonising about whether the nation was musical at all (a degree of insecurity possibly compounded by stronger interest in Welsh, Scottish and especially Irish folk music). While British composers occasionally employed folk material (for example, Macfarren's *Robin Hood* (1860), Stanford's 'Irish' Symphony (1887) and Mackenzie's Second Scotch Rhapsody ('Burns') (1881)[11]), avowedly national art musics only emerged around 1900. In France, self-assurance deriving from the convictions that the French originated and curated most elite European culture, and that Paris was the continent's cultural hub, led perhaps to a belief that art music celebrating its own 'Volk' was unnecessary. As in Britain, initial incorporations of folk material were examples of 'local colour' more than attempts to create a national school (for example, Saint-Saëns's *Rapsodie d'Auvergne* (1884) and *Rapsodie bretonne* (1891), and D'Indy's *Symphonie sur un chant montagnard français* (1886)). D'Indy's promotion of folk music via his Scholar Cantorum, founded in 1894, in some ways parallels activities in Britain but many composers in both countries avoided or rejected folk music, preferring a universalist vein and employing 'local colour' and 'exoticisms' as desired: in England, Londoners Bax and Bantock explored the 'Celtic Fringe', while Holst was inspired by Africa and India as well as English folksong; in France, Ravel, Debussy and Chabrier evoked Spain, and Saint-Saëns several non-European locations. In terms of much twentieth-century thought on national schools of art music, therefore, prior to around 1900 neither Britain nor France sits entirely comfortably. It is unsurprising that Victorian British writers found distinguishing between 'national styles' difficult, especially where composers preferred cosmopolitanism, and that discussions are generalised.

Finally, in this section, a note about terminology. Throughout this study, I typically use 'Britain' and 'British' to indicate the entire nineteenth-century United Kingdom; this is not to ignore or trivialise the significance of the four nations within but is used merely as a shorthand. From the late sixteenth century, London's role as the 'gateway' through which all French culture was passed, examined and approved before dissemination beyond, only grew (see below). British elite culture became increasingly homogeneous, with London society acting as principal arbiter of taste, while Paris played a similar role in France; such was the two cities' dominance in the nineteenth century that the remainders of both states were largely relegated to the status of hinterlands. The distinctive relationships between France and Scotland and Ireland (albeit declining in importance throughout the early modern period) were of less significance in relation to culture.

Two further parameters arise from pragmatic and circumstantial considerations. Firstly, I do not examine music composed before 1825 other than in passing; little is lost as earlier French repertory was virtually unknown in nineteenth-century Britain, being rarely performed or available in print. Secondly, although couched in terms of the Franco-British relationship, this study's focus can be defined primarily as Parisian music in London: the relationship between the two cities, their social elites and musical communities was the lynchpin upon which cultural exchanges depended and they acted as checkpoints on their respective sides of the Channel. Virtually no French music that appeared in Britain did so without passing through Paris (that is, being presented in, and probably written explicitly for, a Parisian audience); most of this music arrived initially in London, gaining a crucial metropolitan imprimatur before dissemination elsewhere. The two cities' distinctive relationship – large, prosperous, capitals in centralised countries – played a fundamental role in the transfer of music and was unequalled in Europe.

Various theoretical and methodological issues have informed this study. Central are theories of cultural transfer and exchange, which examine modes of relocation, networks of interlocutors, trade routes and so on. Michele Espagne's thesis that 'cultural transfer' redefines an object when relocated in its new context, where consumers have different preconceptions, understanding and values, is fundamental. While I use 'nation' and 'country' freely for the sake of variety, Espagne's concept of 'cultural zones' usefully reminds us that communities are not discrete entities; cultural transfers and exchanges (and the movement of people) create 'fuzzy' boundaries between communities in which commodities, values and attitudes intermingle and influence each other. Likewise, theories regarding enclaves, exclaves and agents of exchange are valuable in maintaining an awareness of the existence of networks and locations upon which exchanges depend, for example, the roles of London and Paris as enclaves, ex-patriot communities as exclaves, and composers, performers, impresarios and cultured elites as agents.

Linked to processes of cultural transfer and exchange are aspects of Reception Theory, especially concepts of *Rezeption* and *Wirkung*. More particularly, the notion of the 'horizon of expectations' is of primary importance when interrogating characteristics consumers commonly associated with French music and how these influenced its reception. To demonstrate these perceptions and associated processes, extensive primary source material is cited from newspapers and dedicated theatrical and musical journals, alongside published memoirs and a limited amount of unpublished material. Primarily, the views examined are those of self-appointed connoisseurs and arbiters of taste. While this means that opinions cited were not necessarily widely held and were sometimes deliberately provocative, they are generally those of people (almost invariably men) of some influence (that is, 'agency'), who saw it as their responsibility to shape public opinion. As general practice during the Victorian era was to publish articles anonymously, it is rarely possible to name with certainty authors of individual articles; while many principal critics have been identified, anonymous assistants were regularly employed. Amongst enthusiastic consumers of art music, such connoisseurs' views were not insignificant; as print media rapidly expanded during the nineteenth century, critics' influence upon regular theatre- and concertgoers, however enclosed their own immediate circles, was considerable. While reviews of individual works or composers may have had limited impact, their cumulative effect in creating an atmosphere and what one might term an 'aesthetic superstructure', or broad framework of generalised cultural values, seems certain.

This book comprises five principal chapters, employing a broadly chronological approach. A brief summary of Franco-British political relations is included in each, although it is notable that British consumption of French culture remained resilient even during periods of diplomatic tension. In selecting music for consideration, I have been able to draw only upon a small proportion of the repertory presented; predominantly, I focus on composers and works I believe made the greatest impact, evidenced either by critical acclaim or by sustained performance history.

The first chapter focuses on cultural transfers from the seventeenth century to the beginning of the nineteenth, contextualising subsequent material. I note a sustained association in Georgian minds of France with femininity which, although moderated later, still coloured perceptions of French music. The chapter concludes by considering French music in Britain, the characteristics associated with it, and the perceptions of British visitors to Paris. Chapter 2 examines French art music in Britain from 1830, when French 'grand opera' and *opéra comique* took off in London, to 1862, immediately before the London premiere of Gounod's *Faust*. Although focused primarily on opera, this chapter also examines the arrival of Berlioz's music in London. Chapter 3 covers the period between the first performances of *Faust* in 1863 and *Carmen* in 1878. These became the two most popular operas across Europe until at least 1914 and were well-known throughout Britain, thanks to touring opera companies. The receptions of Gounod and Offenbach, whose *opéras bouffes* arrived in the 1860s, are examined here, as is an emerging interest in French organ music. Chapter 4 explores the period from 1879 to 1900; operas by Massenet and Saint-Saëns are considered, as is French instrumental music, also including works by Saint-Saëns and Massenet. Gounod's 'festival' choral works and the revival of interest in Berlioz in the 1880s are examined, as are entries on French composers in the first edition of *Grove's Dictionary*.

Chapter 5 considers music of the post-Victorian period, especially Debussy and Ravel, alongside older composers such as Saint-Saëns and Fauré. The balance of discussion moves further towards concert music, reflecting both increased French production and British interest.

It is not incorrect to characterise nineteenth-century British musical culture as most strongly orientated towards Germany and Italy. Connections with the former, exemplified by the hero-worship of Beethoven, Mendelssohn and Wagner were intense, and consistently reinforced by composers, critics and the emerging academic establishment, who viewed German music as intellectually and spiritually superior; these links were further strengthened by the incremental consolidation of a performed musical canon within certain genres of instrumental music. Italian opera, meanwhile, though often regarded as an amusement of lesser aesthetic value and subject to whims of fashion and finance, was, nevertheless, recognised as capable of stirring emotions and possessing great beauty. Composers from other European nations, largely ignored before the 1880s, were initially treated as quaint curiosities at best and primitives at worst. For some time, French music existed in a sort of limbo, being neither quaint nor valuable, but its availability and popularity grew throughout the nineteenth century, spurred by both popular demand and critical approval: *Faust* and *Carmen*, the two most popular operas in nineteenth-century Britain, were quite possibly as well known and impactful as *Elijah* or the most famous Beethoven symphonies. Clearly, the presence of French music in Britain needs to be considered more fully; if my thesis is correct, while this study may fill some of the 'gap' in current understanding, it will hopefully raise further questions and stimulate more research.

Paul Rodmell
Birmingham
November 2019

Notes

1 Mary Berry, *Extracts of the Journals and Correspondence of Miss Berry* (3 vols, London, 1865–66), vol. 1, p. 381.
2 For convenience, I refer hereafter to 'Germany', but this should be taken to include composers and musicians from across central Europe whose first language was German and/or who were educated primarily in German-speaking institutions.
3 H R Haweis, *Music and Morals* (19th ed, London, 1900), pp. 58–9.
4 Haweis, p. 59.
5 Haweis, p. 59.
6 See William Weber, *The Great Transformation of Musical Taste: Concert Programming from Haydn to Brahms* (Cambridge, 2008).
7 Thomas Christensen makes a persuasive case for considering the role of piano-vocal scores of operas (both complete works and selections) in the dissemination of new music. See 'Public Music in Private Spheres: Piano-Vocal Scores and the Domestication of Opera', in Kate van Orden (ed.), *Music and the Cultures of Print* (New York, 2000), pp. 67–93.

8 Matthew Riley and Anthony Smith, *Nation and Classical Music* (Woodbridge, 2016), p. 46.

9 Riley and Smith, p. 36.

10 See, for example, Carl Engel's *An Introduction to the Study of National Music* (London, 1866) and Henry Chorley's *The National Music of the World* (London, 1880).

11 Stanford and Mackenzie also published arrangements of Irish and Scottish folksongs respectively.

1 Franco-British cultural relations 1660–1830

Given Great Britain and France's proximity and history, it is unsurprising that cultural transfers and exchanges have occurred between them for centuries. The nature and intensity of these have varied as the nations' self-perceptions and relations developed; the cliché that the Norman invasion of 1066 is one of few historical events embedded in collective English (*sic*) memory demonstrates symbolically the importance of Anglo-French relations, even though neither nation existed in the modern sense.[1] Although simplistic, this date-defined history remains potent as a popular starting point for England's relationship with its nearest continental neighbour.

While looking back to 1066 is excessive, consideration of Franco-British relations prior to 1830 is needed to contextualise later material. This chapter examines processes and manifestations of 'cultural transfer' from France to Britain between 1660 and 1830; many British perceptions of France and channels of communication active in the nineteenth century were established in this period. The relationship was complex and multi-layered, with contradictions and inconsistencies, manifest sometimes even within individuals. The British were concurrently enthusiastic about and hostile toward things French throughout the long eighteenth century. An assumption that these attitudes were proportional to political and diplomatic machinations proves invalid, with both fervent engagement and xenophobic spurning of French culture cohabiting consistently, regardless of whether the nations were at war or peace. This chapter gives illustrative examples of British engagement with French culture and an overarching sense of how perceptions were created and sustained.

Anglo-French political relations 1660–1700

Gesa Stedman puts forward a persuasive case for viewing the seventeenth century, especially the years between the Restoration and Glorious Revolution (1660–88), as the period in which the English elite's fascination with French culture 'took off'.[2] Modern definitions of England, Great Britain, France, and the relationships between them also started to crystallise in a way that remained pertinent in the nineteenth century. Cultural exchanges, including of music, were set in train and reached beyond the narrow world of the royal court.

Charles II's restoration is the most significant catalytic event for the development of England's relationship with France in the early modern period. In the preceding century, Anglo-French relations were typically lukewarm; on occasion, collaborating to counterbalance Spain was of mutual interest, and both France and England dealt with religious reformations that, although they developed differently, involved some common experiences. Despite recurrent French perceptions that England was untrustworthy ('perfidious Albion'[3]), the succession of Scottish James VI to the English throne in 1603 encouraged mutual tolerance;[4] the Stuarts maintained links with France throughout the seventeenth century. Charles I married Henrietta Maria, youngest daughter of Henri IV, in 1625; in 1646, as the British Civil Wars escalated, Henrietta returned permanently to France and was joined by her son, the future Charles II. A formative experience for the prince, aged sixteen when he left England, this led Charles to embrace many aspects of French courtly life and culture.[5] Upon re-establishing the court in 1660, Charles introduced many French interests and conventions, which were embraced by courtiers eager to curry favour. Anglo-French relations strengthened when Charles's sister, Henrietta, married Philippe, Duc D'Orléans, Louis XIV's brother, in 1665. Five years later, Charles and Louis signed the secret Treaty of Dover, in which Charles agreed to convert to Catholicism, and which allied England with France against the Dutch in the conflicts of the 1670s.

This closer relationship was not universally popular: although dogmatic Puritanism was marginalised, England and Scotland remained avowedly Protestant and suspicious of Louis's assertive Catholicism, especially after his revocation of the Edict of Nantes in 1685. Nor was the relationship smooth: petty squabbles and standoffs occurred regularly. Despite his Catholic sympathies, Charles needed to maintain the support of Protestant denominations, especially the Church of England, in order to safeguard his position. Following his younger brother's conversion in about 1668, and with Charles lacking legitimate children, it appeared increasingly likely that Britain would again have a Catholic monarch and so Charles, to assuage Protestant anxieties, ensured that James's daughter Mary, heir presumptive, was raised as an Anglican and married to the Protestant William of Orange, in order to prevent the establishment of a new Catholic dynasty. Charles's death and the end of James's reign both came sooner than expected. The Glorious Revolution, triggered by the birth of James's first legitimate son and his own unwise actions, ended cordial diplomatic relations with Louis, who sided with James; the deposed king was exiled to France, remaining there until his death in 1701.

Cultural transfers from France to Britain 1660–90

Despite this erratic relationship, it was during the reigns of Charles and James that a spirit of Francophilia was instilled in Britain's ruling elite. Reservations notwithstanding, the Sun King's glittering establishment regularly impressed British visitors. French codes of conduct were imported, as were fashions, architectural styles, literature and art, influencing elite taste and culture throughout the eighteenth century.

Charles and James's partiality for French culture played a significant role in this process but was not the only factor. Even during times of conflict, British travellers to mainland Europe often passed through France, Dover to Calais being the shortest and most favoured sea crossing; some encounter with French society, however brief or unrepresentative, was difficult to avoid. More importantly, Paris attracted aristocrats, diplomats, professionals, merchants and artisans. French was the diplomats' lingua franca and any ambitious young nobleman needed fluent French as part of his education.

Before the nineteenth century, interest in and informed knowledge of France was mainly confined to the London-orientated elites and arbiters of taste known later as 'the World' or the *ton*.[6] From 1660 to 1800 this comprised just a few thousand people but still represented a significant increase compared to earlier times. After the Restoration, the *ton* was centred upon the court, aristocracy and landed gentry, but broadened steadily to include the closely connected politicians, financiers, civil servants, clergy, military men and their families; although small and interconnected, the *ton* was neither entirely homogeneous nor static. Elevated social status did not necessarily signify inclusion; mutual acceptability, active participation in social and cultural activities, especially during the London season (and, for several decades, at Bath), were also integral, for it was through shared experiences that taste and culture were determined and disseminated. Suppliers of goods and services were also essential: tradesmen, craftsmen, merchants and servants could all act as agents of cultural transfer.

As Stedman shows, the French customs and culture imported were wide-ranging and varied. Fashions and conventions introduced by Charles were embraced by the prototype elite, and spread to include such people as the Bateliers (vintners) and their friends the Pepyses, 'members of the rising middle ranks who emulated the aristocracy'.[7] Stedman supplies a lengthy list of fashions and practices imported during Charles's reign: the Mollet brothers introduced long straight canals to garden landscapes; several French manuals on horticulture and manuals of French cuisine, such as Pierre de la Varenne's *La cuisinier François* (1651); foods, including salad, casseroles, and fresh fruit (as a dessert) were popularised, as was pall-mall (a forerunner of croquet); plays were presented in translation and often formed the basis of new works by British writers.[8] Trade in books, both in French and translation, further facilitated the transmission of French culture to British society.[9]

Samuel Pepys, a member of London's senior professional class, exemplifies the newly extended community that received these commodities. Pepys, like many of his contemporaries, spoke French well, and noted opportunities for French conversation and the purchase of French books in his diary; more unusually, his father-in-law was a French exile. Likewise, he noted the appearance of French fashions and culture: his patron, the Earl of Sandwich, bought a French suit 'very rich ... with embroidery' (24 April 1661) and the Earl's wife hired a French maid (15 November 1660).[10] Pepys and his wife saw Chapoton's *Mariage d'Orphée et d'Eurydice* at Drury Lane (30 August 1661) and the Duke of Newcastle's *The French Dancing Master*, one of many English plays that satirised French customs (21 May 1662).

Such trends were not universally embraced and provoked a concurrent Francophobic reaction. Much of this was satirical, such as Dryden's lines 'Old English authors vanish and give place / To these new conquerors of the Norman race',[11] though in some instances there was a harder edge. Stedman documents this extensively, showing how several long-lasting stereotypes of Frenchmen and Francophiles were established in this period. The 'fop' was especially popular: Sir Amorous La Foole in Jonson's play *Epicene* (1609) is one of the earliest examples and similar characters appear in several Restoration comedies, including Howard's *The English Mounsieur* (c. 1663), Wycherley's *The Gentleman Dancing-Master* (1673), and Etherege's *The Man of Mode* (1676). 'Fops' were typically affluent young men who embraced French manners and customs, becoming pretentious, vain and dismissive of all things English as inferior and crude although, ironically, their 'sophistication' often resulted in tactlessness and vulgarity. Etherege's Sir Fopling Flutter exhibits all these characteristics:

LADY TOWNLEY: He's very fine.

EMILIA: Extreme proper.

FLUTTER: A slight suit I made to appear in at my first arrival, not worthy your consideration, ladies.

DORIMANT: The pantaloon is very well mounted.

FLUTTER: The tassels are new and pretty.

MEDLEY: I never saw a coat better cut.

FLUTTER: It makes me show long-waisted, and, I think, slender.

...

LADY TOWNLEY: His gloves are well fringed, large and graceful.

FLUTTER: I was always eminent for being *bien-ganté*.

EMILIA: He wears nothing but what are originals of the most famous hands in Paris.

(Act III, Scene 2)

As man-about-town Dorimant says later: 'He went to Paris a plain bashful English blockhead, and is returned a fine undertaking French fop' (Act IV, Scene 1).[12]

Art reflected life: when Pepys met twenty-year-old William Penn (founder of Pennsylvania), recently returned from Paris, he wrote that Penn had 'a great deale, if not too much, of the vanity of the French garbe and affected manner of speech and gait. I fear all real profit he hath made of his travel will signify little' (30 August 1664). Of the composer Pelham Humfrey, also twenty, Pepys was still less flattering: '[L]ittle Pelham Humphreys, lately returned from France … is an absolute Monsieur, as full of form, and confidence, and vanity, and disparages everything, and everybody's skill but his own' (15 November 1667). Being 'frenchified' carried negative connotations, even for the worldly Pepys.

Other archetypes were established at this time, including the cunning French servant or merchant, inspired by their presence in London (such as Lady Sandwich's maid, above); specimens include the duplicitous valet Dufoy in Etherege's *The Comical Revenge* (1664) and scheming cook Ragou in John Lacy's *The Old Troop* (*c*. 1663–65). Both the fop and cunning servant exemplify more generalised stereotyping of French manners and culture. In particular, this associated Frenchmen with effeminacy and vanity, evidenced by exaggerated interest in personal appearance, elaborate manners, and revision of traditional gender roles and spheres of influence (discussed below). Elite French clothing styles included long, curly wigs and decorative fabrics for men (as with Sandwich's coat), while some women's fashions became boyish or androgynous.[13] This association of French culture with aspects of gender identity was sustained in eighteenth-century Britain, affecting perceptions and consumption.

Continuing British interest coincided with French attempts at economic expansion. Jean Baptiste Colbert, France's finance minister, promoted luxury products by establishing the Gobelins tapestry and furniture factory (1662), encouraging manufacture of glassware and mirrors, and introducing rigid quality controls, creating an enduring perception in Britain that French products were of high quality.[14]

While British elite Francophilia was ripe for gentle teasing, there was also some serious concern. Samuel Butler's *Satire upon our Ridiculous Imitation of the French* (1671) lampoons the same targets as Restoration comedies but with a sober point; he condemned 'frenchified' young Englishmen who 'Disdain the country where they were born / As bastards their own mother scorn' and 'Admire whate'er they find abroad / But nothing here, though e'er so good'.[15] Butler, on fashionable society's periphery, amplified Pepys's disdain for the likes of Pelham Humfrey; this perception of English/French dualism became potent in the eighteenth century.

Cultural transfers from France to Britain 1690–1830

Outright Francophilia receded after the Glorious Revolution. Jeremy Black argues that 'the Catholic, autocratic and Francophile tendencies of the Stuart court were seen as evidence of political inclinations and designs',[16] and, as Britain's new Protestant king, William of Orange, distrusted Louis XIV, the court adjusted accordingly. Francophilia was viewed suspiciously; the Nine Years' War (1688–97), War of the Spanish Succession (1702–15) and the French-aided Jacobite rebellions of 1715 and 1745 cemented and then reinforced widespread antipathy between the United Kingdom (from

1707) and France.[17] Conflicting ambitions in North America caused further difficulties.

As Krishan Kumar argues, in the eighteenth century, 'France became the emblem of all that was hated and feared from a Catholic power, the more so as it was seen as actively engaged on the side of the Catholic (Jacobite) interest within Britain itself'.[18] Gerard Newman argues that this hostility was the most significant factor in establishing a distinct sense of English/ British identity in the eighteenth century,[19] while Linda Colley, though more nuanced, also sees perceptions of France as antagonistic 'Other' as a driver in the emerging concept of Britishness, whether based on military rivalry, economic competition, provision of bogus culture or promotion of suspect morals.[20]

Newman nevertheless notes that for the upper echelons of British society – now greater in number and less court-focused but still only a few thousand predominantly aristocratic people – cosmopolitanism was a fundamental part of their ethos.[21] For many British aristocrats, this and Francophilia were two sides of the same coin:

> The intensity of mutual attraction and influence ... has never been greater than it was at the mid-eighteenth century, when, despite dissonant clashes of war in the background, cultivated Englishmen and Frenchmen disparaged local attachments, openly expressed their Francophilism and Anglomania, and moved easily from these affinities to intellectual ideals which embraced the whole of Europe, indeed the whole of mankind.[22]

Wide-ranging disagreements with France did not, in Newman's view, deter Britain's upper classes from internationalist idealism or admiration of other nations' cultures. There was also a selfish dimension: importing goods and services demonstrated wealth and distinctiveness via conspicuous consumption:

> The driving force is the elite's desire to *restrict access* to valued resources ... to itself and its nearest relations ... This results in sharpened cultural differences ... [s]ome of [which] should be *obvious and visible*: e.g. dress, speech, etiquette, taste, intellectual tone, manners, morality.[23]

As in the Restoration period, these luxuries and behavioural codes were predominantly French: cosmopolitanism was persistently if coincidentally Francophilic. Newman cites the British elite's admiration of Voltaire,[24] (German) George II's first language being French, a decline in anti-Catholicism as the Anglican church's influence on the elite declined, and a sense that European aristocrats had more in common with each other than with their respective nations' lower-born citizens. In the words of Scottish Enlightenment philosopher (and Francophile) David Hume: 'where any set of men, scatter'd over distant nations, have a close society or communication together, they acquire a similitude of manners, and have but little in common with the nations amongst whom they live'.[25] According to Newman, English 'cosmopolitan spirit was bolstered by a diffused spirit of Francophilism ... and not infrequently confused with it'.[26]

Colley's thesis of British identity formation draws upon more factors but, like Newman, she views the 'love–hate' relationship with France as highly significant. The consistent perception of France as corrupt 'Other' was important, even as different aspects of Otherness were stressed, starting with Catholicism, Jacobitism and autocracy, and moving later to conflicting imperial ambitions (mainly in North America), and then fear of revolution and Napoleon.[27] Colley also suggests that failures in British government and administration were often blamed on corrupting upper-class Francophilia.[28]

Throughout the eighteenth century, Francophilia was primarily the preserve of the *ton* although, as in Pepys's time, the aspirational classes, especially in London, might also embrace it. Trade continued despite conflicts and French goods, especially luxuries, remained popular. Those hostile to the French state could still respectably obtain goods and services, as, following the revocation of the Edict of Nantes, up to 25,000 Huguenots migrated to Britain, about half of whom settled in London; by 1700, there were 28 French churches in the capital.[29] While the 'Spitalfields weavers' are best-known, of greater significance were up-market craftsmen and merchants (silver- and goldsmiths, watch- and clockmakers, purveyors of food and wine), financiers and ex-military men who resided in the new West End and supplied politically uncompromised French goods and culture.

Modes of conduct in polite society continued to be largely French in origin. Michèle Cohen notes that in Georgian Britain, 'not only the polish of French manners but fluency in French were held to be so indispensable to the fashioning of the gentleman that hundreds of young men from high ranking English families were sent to France to acquire these accomplishments',[30] primarily by undertaking the 'Grand Tour'. Jeremy Black views this as an 'essential feature of eighteenth-century tourism', that played a major role in the 'greater tension between cosmopolitanism and xenophobia'.[31] A visit to France and Italy was regarded as a rite of passage, with a thriftier version taking in Paris and the Low Countries.[32] Newman argues that the Tour became less exclusive due to transport improvements, encouraging the wealthiest to focus upon Italy,[33] but, conversely, the aspirational classes' tendency to imitate those above increased overall traffic; French customs officials estimated that some 40,000 British tourists (employers and servants) arrived in France in 1785.[34]

Trade and tourism flourished most in periods of peace, especially during the longest span, from 1763 to 1792. For British tourists venturing abroad, Paris remained the primary destination; Eagles claims that travel between London and Paris was easier and more comfortable than between London and Edinburgh,[35] and even when France was not the ultimate destination, passing through was almost inevitable as Dover to Calais remained the shortest Channel crossing. France also hosted a substantial ex-patriot British community: Eagles estimates that by the 1780s this comprised 40,000 to 50,000 people, with the biggest concentration in Paris.[36]

Paris's popularity is demonstrated by the publication of English guidebooks, which also indicate activities of greatest interest. Eagles states that

> It was important to be seen, and be perceived to be seen, in the right places at the right time. It was also important to be appropriately dressed depending on the occasion and time of day ... The gardens of the Tuileries were frequented by fashionable society in the evenings, while the 'best company' promenaded in those of the Palais Royal from twelve noon until dinner time.[37]

Conduct and appearance remained important and the link in British minds between Paris and luxury trades was an additional attraction.[38] The city was also acquiring a reputation for less restricted sexual mores; in 1709, Joseph Shaw wrote that French women were 'all Wh---s, or take a great deal of Pains to be thought so ... [S]ome London Strumpets would blush to do what would pass here unguarded ... especially among the Ladies of the Court'.[39] The association of Paris with licentiousness persisted into the nineteenth century and beyond.[40]

Francophobia and upper-class Francophilia continued to rouse satirists and was a recurring topic across the arts. The fop remained alive and well, for example as Tom Rakewell in Hogarth's *A Rake's Progress* (1732–33); Francophilia is mocked in the second painting, in which newly affluent Tom is attended by servants and tutors, including dancing and fencing masters (archetypes of fashionable but unscrupulous French servants) who, like Tom, wear elaborate and implicitly feminising clothes. The fop also appears in plays such as Foote's *An Englishman in Paris* (1753) and *The Englishman Returned from Paris* (1756), mocking the same foibles and pretences as previously.[41] In the 1770s, the fop metamorphosed into the 'macaroni', a wealthy young man typically returned from the Grand Tour, whose affected 'gentility' and interest in fashion exceeded even that of Fopling Flutter: in 1771, the macaroni was described as 'a kind of animal, neither male nor female, a thing of the neuter gender, lately started up among us ... It talks without meaning, it smiles without pleasantry, it eats without appetite, it rides without exercise, it wenches without passion'.[42] Macaronis were subjected to sustained ridicule: John Moores argues that 'despite the Italian origin of 'macaroni', the word came to refer almost exclusively to French tastes ... The effeminacy of Frenchmen (and their English imitators) is a defining, almost constant, theme in [Georgian] satirical prints'.[43] As in other cases, macaronis were also found in the aspirational classes; prints depicted lawyers, artists, teachers and apprentices, a further consequence of improved transport which 'increasingly permitted a broader cross-section of society to experience what had previously been a perquisite of the elite ... The cosmopolitan trend of the century increased rather than diminished with the Macaroni phenomenon'.[44]

Such portrayals consistently emphasise superficiality and vacuity, presenting the subjects as un-English: in Fanny Burney's novel *Evalina* (1778), Paris is enticing yet corrupt but Francophile London no better; not only are the French at fault, but also the English aristocrats seduced by French decadence.[45] Joseph Shaw and man of letters John Andrews were more politically motivated than Burney but, although writing almost 80 years apart, reiterate similar themes. Shaw attacked autocracy, Catholicism, French duplicity and English Francophilia:

> The Government of France, whose Condition is miserable and deplorable, whether we regard the firm Establishment of the Romish Religion, so manifestly destructive both to the Increase of Trade, and of Mankind it self [*sic*]; or that despotick arbitrary Government, where the Lives and Estates of so many Millions of Mankind are subjected to the lawless Will of one single Prince ...
>
> The Interest[,] Religion and Friendship of France, hath ever been fatal and ruinous to this Nation; and therefore, especially now we are at War with it, I think it a piece of good Service to wean and take off that pernicious Fondness of many English Gentlemen, whom nothing pleases so much as the French Tongue, French Ayr, French Wine, French Cooks, French Carriage, French Servants, French Mistresses, French Dances, and too often French Surgeons too.[46]

Andrews likewise believed that France was corrupted by its aristocracy and absolute monarchy: its 'people of rank' were 'prodigiously fond of exterior marks of grandeur', and Andrews also ridiculed 'the excessive and absurd regard shewn ... to secondary qualifications, such as a skill in singing, dancing, [and] musical instruments'.[47] Andrews's portrayal of Francophilia as unpatriotic recalls both Butler and Shaw:

> Some of the English ... become so enamoured of France and its inhabitants, as to forget the superior ties that bind them to their own nation; and in the enthusiasm of their attachment to that country, as so lavish and profuse in its praises, as to prefer it to their own, even in those things wherein its inferiority is apparent.[48]

Effeminacy was also a recurring theme. Although not associated solely with the French, regular reiteration reinforced broader ambivalence towards France to such an extent that parts of the *ton* reacted against long-accepted norms of cosmopolitanism. Concern that imported goods, cultures and codes of behaviour undermined British masculinity bolstered suspicions that Francophilia emasculated the wealthy, resulting in a corrupt and indolent lifestyle.[49] This view accorded with residual Puritanism: its advocates 'attacked fashionable recreations because they distracted people from work, civic duties and public responsibilities. The leisure time required to attend the theatre or to appreciate painting was condemned as "idleness"'.[50] It was a neat coincidence that the nation most associated with luxury and leisure was France.[51] Brewer suggests that several commentators viewed this as a conspiracy: 'Foreigners in general, and the French in particular, had an interest in spreading effeminacy because it sapped the patriotism and public-spiritedness that protected the rights of Englishmen at home and kept such despotic powers as France at bay'.[52]

Such concerns were partly countered by the emerging ideology of 'separate spheres'. Colley argues that, in the late eighteenth century, British gentlemen were encouraged to pursue 'masculine' activities, leaving cultured accomplishments to women and creating greater separation of the sexes.[53] An avowed purpose of the expanding public schools was the creation of a 'warrior caste' of soldiers and colonial administrators, forged 'on the playing fields of Eton' (to misquote Orwell and Wellington); indoor pursuits such as music and art were replaced by outdoor activities such as foxhunting. While the British 'man of letters' could still pursue his interests, fine arts were more commonly associated with women and, while artistic pastimes did not become *infra dig* for men, they had to be pursued judiciously and proportionately.[54] The French language was also affected: Cohen shows that, between 1750 and 1850, it gradually became a 'gendered' language preferentially studied by girls; for boys, Latin, thought to be more intellectually demanding, replaced it.[55] Meanwhile, in both Britain and France, noblemen's dress lost its 'feminine' associations, largely discarding lace, embroidery, powder and wigs, and favouring (superficially) plainer styles.[56] Broadly speaking, the 'threat' of effeminising Francophilia was neutralised not by outright rejection but by transforming it into laudable femininity.

'Separate spheres' also regulated social interactions and women's engagement with politics and intellectual pursuits.[57] Francophobic writers such as Andrews noted disapprovingly the role Parisian women played in polite society, which implicitly diminished the status of men:

> In England, the glory of the [female] sex is modesty in their behaviour, and discretion in their words. Though possessed of an exquisite share of wit and sense, they have too much prudence to make a parade of either …
>
> Far different is that of the French women: no country producing such a restless, busy race; ever on the *qui vive*, ever seeking how to employ their active spirits, and never satisfied, unless immersed in the prosecution of some scheme.[58]

John Moore, a more sympathetic commentator, was also clear that English distinctiveness had to be maintained. Conversely, though, he commended the conduct of women at a dinner party in Paris:

> There were some very ingenious men present, with an admirable mixture of agreeable women, who remained to the last, and joined in the

conversation, even when it turned on subjects of literature; upon which occasions English ladies generally imagine it becomes them to remain silent. But here they took their share without scruple or hesitation. Those who understood any thing of the subject delivered their sentiments with great precision, and more grace than the men.[59]

Likewise, the musician George Smart, who visited Paris in 1802, noted that '[t]he French young ladies in their conversation seem to wish to make themselves agreeable and not to study to gain admirers. We are all charmed with the French women in general, they move with such ease'.[60] Nevertheless, Moore still argued that 'no other country but Great Britain is proper for the education of a British subject ... The most important point ... is to make him an Englishman, and this can be done nowhere so effectually as in England';[61] he cautioned that, 'I can scarcely remember an instance of an Englishman of fashion, who has evinced in his dress or style of living a preference to French manners, who did not lose by it in the opinion of his countrymen'.[62] Moore's tolerance did not extend to 'frenchification'.

While concerns about cosmopolitanism and Francophilia were partially countered by changes in social values and modes of conduct, anxieties reduced further during the French Revolutionary Wars as travel again became difficult and sometimes impossible. Interest in French culture and fashion remained, however, and in the 1790s London received a new wave of immigrants, this time anti-Revolutionaries, including nobles and servants, priests, craftsmen and merchants. Kirsty Carpenter estimates that up to 25,000 exiles settled in London; like the Huguenots, they were welcomed by affluent London society. Although most returned to France during the Peace of Amiens (1802–03), 'the Emigration was a meeting of two cultures with much in common and the emigration years served to demystify and whittle away prejudices which had shallow foundations'.[63] French servants became fashionable again and other émigrés established successful careers in occupations such as hat-making and miniature painting.[64]

The Peace of Amiens also enabled the British to visit France again, with travellers including Charles James Fox, William Hazlitt, J M W Turner and George Smart before the Napoleonic Wars resumed. Following the Congress of Vienna, French power was thought to have been contained; under Louis XVIII, who had been exiled to England from 1807 to 1814, the Bourbon monarchy pursued a pro-British foreign policy and diplomatic relations improved and, by 1830, both British Francophilia and Francophobia had been moderated. From about the 1780s, Francophilia was also steadily regendered, becoming an attribute associated primarily with women, with a concomitant emphasis on domestic occupations and commodities, replacing threatening effeminacy with genteel femininity. To speak French, to be interested in French culture, or to visit France, were not endangering, but neither were they necessarily evidence of good breeding or fashion. Old stereotypes remained but were toned down; clichéd views of France and the French lived on.

British attitudes to French music 1660–1830

Within this overall milieu, the position of music and musicians is less prom-inent than other occupations and commodities.[65] Moreover, while imports of culture, fashion and conduct were persistent from the Restoration onwards, the transfer of music declined significantly in the eighteenth century.

Like other cultural commodities, French music arrived first in royal courts in the early seventeenth century. In 1626, Queen Henrietta Maria brought several French musicians to London, including lutenist Jacques Gaultier;[66] French dancing masters such as Jacques Cordier, who worked at James I's court, influenced the development of the English masque.[67] It was during the Restoration period, however, that the presence of French music and musicians grew significantly. As early as 20 November 1660, Pepys noted that

> I found my Lord [the Earl of Sandwich] in bed late, he having been with the King, Queen, and Princess, at the Cockpit all night ... [T]he King did put a great affront upon [John] Singleton's musique, he bidding them stop and bade the French musique play, which, my Lord says, do much outdo all ours.

Contextualised, however, this incident is not so remarkable: Peter Holman has shown that Charles's replication of the Vingt-Quartre Violons du Roi has emblematic significance but was not a wholesale import of French musical culture;[68] the ensemble was staffed entirely by Englishmen until Louis Grabu was appointed Master of the Musick in 1666. Nevertheless, the Twenty-Four Violins played a prominent role at major court functions.[69]

Charles's preference for the violin and French dance music demonstrates the monarch's ability to direct elite culture and taste. Their introduction to the Chapel Royal was striking; Pepys recorded hearing 'Captain Cooke's new musique' on 14 September 1662, being 'the first day of having vialls and other instruments to play a symphony between every verse of the anthem; but the musique more full than it was the last Sunday, and very fine it is'.[70] Pepys noted other performances, though not always positively:

> [At the Chapel Royal I] heard a fine anthem, made by Pelham [Humfrey] (who is come over) in France, of which there was great expectation, and indeed is a very good piece of musique, but still I cannot call the Anthem anything but instrumentall musique with the voice, for nothing is made of the words at all.
>
> (1 November 1667)[71]

In Spink's view, neither Humfrey's nor Cooke's compositions for the ensemble were truly French in style.[72] Rather, it was Henry Purcell who developed an approach open to French influence, used in both sacred and secular spaces; the characteristics of French music taken on by Purcell and others were 'liveliness of rhythm, a more obvious tunefulness and regularity of melody, and clarity of form'.[73] Examples include the recently arrived bourrée, gavotte and minuet, featured in collections such as the *Tripla Concordia* (1676), and Purcell's symphony anthems for the Chapel Royal, which often exhibit French characteristics, including dance-like rhythms, and dramatic and virtuosic vocal solos, all contrasting with the measured polyphony of earlier Stuart composers.

Wider London audiences also had occasional opportunities to hear French music. Following Grabu, Robert Cambert and Jacques Paisible both moved to London in 1673; Cambert lived only four more years but Paisible remained until his death in 1721.[74] Cambert's opera *Ariane*, possibly revised or augmented by Grabu, was given in 1675, and Grabu also set Dryden's *Albion and Albinius* in 1685. Lully's *Cadmus et Hermione* followed in 1686, while Paisible, in addition to performing, composed regularly for London theatres. Doubtless anticipating criticism, Dryden stressed Grabu's skills:

> He has so exactly expressed my sense in all places where I intended to move the passions, that he seems to have entered into my thoughts, and to have been the poet as well as the composer. This I say, not to flatter him, but to do him right; because amongst some English musicians, and their scholars, who are sure to judge after them, the imputation of being a Frenchman is enough to make a party, who maliciously endeavour to decry him ... When any of our countrymen excel him, I shall be glad, for the sake of old England, to be shewn my error; in the mean time, let virtue be commended, though in the person of a stranger.[75]

Following the Glorious Revolution, French musical presence and influence in England declined. The Twenty-Four Violins did not, according to Thomas Tudway, appear in the Chapel Royal after Charles II's death: James II had little interest in the Chapel and William III appears to have removed the ensemble entirely in 1691,[76] also reducing the court's musical establishment and favouring martial instruments.[77] Wider English taste turned to Italian music: in the early eighteenth century, fashionable Londoners became obsessed with Italian opera, enjoying the graceful, melody-driven style and the 'star quality' of its singers; opera had the further advantage of demonstrating 'conspicuous consumption'. Although it declined in the 1730s, replaced by Handelian oratorio, significantly, neither genre was in any sense French. While the Hanoverian court exercised less influence as an arbiter of taste than its Stuart predecessor, George II's support of Handel increased his prominence. In the 1770s, London's musical culture shifted towards concerts, but French music remained marginalised as Italian and German repertory and musicians vied for the *ton*'s attention alongside indigenous talent. The Concerts of Antient Music, founded in 1776, focused on Handel and Italian composers such as Corelli and Geminiani; its activities constitute an early instance of the emerging process of the formation of a British canon of performed art music, a corpus of works allegedly determined by reference to aesthetic quality (as opposed to fashionableness), but a collection from which French music was consistently excluded.[78]

Only in dance music did French influence persist, this being true of both social dancing and ballet. Anthony L'Abbé arrived in London in 1698, and 'became the foremost choreographer of his day, creating some of the most beautiful (and still extant) dances for the London stage'.[79] L'Abbé's notations of social dances were published, ensuring that 'in the ballroom a knowledge of the etiquette and form of French-inspired dances like the formal minuet was considered essential to the education of a gentleman and his family, taught by a French or at least a French-trained dancing-master'.[80] The virtuoso Auguste Vestris was hugely popular in the 1780s, and the King's Theatre 'was remodelled to cater for the demand for full-length ballets danced between the acts of Italian operas. The carefully constructed narrative ballets of Jean Dauberval and his former pupil from Paris, Charles-Louis Didelot ... led the way towards the later era of romantic ballet'.[81] Surviving information does not, however, indicate the origins of the accompanying music, implying that it was little valued by audiences.[82]

Simon McVeigh notes that performances of French music made little headway: a 'Concert François' organised by Noverre in 1783, including extracts from Grétry's operas, failed, and McVeigh argues that 'it appears that the broad-brush French idiom, lacking Italianate melodic sensuousness, was of only passing attraction'.[83] French music was heard in London only sporadically, comprising occasional performances of symphonies by Gossec and Le Duc, and concerts by French musicians who came to England after 1789. Arriving in 1792, François-André Philidor was the only prominent Parisian composer to settle in London, but he died in 1795. French music appears to have held no fascination for the *ton*; indeed, McVeigh argues that 'to describe music as French in style was tantamount to an insult, a synonym for shallow charm and empty virtuosity'.[84] Kirsty Carpenter notes that the comte de Marin, a Revolution refugee, made a successful living as a violinist, and that Sebastien Érard spent two fruitful spells in London (1792–96 and 1808–12) but that a talented harpist, Mdlle Mérelle, 'gave concerts which were sparsely attended, in freezing venues, and was thrown into the debtors' prison'.[85] Musical French émigrés resident in the 1790s focused mainly on teaching.

It was in theatres that London audiences were most likely to hear French music. Theodore Fenner and William Smith record occasional performances of several Parisian operas including Gluck's *Orfeo* (1773), *Alceste* (1795 and 1797), and *Iphigénie en Tauride* (1796); Grétry's *Zemira ed Azor* (1779 and 1796) and *Richard, Coeur-de-lion* (1786); Gresnick's *Alceste* (1787); and Monsigny's *La belle Arsène* (1796). Of these, though, only *Richard* and Gluck's *Alceste* received positive receptions.[86] Works were often extensively modified, with plot alterations and other composers' music added or substituted; *The Times*'s lengthy review of *Richard* mentioned neither the music's character nor its origins.[87]

In part, English perceptions of French music being unattractive arose from generalised established prejudices. In 1762, John Potter, assessing the merits of Italian, German, English and French styles, dismissed the latter. German music he considered 'rough and martial ... [with] strong effects produc'd, without much delicacy, by the rattle of a number of instruments', while 'Some of the best Italian masters ... have so deeply enter'd into all the different sensations of the human heart, that they may almost be said to have the passions of mankind at their command'.[88] French music, though, was excoriated:

> Their taste is intolerable, a strict sameness runs thro' the whole; delicacy they have none, nor do they seem to be sensible of the powers of harmony. Indeed it seems admirably well suited to please the gloomy dispositions of those whose minds are enslav'd with bigotry, superstition and priestly power; and therefore never has, nor it is hop'd never will be admir'd by a great and free people.[89]

English music, meanwhile, was a Handel-created fusion: 'He has join'd the fullness and majesty of the German music, the delicacy and elegance of the Italian, to the solidity of the English; constituting in the end a magnificence of stile superior to any other nation'.[90] This argument handily ticks many chauvinistic and exceptionalist boxes, while not being wholly specious: the popularity of Handel and Italian and German music generally are recognised but the extra fillip only the British could provide is essential; even better, French characteristics are excluded.

Such polemic was not universal. The music historians John Hawkins and Charles Burney presented evidenced-based arguments that modern French music was regressive and less significant than either German or Italian. Burney stated that 'The long and pertinacious attachment to the style of Lulli and his imitators in vocal compositions ... doubtless more impeded [music's] progress than want of genius in this active and lively people', a view Hawkins had also asserted.[91] Both believed Rameau the greatest modern French composer and acknowledged him as a theorist; Hawkins also held Leclair in high regard. Nevertheless, Burney blamed Rameau's success and longevity for France's apparent musical isolation:

> Rameau's style of composition, which continued in favour almost unmolested for upwards of forty years, though formed upon that of Lulli, is more rich in harmony and varied in melody. The genre [Rameau's operas], however displeasing to all ears but those of France ... was carried by the learning and genius of Rameau to its acme of perfection.[92]

In his commentary on *Castor et Pollux* (1737), Burney was more detailed, criticising 'eternal changes of the measure', and the use of appoggiaturas which, 'being so frequently incorporated into the harmony, renders it crude, and the hanging on every note, as if unwilling to relinquish it, checks and impedes the motion of the air, and gives it a slow and languid effect, however lively the theme'.[93]

Burney viewed Italian influence in Paris in the 1750s and '60s as beneficial but, recalling a recent visit to Paris's Théâtre Italien, he wrote:

> One of these pieces was new, and meant as a comic opera ... [T]he com-
> poser, M de St Amant, was very much to be pitied, for a great deal of real
> good music was thrown away upon bad words ... But this music ... was
> not without its defects; the modulation was too studied, so much so as to
> be unnatural, and always to disappoint the ear. The overture, however,
> was good music, full of sound harmony, elegant and pleasing melody,
> with many passages of effect.[94]

Burney thought Gluck's presence was another step forward but worried that he had compromised with French values, limiting his appeal elsewhere.[95] Another problem was French vocal technique, a forced sound produced far back in the throat, necessitated, Burney thought, by the French language, but creating too unpleasant a sound for those accustomed to Italian singing.[96] Referring to Piccini's appointment at the Royal School of Music (forerunner of the Paris Conservatoire), Burney stated that, unless Piccini expelled all French influence and practice, 'it may be safely predicted, that many ages will elapse before any scholars will be produced that foreigners will hear with pleasure'.[97] Burney thought Grétry's music was 'fertile and pleasing', but believed his virtues Italian and partially undone by French audiences, noting that, 'he has, at least, improved the French taste as much as they have corrupted his'.[98] Burney's overarching view was that Parisian insularity and sense of superiority caused its music's failure to transfer to other cultures.

A widespread criticism was that, while Parisian operas were visually sump-tuous, 'these are all objects for the eye, and an opera elsewhere is intended to flatter the ear'.[99] Joseph Shaw wrote in 1709 that 'I have been at several Opera's [*sic*], whose Musick pleased not my Ears, and is much inferior to the English and Italian, but their dancing superior',[100] while the diplomat Sir Andrew Mitchell, writing in 1731–32, commented that, while the opera was 'the most frequented of all the spectacles, the connoisseurs in music cannot bear it, [though] the lovers of dancing admire it ... The scenes and decorations are very beautiful and the dresses of the actors very rich'.[101] When the actor David Garrick heard Mouret's *Le triomphe des sens* in 1751 he thought it 'a very raw Entertainment ... the scenes were well conducted and had a good Effect, the habits seemingly rich, the singers and dancers very numerous; but the singing abominable to me, and the dancing very indifferent'.[102] In a similar vein, Robert Wharton wrote in 1775 that

> [of] the opera with the old style of French music ... nothing in nature can
> be more disagreeable; For my part I could not help asking the Gentleman

who sat next to me whether they were singing an air or a Recitative it mattered not which for both were equally detestable ... the eye is the only organ to be pleased at the French opera ... .[103]

Ten years later, William Bennett concurred when seeing Gluck/Salieri's *Les Danaïdes*: 'The music loud and noisy in the French taste, and the singers screamed past all power of simile to represent. The scenery was very good, no people understanding the *jeu de theatre* or the tricks of the stage so well as the French'.[104]

Frances Crewe and Richard Edgbcumbe, both with strong musical interests, largely agreed with their predecessors. In 1786 Crewe wrote from Paris:

Gluck and Piccini are now the favourite composers here. [The French] taste in music is, I think, much improved with these ten or twelve years, and their theatres on that account much worth going to. I still think, however, one may trace a great deal of the abominable French stile of composition: but there is more, perhaps, in the manner of expression, than in the composition itself. The dancing is very fine.[105]

Like Burney, Crewe appreciated the move towards a more Italianate style. She found Grétry's *Richard, Coeur-de-lion* 'a more beautiful, and splendid Opera ... than ever was presented in England ... [A]s I heard a French say on the Stair Case, "there is a Gradation of Interest from the beginning to the End of it"'.[106] She also approved of Sacchini's *Dardanus* though, like others, found the visual aspects most appealing:

[S]ince the performers have left off the strange and disgusting French manner of singing, it is impossible not to be often delighted with the great opera at Paris ... [*Dardanus* is] a piece tho not remarkably well written, yet full of interest ... The scenery of this theatre is remarkably magnificent and the machinery is managed with infinite dexterity.[107]

Edgcumbe, arguably the most well-informed dilettante commentator of the period, was less positive. Tellingly, he wrote nothing about French operas performed in London; recalling two visits to Paris, his views barely changed: in 1771, '[T]he grand opera to all ears but French can give only pain', and in 1802, 'Of French music the less that is said the better ... The *grand opera* was in no respect improved: that human ears can bear it is marvellous'.[108]

Further corroboration comes from Smart: upon seeing *Iphigénie en Aulide* in 1802, he wrote: 'The dancing and decorations are far better than ours, the choruses go extremely well, but the recitatives and singing are horrid, nothing but ranting, squalling and bawling'.[109] He later found an unspecified opera by Grétry 'charming', and the Théâtre Feydeau, 'very good both in actors and singers', with 'a most excellent band'.[110] When Smart returned in 1825, he remained largely unconvinced: he enjoyed Rodolphe Kreutzer's music for the ballet *La servante justifiée* and Méhul's *Joseph*, but thought Auber's *Emma* better in London and general performance standards higher in Berlin.[111] Shortly afterwards, the Irish novelist, Lady Sydney Morgan, opined that, thanks to Rossini, French music had improved in at least one instance:

> Auber seems to me to have most perfectly thrown off the mannerism of the old school, and to have imbued himself with the genius of Italian melody. The music of his opera *Masaniello* is as influential on the senses and imagination as any I ever heard.[112]

Recurring across a century, such views effectively became self-reinforcing tropes, just as French clothing and furniture was unquestioningly deemed fashionable, and the fop a 'frenchified' fool. The Parisian preference for opera, while London shifted towards concerts, may also have contributed to French music's failure to become popular in England. Given also the expanding role of women as musical consumers, whose locus was increasingly domestic, with a concomitant focus on singing and the piano (an instrument the French embraced much more slowly than the British), it appears that, as regards music, British and French elite fashions simply failed to align, and the British found music from elsewhere more to their taste.

Conclusion

Despite well-established processes of cultural transfer, covering many trades, commodities and services, together with intellectual exchanges across numerous subjects, transfers of French music to Britain were atypically uncommon. There is suggestive evidence that, despite the *ton*'s long-standing Francophilia, the appeal of French music was limited after 1700. This was not due entirely to British ignorance; for British visitors to Paris, opera was an integral activity but one which was, so far as music was concerned, received indifferently. For British people who did not visit France but engaged broadly with French culture, opportunities to experience French music in performance were extremely limited, doing little to incentivise the purchase of printed music for private use, especially when Italian and German alternatives were accompanied by widespread approbation. More likely, general ignorance or a specific perception that French music was unattractive produced a self-reinforcing paradigm, summarised as 'if it's French music it must be bad, and if it's bad music it must be French'. In the early nineteenth century, extended lack of exposure and enthusiasm meant that by 1830 knowledge of French music, within both the *ton* and the music profession was minimal. Concurrently, many stereotypical perceptions of France and the French were diluted but not forgotten. Coupled with strong British interest in Italian opera and German orchestral and domestic music, it is unsurprising that the dissemination of French music in nineteenth-century Britain started hesitantly.

Notes

1 Archetypally illustrated by Sellar and Yeatman's satirical history *1066 and All That* (London, 1930), which inspired Arkell and Reynold's 1935 musical comedy; the title has inspired many retakes and spoofs.
2 Gesa Stedman, *Cultural Exchange in Seventeenth Century France and England* (Aldershot, 2013).
3 A phrase commonly attributed to the eighteenth-century playwright Auguste Louis de Ximénès but originating in the thirteenth century.
4 James's mother, Mary, Queen of Scots, was briefly queen of France following her marriage to Francis II. Mary's mother, Marie de Guise, was French.
5 Even though Louis XIV made an alliance with Cromwell in 1654, resulting in Charles's removal to the Spanish Netherlands.
6 '(Le bon) *ton*' was superseded in the nineteenth century firstly by 'le beau monde', and then by the American 'Upper Ten (Thousand)'.
7 Stedman, p. 63.
8 Stedman, pp. 69–85.
9 Stedman, pp. 93–5.
10 This, and all subsequent references, from www.pepysdiary.com.
11 Prologue, spoken at the Opening of New House, 26 March 1674, quoted in Stedman, p. 16.
12 Dryden's *Marriage à la Mode* (1671–72) take this a stage further by presenting a female fop: Melantha is 'an English *Madame* who loves French culture and especially the French language (or what she thinks is French) … [S]ignificantly, [she] is not a silly aristocrat … but a lady from the town who tries to imitate what her social superiors do – or what she thinks they do' (Stedman, p. 143).
13 Stedman, pp. 177–9.
14 Stedman, p. 162. The establishment of the porcelain and china factories at Chantilly (1725) and Sèvres (1756) reinforced and extended this perception.
15 Samuel Butler, *The Poetical Works of Samuel Butler* (2 vols, London, 1835), vol. 2, p. 203.
16 Jeremy Black, *Natural and Necessary Enemies: Anglo-French Relations in the Eighteenth Century* (Georgia, 1989) p. 1.
17 Diplomatic flexibility, though, is demonstrated by the Anglo-French Alliance of 1716–31, a pragmatic attempt to contain Spain and Russia.
18 Krishan Kumar, *The Making of English National Identity* (Cambridge, 2003), p. 162.
19 Gerald Newman, *The Rise of English Nationalism: A Cultural History 1740–1830* (London, 1987).
20 Linda Colley, *Britons: Forging the Nation 1707–1837* (London, 2005).
21 Henry Fielding (1707–54) believed the elite comprised around 1,200 people, while the playwright Samuel Foote estimated in 1747 that London's regular theatre-going audience (i.e. more affluent consumers of culture) was around 12,000 out of a population of 700,000. See Robin Eagles, *Francophilia in English Society 1748–1815* (Basingstoke, 2000), p. 15.
22 Newman, p. 2.
23 Newman, p. 28.
24 Voltaire's house at Ferney was a popular stopping point for Britons undertaking the Grand Tour to Italy; Charles Burney was one such visitor.

25 Quoted in Newman, p. 13.
26 Newman, p. 17.
27 A view supported by Kumar (p. 162).
28 Colley, pp. 86–90.
29 See Robin Gwynn, *The Huguenots of London* (Brighton, 1998); Huguenot refugees had been arriving in England in small numbers since the late sixteenth century.
30 Michèle Cohen, *Fashioning Masculinity: National Identity and Language in the Eighteenth Century* (London, 1996), p. 38.
31 Jeremy Black, *The British Abroad: The Grand Tour in the Eighteenth-Century* (Stroud, 1992), p. 1.
32 Black, *British Abroad*, p. 10.
33 Newman, p. 42.
34 Newman, p. 42.
35 Eagles, p. 121.
36 Eagles, pp. 98–100.
37 Eagles, p. 135. See also Thomas Martyn, *The Gentleman's Guide in his Tour through France* (London, 1787).
38 Black, *British Abroad*, p. 21.
39 Joseph Shaw, *Letters to a Nobleman* (London, 1709), p. 134. The 'nobleman' was Anthony Ashley-Cooper, 3rd Earl of Shaftesbury; nothing is known of Shaw.
40 Black, *British Abroad*, p. 208.
41 In the former, John Buck goes to Paris to polish his manners, but becomes outrageously 'frenchified'. On returning, he has to address his earlier betrothal to Lucinda, who personifies English virtue. She tricks him into destroying his French possessions and sending his friends and servants back to Paris but still rejects him and marries instead a sensible Englishman. For further discussion, see Elaine McGirr, *Eighteenth Century Characters: A Guide to the Literature of the Age* (Basingstoke, 2007), pp. 37–51.
42 *The Treasury, or Impartial Compendium*, quoted in Susan C Shapiro, '"Yon Plumed Dandebrat": Male "Effeminacy" in English Satire and Criticism', *The Review of English Studies*, **39** (New Series) (1988), p. 410.
43 John Richard Moores, *Representations of France in English Satirical Prints 1740–1832* (Basingstoke, 2015), p. 37.
44 Eagles, p. 21.
45 See Newman, p. 136. Burney exemplifies British inconsistency; *Evalina*'s satire notwithstanding, Burney married a French émigré, Alexandre D'Arblay, in 1793, despite her father's disapproval.
46 Shaw, pp. xiii–xiv and xix–xx.
47 John Andrews, *A Comparative View of the French and English Nations, and their Manners, Politics and Literature* (London, 1785), pp. 66 and 79–80.
48 Andrews, pp. 104–5.
49 See John Brewer, *The Pleasures of the Imagination: English Culture in the Eighteenth Century* (London, 1997), pp. 72–86.
50 Brewer, p. 74.
51 In Georgian Britain, contemporaneous Italian culture, especially opera, was perceived similarly but, although writers such as Jonathan Swift and Aaron Hill railed against the 'effeminacy' of Italian opera, its popularity in London was never seriously undermined on these grounds; see Gillen D'Arcy Wood, *Romanticism and Music Culture in Britain 1770–1840* (Cambridge, 2010), pp. 95–8.

52 Brewer, p. 83.

53 Colley, pp. 167–72.

54 It is, perhaps, no coincidence that the regulating concept of 'taste' developed in parallel; see Brewer, pp. 87–92.

55 Cohen, pp. 82–8. Although French was still widely taught in boys' schools, it was generally perceived to be 'easier', less relevant and, like music, effeminate.

56 In Britain, Beau Brummell personified the new style but needed several hours to create his 'understated' appearance.

57 Brewer, pp. 75–80.

58 Andrews, pp. 85–86.

59 John Moore, *A View of Society and Manners in France, Switzerland and Germany* (Dublin, 1780), p. 16.

60 George Smart (ed. H Bertrand Cox and C L E Cox), *Leaves from the Journal of Sir George Smart* (London, 1907), p. 34.

61 Moore, pp. 197–8.

62 Moore, p. 200.

63 Kirsty Carpenter, *Refugees of the French Revolution: Emigrés in London 1789–1802* (Basingstoke, 1999), p. 180.

64 Carpenter, pp. 71 and 162.

65 Notably, music features only briefly in Stedman's work.

66 See Ian Spink (ed.), *Music in Britain: The Seventeenth Century* (Oxford, 1992), p. 386.

67 Spink, pp. 289–90.

68 Peter Holman, *Four and Twenty Fiddlers: The Violin at the English Court 1540–1690* (Oxford, 1993).

69 In the 1670s, Anthony Wood claimed that 'the king according to the French mode would have 24 violins playing before him, while he was at meales, as being more airie and briske than viols' (quoted in John Spitzer and Neal Zaslaw, *The Birth of the Orchestra: History of an Institution 1650–1815* (Oxford, 2004), p. 268). See also Holman, pp. 303–13.

70 John Evelyn was less convinced, writing that 'the antient, grave and solemn wind musique accompanying the organ' had been replaced by 'a concert of 24 violins … after the French fantastical light way, better suiting a tavern or playhouse than a church' (Diary, 21 December 1662, quoted in William Bray (ed.), *The Diary of John Evelyn* (London & New York, 1901), p. 366).

71 In addition, on 1 October 1667, after hearing a work by Grabu at Whitehall, Pepys wrote: 'I never was so little pleased with a concert of musick in my life. The manner of setting of words and repeating them out of order, and that with a number of voices, makes me sick, the whole design of vocall musick being lost by it.'

72 Spink, p. 126.

73 Christopher Field and Michael Tilmouth, 'Consort Music II: From 1660', in Spink, p. 253.

74 Paisible spent five years at James II's court-in-exile but returned to England when appointed composer to Princess, later Queen, Anne.

75 John Dryden, Preface to *Albion and Albinius*, in *The Complete Works of John Dryden* (18 vols, London, 1808), vol. 7, pp. 221–2.

76 Holman, pp. 413–4.

77 Holman, pp. 431–5.

78 For further discussion, see William Weber, *The Rise of Musical Classics in Eighteenth-Century England* (Oxford, 1992).

79 Paul Boucher and Tessa Murdoch, 'Montagu House, Bloomsbury: A French Household in London 1673–1733', in Debra Kelly and Martyn Cornick (eds), *A History of the French in London: Liberty, Equality, Opportunity* (London, 2013), pp. 62–3.

80 Boucher and Murdoch, p. 67.

81 Boucher and Murdoch, p. 67.

82 See William Smith, *Italian Opera and Contemporary Ballet in London 1789–1820* (London, 1955). Ballets performed, normally with French titles, are listed but composers' names, where given, are almost always Italian.

83 Simon McVeigh, *Concert Life in London from Mozart to Haydn* (Cambridge, 1993), p. 126.

84 McVeigh, p. 127.

85 Carpenter, p. 72.

86 See Theodore Fenner, *Opera in London: Views of the Press 1785–1830* (Carbondale, 1994), pp. 103–5; Smith, pp. 34–43. The *Morning Chronicle* stated that *Alceste* was 'so different from the common race of Operas, that it requires to be judged of, only, by a master in the science. Its character is dignity and pathos. There is a solemn air in the music finely adapted to the subject, and the passion is carried to a height that is irresistible in its effects on our emotions' (quoted in Smith, p. 34).

87 *The Times*, 25 October 1786, p. 3. Unusually, a vocal score was issued by Longman & Broderip.

88 John Potter, *Observations on the Present State of Music and Musicians* (London, 1762), p. 40. Little is known of Potter; his book's preface claims that its contents were based on lectures delivered at Gresham College in 1761, although he was not a Gresham Professor.

89 Potter, pp. 40–2.

90 Potter, pp. 44–5.

91 Charles Burney, *A General History of Music from the Earliest Ages to the Present Day* (4 vols, London, 1776–89), vol. 4, p. 607; John Hawkins, *A General History of the Science and Practice of Music* (2 vols, London, 1875), vol. 2, p. 898.

92 Burney, vol. 4, pp. 610–1.

93 Burney, vol. 4, p. 612.

94 Charles Burney, *The Present State of Music in France and Italy* (London., 1771), pp. 16–18.

95 See Burney, *General History*, vol. 4, pp. 618–9.

96 In the anonymous work *Euterpe; or, Remarks on the Use and Abuse of Music as a Part of Modern Education* (London, ?1778) aspects of French syntax are also cited as they rendered the language 'utterly unfit for music expression' (p. 13).

97 Burney, *General History*, vol. 4, p. 621.

98 Burney, *General History*, vol. 4, p. 624.

99 Burney, *Present State*, p. 31.

100 Shaw, p. 105.

101 Quoted in Black, *British Abroad*, p. 280.

102 David Garrick (ed. R C Alexander), *The Diary of David Garrick, Being a Record of his Memorable Trip to Paris in 1751* (Oxford, 1928), p. 6. Garrick marginally preferred Rameau's *Les Indes Galantes* (p. 8).

103 Letter to Mary Lloyd, 29 February 1775, quoted in Graham Rodmell, 'An Englishman's impressions of France in 1775', *Durham University Journal*, **61** (1968/69), p. 79. Wharton, from a prosperous Co. Durham family, was undertaking the Grand Tour prior to training for the priesthood.

104 Quoted in Black, *British Abroad*, pp. 280–1. Bennett was Senior Tutor at Emmanuel College, Cambridge, and later Bishop of Cloyne (p. 9).

105 Frances Crewe (ed. Michael Allen), *An English Lady in France: The Diary of Frances Anne Crewe, 1786* (St Leonard's, 2006), p. 93.

106 Crewe, p. 97.

107 Crewe, p. 105

108 Richard Edgcumbe, *Musical Reminiscences of an Old Amateur, Chiefly Respecting the Italian Opera in England* (2nd ed, London, 1827), pp. 44 and 90–1. Edgcumbe gave some grudging praise to the singer Antoinette Saint-Huberty on his first visit, and to two male singers, Elleviou and Martin, at the Théâtre Feydeau, during his second.

109 Smart, p. 27. See also Mary Berry, *Extracts of the Journals and Correspondence of Miss Berry* (3 vols, London, 1865–66), vol. 2, pp. 137–9 and 161–2.

110 Smart, p. 38.

111 Smart, pp. 226–36.

112 Sydney Morgan, *France in 1829–30* (2 vols, London, 1831), vol. 2, pp. 342–3.

2   From Auber to Meyerbeer, 1830–62

The period 1830 to 1862 witnessed a steady transformation of the representation of French music in Britain, especially London. Opera dominated, starting with the establishment of Auber, followed by a range of *opéras comiques* and Meyerbeer's 'grand operas'. By the 1850s, Parisian opera was an integral part of West End repertory, together with a modest provincial presence. Performances of authentic concert music were rare but public concerts played an increasingly important role, especially in disseminating opera extracts to audiences outside the West End. This activity parallels a widening British interest in French culture and improving political relations; residual diplomatic tensions had little impact on British partiality for French goods or increasing interest in French music. While timeworn clichés ridiculing its manners and culture remained common, British regard for France was higher in 1860 than at any time since the Restoration.

Franco-British political relations

After 1815, Franco-British relations improved and stabilised, with both sides desiring friendship. Differences still arose, but France generally pursued a cautious foreign policy, not wanting to antagonise her neighbours, especially newly confident and increasingly prosperous Prussia. Synergies between France and Britain were reinforced up to 1851 as both states functioned, albeit with significant differences, as constitutional monarchies; neither the 1830 nor the 1848 revolutions undermined that basic premise. In the 1850s, the two states, for reasons of *Realpolitik* on the British side, were allied against Russia in the Crimean War (1853–56) and China in the Second Opium War (1859–60). Britain maintained and France redeveloped imperial ambitions but generally in different territories, rivalries in North America having dissipated earlier. Many Britons were still inclined to distrust France and viewed her as a likely antagonist, but the desire for peaceful co-existence kept these sentiments in check; while the 'Oriental Crisis' (1840) and 'Affair of the Spanish Marriages' (1846) both raised tensions, these were resolved more or less amicably.

Louis-Napoléon Bonaparte's election as president after the 1848 Revolution unnerved sections of the British establishment, partly due to his ancestry, but also because he pursued a more expansionist foreign policy. His *coup d'état* in 1851, which established the Second Empire, heightened anxieties considerably, but Napoléon, following periods of exile in Britain in the 1830s and '40s, remained an Anglophile, and declared that 'L'Empire, c'est la paix'. Inclined to pursue amicable relations with Britain, he maintained a friendship with the Foreign Secretary and later Prime Minister, Viscount Palmerston. Harbour work at Cherbourg strained relations, inducing the construction of improved defences on Alderney and at several southern British ports, but, while Alderney's fortification continued in the 1860s, alliances in Crimea and China showed that collaboration was possible. An effective demonstration of this concordant spirit was the Cobden–Chevalier Treaty (1860), which lowered tariffs and resulted in expanded trade.

Cultural transfers from France to Britain

Cultural exchanges were largely unaffected by political disputes and rapprochements. Earlier, sometimes virulent, Francophobia steadily receded, replaced by more nebulous mistrust and a chauvinistic sense of superiority. Positive feelings remained strongest within the *beau monde* and upper bourgeoisie, but this positivity also gradually percolated down to the increasingly affluent middle classes of urban and suburbanising Britain. Engagement with French culture remained indicative of good taste or wealth.

It was entirely possible for French and British citizens to make dismissive criticisms of each other whilst simultaneously engaging positively with the others' cultures.[1] As English/British exceptionalism strengthened, driven by superior economic power and a foreign policy that presented Britain as rising above petty squabbles between lesser nations, perceptions of the 'continent' representing a dualistic 'Other' remained strong. Conceptions of the French were especially prone to this. In literature, Nicholas Dames demonstrates how English Protestantism was often presented in opposition to continental Catholicism, often represented as French, such as in Trollope's *La Vendée* (1850), Charlotte Brontë's *Villette* (1853) and Dickens's *A Tale of Two Cities* (1859).[2] More generalised satire is seen in Thackeray's mildly mocking portrait of the elderly Matilda Crawley in *Vanity Fair* (1848–49), who 'had been in France ... and loved, ever after, French novels, French cookery, and French wines. She read Voltaire, and had Rousseau by heart; talked very lightly about divorce, and most energetically of the rights of women'.[3] Meanwhile, Mrs Forrester, in Gaskell's *Cranford* (1851–53), worried that 'There could be no doubt Signor Brunoni was a Frenchman – a French spy come to discover the weak and undefended places of England ... French people had ways and means which, she was thankful to say, the English knew nothing about'.[4] Ceri Crossley and Ian Small convincingly argue that, for much of the nineteenth century, France was viewed by many as a haven, due to perceived 'quite different French sexual ethics. "Naughty" Paris and France ... came to figure in the works of such writers as Charles Dickens and Wilkie Collins quite literally as an escape from the claustrophobia of British social and domestic life'.[5]

Interest in French culture was still regarded as characteristic of the wealthy and those with social pretensions. Valerie Mars argues that 'French *haute cuisine* was still both loved and hated. This was in part due to its political role in symbolising recurrent views of all things French; but it was, at the same time, the cuisine of Europe's elites'.[6] Varenne's *La cuisinier François* (1651) remained a reference point in affluent British homes, and *service à la russe* was imported from France after becoming fashionable there in the 1810s. The status of the French language also changed. The anonymous author of *Advice to a Young Gentleman* (1839) stated that for a man of the world, 'Italian and German, also Latin and Greek, are for distinction; French for convenience. It is honourable to know the former; disgraceful not to know the last'.[7] This is illustrated in novels: both Dickens's Nicholas Nickleby (1838–39) and Disraeli's Coningsby (1844) speak French well, demonstrating their social status. Coningsby is told by his grandfather that while

> A classical education was a very admirable thing, and one which all gentlemen should enjoy ... Coningsby would find some day that there were two educations, one which his position required, and another which was demanded by the world. 'French, my dear Harry ... is the key to this second education'.[8]

Twenty years later, however, Lady Theresa Lewis opined that, 'Not many Englishmen are capable of speaking French with tolerable ease. Amongst the upper and best educated classes generally some efforts are made by parents to secure that power for their daughters, but rarely for their sons',[9] confirming Michèle Cohen's theses regarding the decline and feminisation of French in nineteenth-century Britain.[10] These changes notwithstanding, however, West End seasons of French drama in the original language were given through much of the century.

Easier travel was also significant in altering British attitudes. After 1815, Paris again became a primary destination for Britons travelling overseas. As railways developed, other parts of France became accessible; Pau, in the Pyrenean foothills, became a popular spa resort in the 1840s, complete with golf course from 1856. Continuing the late eighteenth-century trend, more people, from more varied backgrounds, were able to travel for both business and pleasure. Although France's rail network developed more slowly than Britain's, Boulogne and Paris were linked in 1848, only five years after London was connected to Folkestone and Dover. In 1855, Thomas Cook organised his first group overseas excursions, climaxing with visits to the Exposition Universelle in Paris (the French riposte to the Great Exhibition of 1851). Cook's took some 70,000 British tourists to France between 1863 and 1868, and between 1830 and 1870 the number of British passengers disembarking at Calais, Dieppe and Boulogne rose from approximately 18,000 to 72,000 per annum.[11]

Making a still greater impact on British attitudes were developments in trade. Prior to the Cobden–Chevalier Treaty, French protectionism had had the inadvertent consequence of inhibiting industrialisation, a process also hampered by the lack of coal. Whitney Walton examines the French contribution to the Great Exhibition and reactions to it;[12] the Crystal Palace show having been inspired by France's Expositions des produits de l'industrie française, the French took pains with their display. Due to its robust internal market, driven primarily by the prosperous Parisian bourgeoisie, Walton argues, production of high-quality, non-generic goods by independent artisans was characteristic and French wares maintained an air of bespoke design. At the Crystal Palace, French exhibits were 'simple, elegant, delicate, charming, harmonious, pure, [and] perfect in detail or finish',[13] such qualities allegedly arising from the 'discriminating standards of French consumers ... French commentators liked to believe that they, and especially French women, were inherently more tasteful, [and] more sensitive to beauty, than other nationalities'.[14] This accorded with British associations of France with femininity, whose products and culture best suited lighter, domestic settings. This French success helped secure the Cobden–Chevalier Treaty; French politicians became confident that expanding exports would offset any increase in imports of cheap, mass-manufactured and low-quality British goods. Walton is circumspect about the extent to which French tastes influenced British consumers,[15] but the association of French goods with luxury, delicacy, femininity and acceptable self-indulgence was maintained.

Compared to the pre-Waterloo period, British perceptions of France had undergone significant change. Despite a nebulous suspicion that France was an exotic, seductive, yet untrustworthy and inferior Other, vicious Francophobia diminished and, among the *beau monde* and upper bourgeoisie, enthusiasm for French culture was common. Many earlier stereotypes continued but were tempered, while French goods became more easily accessed, as did France itself. Conversely, some aspects of French culture became more distant, confined to a small, wealthy and educated minority; knowledge of the French language became a more female preserve, and consumption of literature, especially untranslated, declined, as British exceptionalism and residual Puritanism combined to view French morals as less than respectable.[16]

The success of Auber

Operatic activity in London during the 1830s and '40s was both dynamic and unstable. The King's Theatre (Her Majesty's from 1837), together with the patents at Drury Lane and Covent Garden were the main centres of production,[17] but many other theatres produced 'opera' in various guises; competition was intense, with regular company failures and management bankruptcies.

Between 1830 and 1848, French opera in London was dominated by Auber. Previously, performances had been infrequent and comprised only a few works; in these two decades the situation was transformed.[18] New works came principally from the *opéra comique* tradition, although the nascent 'grand operas' of Auber and Meyerbeer also appeared. While relatively few made a lasting impression, Auber's operas brought French music to a level of prominence unseen since the seventeenth century.

As documented by Christina Fuhrmann, prevalent practice was to perform foreign operas with substantial alterations, little value being placed on fidelity to the original source.[19] Standard practices included translation into English, replacement of recitative with spoken dialogue, omissions, interpolations and overall compression, all undertaken to render works amenable to London audiences and executable by under-rehearsed performers.[20] The absence of robust copyright and performing right laws largely prevented composers and librettists from insisting upon 'accurate' productions;[21] popular works sometimes existed in several versions, running concurrently at different theatres and catering for different audience demographics; managers often competed to get new works on stage first.

Although now generally deemed the first 'French grand opera', Auber's *La muette de Portici* was not regarded as especially distinctive when introduced to London (**1829**-1). First presented at the King's Theatre as an afterpiece ballet under the title *Masaniello*,[22] Thomas Cooke's English sung version followed at Drury Lane. Although critical reception was mainly positive, the stage business proved of greatest interest. *The Times* stated that

> The music, which is extremely beautiful and characteristic, was very well executed ... The fishermen's *barcarole* and a hymn which is sung by the whole populace, kneeling, both of which are delightful compositions, produced great effect ... As a drama the piece has no great pretensions ... but as a scenic representation it has a peculiar merit, and one which has been hitherto almost unknown to the English stage. The crowds of persons that are introduced, and the way in which their various actions are arranged, engage and keep up in the attention of the audience, in a very striking and agreeable manner.[23]

Later perceived as a genre-defining characteristic, the crowd scenes made a significant impression; the *Morning Post* noted that sometimes over 150 people were on stage but only said that Auber's music was 'among his most fortunate efforts'.[24] The *Spectator* was less enthusiastic:

> A French opera is, generally speaking, but a barren field to cultivate. The opera of the French has no musical style or character: their compositions (with the exception of their vaudevilles ...) are a compound of the worst parts of the German and Italian schools: like bad champagne, froth but no flavour. *Masaniello* has scarcely redeeming qualities sufficient to form

an exception to this rule. In the first act there is not a melody that we can remember: abundance of noise, but nothing to make an impression on the memory; nothing like the gleams which break through the murky atmosphere in which the German writers love to revel and which, once heard, are fixed in the remembrance forever.[25]

The writer conceded the work's success, and in the 1830s *Masaniello* was also performed occasionally outside London (see below) but did not become a core part of the repertory; it reappeared in the West End periodically, including in Italian at Covent Garden in 1849, and was revived there periodically until 1873.

Several London managers saw potential in this new source of entertainment. Auber's productivity meant that new works became available regularly (see Appendix) and French operas were regarded as light, untaxing and ripe for adaptation: while some critics pushed for faithful performances of German and some Italian works, French operas were regarded as possessing lower aesthetic value, and adaptation, unless extreme, continued to be acceptable.[26]

While most French operas introduced in the 1830s roused only brief interest, Auber's *Fra Diavolo* and *Gustave III* were exceptions. Like *Masaniello*, *Fra Diavolo* was at first heavily adapted (**1830**-2). The Drury Lane production in February 1831 was an 'indifferent success', according to the *Literary Gazette*: 'the musical portion of the audience, attracted by the announcements in the bills that the original music, by Auber, would be sung ... was disappointed; two songs out of Mrs Waylett's four being the entire composition of [Mr Lee]; and Mr Sinclair's and Mr Harley's songs also were foreign to the opera'.[27] The *Spectator* opined that 'we are not very outrageous in our admiration of [Auber] but, comparing him with the author of the [interpolated numbers] ... he rises into a Mozart or a Weber'.[28] A more complete version at Covent Garden starring John Braham also drew varied critical reaction; the *Tatler* declared that 'Auber's music, taken altogether, disappointed us',[29] and the *Standard*, although more positive, remained equivocal:

> There are several light and graceful passages ... in the lesser concerted pieces of the opera ... [but] we cannot say that any of the songs allotted to Mr Braham was particularly fine ... The elaborate opening of the third act ... aimed at extraordinary variety of style – recitative – the martial – the cavatina, and the rondeau, and contained certainly some interesting passages, but, on the whole, was not so effective as it was ambitious.[30]

The *Morning Post* and *The Times* were both positive, the latter declaring that '[t]his opera will place Auber's character as an elegant and highly scientific composer in a far more elevated position than it has hitherto attained in this country. It abounds in concerted pieces of unquestionable merit, and there are to be found in it many delightful melodies, both lively and pensive',[31] with

Diavolo's extended *scena* in Act III highlighted. The opera proved popular outside London (see below) and became the most frequently performed of all of Auber's operas in the provinces, remaining in the repertory until the century's end. An Italian version appeared at Covent Garden in 1858 and returned regularly until the mid-1880s.

Whilst ultimately short-lived, the immense success of *Gustave III* (**1833-5**) further strengthened Auber's British reputation. Greatest admiration was aimed, though, at the *mise en scène*, especially the *bal masqué*; the invitation of select audience members to join the cast on stage became an integral feature and caused much excitement. *Gustave* was brought to London by writer-manager Alfred Bunn, who had seen it in Paris and noted privately that it was 'splendidly "got up" – music better than I was led to expect. Sure to please our gude folk, and some parts of it shall be better done.'[32] Bunn later claimed that malcontents complained about him presenting foreign works, but wryly noted that 'Give "John" [Bull] anything to please him, and not one penny does he care if it be the invention of his greatest enemy (and in his heart there is none *so* great as a Frenchman)'.[33]

Adapted by Cooke and James Planché, *Gustave* was compressed into three acts while retaining most of the music.[34] Critical reaction was less enthusiastic than that of theatregoers. The *Theatrical Observer* attributed the work's success to

> The Masquerade scene ... [which] is beyond doubt the most splendid *coup d'oeil* we ever saw in a Theatre; it represents a saloon of immense size, illuminated in the most brilliant manner, and crowded with masqueraders; when the scene opened on this gorgeous display, the audience testified their delight by repeated cheers, which were repeated when the green curtain fell.[35]

The *Morning Chronicle* viewed the music as 'decidedly inferior to [Auber's] other works'; it conceded the ball scene's magnificence but doubted whether 'it is worth sitting out a whole opera for that and that alone'.[36] The *Spectator* thought *Gustave* 'a worse failure even than *Robert the Devil*' (see below),[37] but *The Times* stated that 'the music, which is throughout dramatic and expressive, contains some passages of extraordinary beauty'.[38]

Despite critical reservations, *Gustave* topped 100 performances before it was withdrawn early in 1835.[39] Short-term interest was almost unparalleled and driven by audiences, against the judgement of most critics. *Gustave* also appeared successfully outside London, making a great impression in Edinburgh, and running for several weeks in Birmingham in 1835.[40] Although quickly discarded, *Gustave* was successfully revived by Benjamin Lumley at Her Majesty's in 1851; *The Times*'s review, almost certainly by James Davison, is indicative of Auber's later reputation:

> No French composer, Boïeldieu not excepted, has displayed the power of continuity and symmetry of plan ... to so high a perfection; none have

written such elaborate and masterly concerted pieces and finales, and none have manifested so comprehensive a knowledge and such a variety of orchestral treatment. We leave Auber's inexhaustible vein of melody out of the question, as too often acknowledged to admit of controversy.[41]

In British minds, Auber became the perfect representative of *opéra comique*, indelibly associated with gaiety and levity, and a welcome relief from the exciting but weighty and complex Meyerbeer.

Meyerbeer in London 1832–42

While Auber was more immediately popular, Meyerbeer made the more profound impression. Initially, British critics were ambivalent, as they were with much new music; the consensus was that Meyerbeer merged aspects of the German and Italian 'schools', both of which he knew intimately. Insofar as his operas were regarded as French, it was due to their being composed for Parisian audiences.[42]

Meyerbeer's first high-profile exposure in London was the production of *Robert le diable* (**1832**-1). Its Parisian success attracted considerable attention and an intense competition to give the first London performance augmented popular interest. Six versions appeared in six months, starting at the Adelphi with Fitzball and Buckstone's burlesque parody in January,[43] with more faithful but still substantially modified English versions following at Drury Lane and Covent Garden on consecutive days in February. Greatest critical attention, however, was paid to the King's Theatre's production which was sung, unusually at this time, in French, by substantially the original Paris cast. Unfortunately for Meyerbeer, who travelled to London to supervise rehearsals but, due to continual delays, left after perhaps only one,[44] the King's production was the least well received.

Initial prospects appeared promising. The *Harmonicon* published a substantial article on both composer and opera in anticipation of the Drury Lane and Covent Garden performances;[45] it later admitted to disappointment in both but other reviewers were more positive.[46] Meyerbeer later claimed that the theatres had used incomplete vocal scores, with orchestration undertaken in-house.[47] Nevertheless, Covent Garden's version was sufficiently well received to justify several repetitions.

The King's production came late in its season; reactions were polarised although, despite shortcomings, many critics defended both work and performance. Most believed the opera too long for British audiences, who expected works not to exceed two-and-a-half hours. A hostile review in the *Tatler* dismissed Meyerbeer's melodies as 'common-place or fantastic – rarely elegant, and frequently frivolous and contemptible', the orchestration as 'constantly injudicious', and argued that there was 'almost utter discrepancy between the sentiment of the words and their musical expression', before concluding that 'we shall never go to this opera again'.[48] Such outright condemnation was atypical; the *Literary Guardian* thought *Robert* challenging and reckoned that its 'excellencies ... have not, we must confess with shame, been appreciated by the public'.[49] The *Athenaeum*'s review (possibly by Chorley, a Meyerbeer enthusiast) asserted 'how scrupulously the composer has attended to the character of the drama and its detail in effect ... [I]t has one feature throughout ... viz. its appropriateness to the scene', and continued, 'the sublime effect of the music of the fifth act surpasses all we have ever heard on the stage, and is sufficient to rank Meyerbeer with the first musical geniuses of the age'.[50] Financially, though, the production was disastrous, costing over £6,000 but lasting only six performances.[51] Critical and popular reaction is informative: as Fuhrmann argues, it shows that London audiences were not ready for 'faithful' productions if they strayed far from established expectations; excepting a few enthusiasts and critics (who may have seen the opera in Paris), *Robert* was found to be musically, thematically and dramatically too radical and, unlike *Gustave III*, it did not have a moment of overwhelming appeal to counter perceived weaknesses.[52]

Increased interest in French opera led some to consider its place in national schools and traditions but Meyerbeer's cosmopolitanism defied easy categorisation. The *Spectator*, unenthused by *Robert*, viewed him as fundamentally German:

> It would be just as absurd ... to perform Weber's *Oberon* at Paris as a specimen of the English opera. Intrinsically, *Robert le diable* has not a particle of the French school about it – if, indeed, such a thing as a French school exists. Meyerbeer's operas bespeak their German origin, with an endeavour to engraft upon the native stock some of the gay flowers of modern Italy.[53]

In the *Court Magazine*, 'C', a Meyerbeer advocate, took a similar position, but gave more weight to the Italian influence, and credited the composer with a beneficial effect on French music:

> The first years of his manhood were spent in Italy, of whose music he imbibed the precepts, and pursued the studies, but he brought to them the genius of German instrumentation, and the feelings and associations of a German poet ... *Robert le diable*, every scene of which is in a separate and distinct style, beautifully appropriate to each, places him in the highest rank of the French musical drama. In the latter, he has made the most daring and successful innovations – having altered the mode of recitative, and by his prosodical arrangements imparted a power and energy to French musical declamation to which it could never before attain.[54]

The *Harmonicon* went much further, reckoning that France was rapidly approaching the sophistication and depth of Germany:

Meyerbeer composed *Robert* for the meridian of Paris; his melodies then are French, and he has succeeded in pleasing those to whom he has addressed them ... [Notwithstanding] all our national prejudices against the music of our neighbours ... it will be admitted, by impartial judges, that of late years the French have made vast strides in composition, particularly in that for the stage; they have left the living Italians, Rossini excepted, far behind, and are nearer and nearer approaching the best school of Germany.[55]

Such positivity was unusual; the dominant thesis was that, if French music was distinct at all, it remained inferior to that of Germany and Italy. Meyerbeer's provenance was left open, with the *Harmonicon*'s writer averring that he could adapt to the tastes of his audience.

The failure of the King's production almost certainly deterred the production of *Les Huguenots* which, although rumoured several times, did not appear in London until six years after its Paris premiere (1842-1). Like *Robert*, *Les Huguenots* appeared late in the season, given by a visiting German company that competed against Lumley's Italian troupe at Her Majesty's and other attractions.[56] Critical reactions were unusually polarised. Chorley took exception to the extensive cuts and listed them,[57] while others either did not comment or advocated still more excisions. The *Musical World* was enthusiastic, deeming *Les Huguenots* 'beyond comparison, the most complete lyric drama that has ever been put on the stage', due to consistent strength across its constituent parts.[58] Charles Gruneisen, another supporter, also eulogised Meyerbeer and his librettist, Eugène Scribe.[59] The *Spectator*, though, wrote of the opera's 'strange medley of faults and beauties, of absurdity and horror, of fun and fury, of dancing and murdering, spun out to the tedious length of five acts'.[60] *The Times* condemned the work, arguing that

it has no dramatic unity, ... no dramatic interest, [and] no really dramatic situation ... [T]he composer has attempted to introduce every variety of composition, every character of song, every concerted piece, Protestant hymns and Catholic hymns, and festival choruses, and rollicking choruses of lawless soldiers, and ballets, [and] the chorale of Luther.[61]

The writer bemoaned 'the constant aim at variety and new effects [which become] ... at last monotonous, and the ear vainly longs for something like a cessation from the continual effort and crash'. The novelty of *Les Huguenots* could not save the German season which closed, on financial grounds, after less than three weeks.

Relatively few critics commented on the opera's origins; those that did viewed *Les Huguenots* as French, or at least Parisian. The *Spectator* returned to France as Catholic 'Other', expressing incredulity that French audiences 'should not only tolerate but welcome and applaud, the scenic representation of a transaction so base, so cowardly, so bloody, so disgraceful to the French character, as the massacre of St Bartholomew', and derided Meyerbeer for adopting

> the fleeting fashion of any country in which he might happen to be resident, whether good or bad ... In 1822, Weber, his early friend and instructor ... said 'Meyerbeer has grown quite Italianised: what are become of all our fine dreams and flattering hopes?' Poor Weber little dreamed that a yet lower degradation awaited his pupil, and that he had to become Frenchified.[62]

The *Morning Chronicle* recounted the Weber story to a different end: it thought the German production bound to fail as *Les Huguenots* 'is German in little more than the name and country of its composer', while the focus on conflict and representations of religious ceremonies and music were all antagonistic to English sensibilities.[63] Such comments, however, were atypical; the *Musical World* declared the piece 'essentially a French opera – a work teeming with that *chaleur* and *esprit* which is totally incomprehensible by the slow phlegmatic process of German intellect',[64] as a justification for criticising the performance while admiring the work.

Meyerbeer's supporters proposed several explanations for *Les Huguenots'* failure but, as audiences had become more receptive to French music during the 1830s, its poor reception was disappointing: why had a major success in Paris failed in London? For advocates, the incongruity of a Parisian work appearing translated into unfamiliar German, and in an uneven and truncated performance, must have been contributory factors. For detractors, the work was just incoherent and unpleasant. It was another six years before Meyerbeer became firmly established in London.

French opera seasons 1845–6

London's first dedicated 'French opera' season was given by the company of the Théâtre de la Monnaie, Brussels (Covent Garden and Drury Lane, 6 June to 25 July 1845). It was a risky undertaking; the troupe planned a modest six-week season (later adding a seventh), to limit its exposure. London's critics welcomed the company enthusiastically. Most works had been seen before,[65] but *La reine de Chypre* (Halévy; **1845**-6), *La part du diable* (Auber; **1845**-5), *Le maître de chapelle* (Paer; **1845**-4) and *Le chalet* (Adam; **1845**-3) were new. The novelty was hearing French opera in French, performed more completely than previously. Attendance picked up after a slow start;[66] the support of the queen and Prince Albert burnished its fashionable credentials.[67]

While not uncritical, reviewers praised the company extensively, principally due to growing appreciation of French repertory, alongside a genuine desire to promote its 'faithful' performance, while implicitly criticising the Italian seasons' reliance on 'star singers'. Common themes were the troupe's *esprit de corps*, high production values and authenticity. The repertory's increased aesthetic worth challenged the established view that French 'grand operas' deserved adaptation, replacing it with a preference for fidelity to an authoritative source.

An early review in the *Spectator* exemplifies the positive impression:

> The audience were quite captivated ... The entire performance seemed the work of an assemblage of artists, playing indeed, up to one another, but without desire of undue prominence; and, from this ambition of general effect, the result ... satisfied the *ideal* in the mind of the spectator.[68]

The *Critic* contrasted the chorus's naturalism with stilted Italian performances: in one scene in *Les diamants de la couronne* 'the company ... instead of standing painfully about, silent, and with long faces ... are grouped comfortably and easily about the stage on chairs, on sofas, on ottomans, chatting, laughing and playing as they would at a real soirée'.[69]

Reception of individual works varied; the primary beneficiary was Meyerbeer, with *Robert* and *Les Huguenots* meeting even Chorley's expectations,[70] and was a major step towards Meyerbeer's Parisian works becoming established in London. *The Times* and others argued that the more complete version of *Robert* (finally seen in its five-act format) would enhance audience appreciation: 'it is needless to utter a word on the grandness and eccentricity of its structure, the fullness of its colouring, its elaborate working, and varying character it assumes in its lengthened progress'.[71] In a broad-ranging review, the *Musical World* recognised the impression made by *Les Huguenots*, despite remaining unconvinced:

> Never was anything witnessed within the walls of any theatre in London, more important than the representation of this *chef d'oeuvre* ... Meyerbeer's *forte* seems to be a great knowledge of contrast, which he applies in every possible manner in his operas. There is no doubt that at times this produces very startling effects, and when we hear his music for the first time, it has a certain hold on the ear, which surprises us into a kind of gratification. But this contrast, or opposition of colouring, is carried to such an extent in the *Huguenots* as to become extravagant and incongruous. The absence of melody, too, is greater in this opera than any other of the composer's ... Meyerbeer we consider a man of very great abilities, but totally deficient in inspiration.[72]

Halévy, though, was received only politely: he was generally deemed tasteful and an excellent craftsman but lacking in melody and originality. The *Observer* praised the orchestration of *La reine de Chypre*, but continued, 'Melodies it has few or none ... [T]here is power and breadth in the choruses, if not sufficient to compensate for the want of soul in the music'.[73] *The Times* was still less complimentary, but praised the Brussels company's decision to present Halévy's work.[74]

Although commentary on the company and the 'grand operas' occupied much space, the *opéras comiques* received greatest praise, and appealed most to audiences. Here, 'faithful' performance was demanded less often and the music less deeply scrutinised; the affirmative words 'light', 'airy', 'sparkling' and 'graceful' appeared regularly. London critics rarely considered such works as high art but recognised their appeal. *The Times* commended *Les diamants de la couronne*:

> What an admirable opera of the comic genre is this work of Auber's. What piquant melodies – what ingenious combinations – what dramatic conception! The train of gaiety and brilliance is fired at the commencement, and goes sparkling merrily along through three long acts without causing an inkling of weariness.[75]

The sense that French opera was of sufficient artistic value to be taken seriously drew Chorley's approval, who claimed that 'A fondly-treasured national prejudice has been overthrown by [the Brussels troupe's] performance'.[76] This is hyperbole but reflects the direction of travel: significantly aided by the first dedicated season mounted in London, modern French opera was gaining popular and critical acceptance to an extent previously unknown; by 1850, casual and dismissive evaluations of Parisian opera had almost disappeared.

The Brussels company returned (Drury Lane, 15 July to 15 August 1846) but was less successful. Three reasons were given: illness amongst principal singers, a weaker orchestra (comprising a core from Brussels supplemented by local players unfamiliar with the music), and performances too late in the social season.[77] New productions did not prove sufficiently attractive; adapted versions of Auber's *Le domino noir* (**1838**-1) and *Le philtre* (**1831**-1) had already been heard, although Lebrun's *Le rossignol* (**1846**-1) and Halévy's *La juive* (**1846**-2) and *Les mousequetaires de la reine* (**1846**-3) were introduced to London.

Reviewers were also more inclined to find fault. Halévy was dismissed on the same grounds as before: *The Times* called *La juive*, 'the most characterless and insipid of all the [Parisian] Grand Operas' adding that '[t]here is not a melody which the ear can retain, nor is the attempt at originality in harmony and orchestration anything better than a poor imitation of the vices of Meyerbeer's style'.[78] *Les mousequetaires* fared no better.[79]

The *Spectator* reflected overall opinion by stating that it was 'not that the company was not good, or would not stand a comparison with most musical companies we have met with; but it has not been quite able to stand a comparison with itself'.[80] The Brussels troupe did not return. The perception that Halévy was a 'poor man's Meyerbeer' took root and, despite subsequent attempts, his operas never succeeded in London (see below). But, although this season was less successful, London's interest in French opera continued to grow.

French opera – as Italian opera

The crucial imprimatur for French opera in London was, ironically, production by the city's 'Italian' troupes, a process inaugurated by Jenny Lind's British debut in 1847. Contracted by Benjamin Lumley, Lind's appearance was eagerly anticipated and became *the* social event of the season. She selected the role of Alice, in *Robert le diable*, for her *entrée* on 4 May at Her Majesty's (see Figure 2.1).[81] The presence of Victoria and Albert lent further prestige and reviews focused almost entirely on Lind. The queen herself was impressed by Lind though critical of other aspects: 'It is a most beautiful Opera. The Choruses were bad, & the Orchestra very often went wrong, but Jenny Lind was absolutely perfection'.[82] Lind subsequently appeared in Italian repertory, including the world premiere of Verdi's *I masnadieri*, conducted by the composer; she sang in *Robert* for Lumley again in 1848.

Lind's performances may not have greatly altered perceptions of Meyerbeer's music, but they transformed his status in London to that of fashionable composer. Prompted by the queen, *Les Huguenots* was given (as *Gli Ugonotti*) at Covent Garden in 1848, a command performance burnishing its status. Many press reviews were lengthened and, although they often devoted most space to the royal presence, neither performance nor work was neglected. Chorley, still supporter-in-chief, claimed confidently that *Les Huguenots* 'will have a popularity as unprecedented as the luxury with which it has been produced'.[83] The following week, while acknowledging Meyerbeer's unevenness, Chorley argued that his strengths were more than sufficient:

> We imagine it will be hard for him to out-do *Les Huguenots*. Others have far exceeded him in melody ... [and] most writers surpass him in construction ... but as regards colour [orchestration] he is unsurpassed. There have been few specimens of contrast more enticing than the antiphony and mixture of the *Rataplan* Huguenot chorus with the Catholic litany in the *Pré aux Clercs* – or than the minuet in the ball scene of the last act as coming before the final trio ... Effect, then, is Meyerbeer's greatest merit.[84]

In the *Observer*'s view, Meyerbeer wrote for ensembles more effectively than for intimate scenes between individuals; while recognising 'remarkable originality and immense graphic power', the writer found 'diffuseness of style, excessive elaboration of minute points, constant experimentalism in orchestration, and a tendency to mistake oddity for novelty and triteness for simplicity'.[85]

LIND AS "ALICE," AND HERR STÄUDIGL, AS "BERTRAM," IN MEYERBEER'S OPERA OF "ROBERTO IL DIAVOLO," AT HER MAJESTY'S THEATRE.—(SEE PAGE 301.)

Fig 2.1 Jenny Lind as Alice in Meyerbeer's *Robert le diable*, Her Majesty's Theatre
(*Illustrated London News*, 8 May 1847, p. 289)

Davison, meanwhile, thought the opera's success due solely to the performance, although he later moderated his view:

> Tune, which is the very essence of all lyric works, appears to have been
> dispensed with ... No pleasing arias, no striking duets, no brilliant cava-
> tinas are exhibited. Simplicity is eschewed ...

Something of these opinions remains after a second hearing, but most of them vanish as the ear becomes familiar with the music. Phrases, which were at first considered harsh and forced, become pleasing on repetition. Harmonic combinations, which were found intricate and purportless, are recognised as clear and fraught with meaning. Acquaintance is certainly favourable to the *Huguenots* ... We are nevertheless satisfied that [it] can never become a popular work – at least in this country.[86]

Davison was wrong: *Les Huguenots* appeared ten times in the 1848 season and was jointly the most frequently performed opera at Covent Garden under Gye's management (see below).

From 1848, Meyerbeer was fully appropriated into the Italian repertory. Gye moved unusually quickly to introduce *Le prophète* (**1849**-4), just over three months after its Parisian premiere (see Figure 2.2). Interest was augmented by reviews from Paris,[87] and opening night was invested with great importance in fashionable London. The previously sceptical *Musical World* devoted over four paeanistic pages to its review:

[T]here is a greater unity of style, a more evident simplicity of purpose, than in any other work of the author. The orchestration has all the peculiarities of the *Robert* and the *Huguenots*; but in the *Prophète* these peculiarities are no longer the product of a wayward genius, but the eccentricities of one fully acquainted with the resources of his art. As with the *Huguenots*, Meyerbeer has gradually worked up the interest of his music until the third act [Act IV; see note] ... but [while] the last act of the *Huguenots* is by many degrees the weakest (musically speaking) ... the last act of the *Prophète* contains some of the most striking pieces of the opera.[88]

Earlier criticisms of excessive intricacy dropped away and the use of contrasting styles for different characters was now seen as a strength; the portrayal of Fides was highlighted for its power and subtlety. With *Le prophète*, Meyerbeer was wholeheartedly accepted on London's operatic stage.

For 30 years from 1850, Meyerbeer's operas were pillars of London's Italian repertory. *Les Huguenots* and *Don Giovanni* were the most frequently performed works at Covent Garden under Gye's management, each clocking up 156 performances in the spring opera seasons from 1848 to 1878 inclusive, far ahead of other works.[89] *Robert* was added to Gye's repertory in 1849, followed by *L'étoile du nord* (**1855**-1), *Dinorah* (**1859**-2) and *L'Africaine* (**1865**-3). By the end of his tenure they had been given 41, 45, 44 and 43 times respectively.[90]

Covent Garden's significance is demonstrated by Meyerbeer's visiting to advise on productions of *L'étoile* and *Dinorah*; having turned to *opéra comique*, Meyerbeer set the spoken dialogue to recitative to accommodate Italian practice.[91] The 1855 visit was a triumph: Meyerbeer appeared at Her Majesty's Theatre, John Ella's Musical Union, and was honoured at an exclusive salon concert given by Julius Benedict.[92] Now comfortable with his approach, critics

Fig 2.2 Meyerbeer's Le prophète *(Illustrated London News, 28 July 1849, p. 56)*

had relatively little substantive to say about *L'étoile* other than that, at four hours, it might be shortened.[93] *Dinorah*'s scenario was thought slight and incredible; the *Observer* deemed it 'scarcely good enough for the music which is employed to illustrate it',[94] while the *Examiner* unsurprisingly perceived a retreat from 'grand dramatic themes and ... massive choral effects'.[95] Despite broadly positive comments, a sense that Meyerbeer had not advanced is apparent; the *Musical World* concluded that the music, 'if less gorgeous, grand, and lofty than much he has wedded to more absorbing subjects, has not been surpassed in grace, invention, melodic beauty, newness of idea, originality of treatment, and finesse of colouring'.[96]

Meyerbeer's acceptance by the Italian operas conferred precious artistic worth. Critical opinion, originally equivocal or overtly hostile, shifted decisively in his favour from 1848; despite turning to *opéra comique* and being perceived as 'standing still' in the 1850s, he was widely regarded in London as the most effective living opera composer. This partly reflects acclimatisation and wider changes in practices and values; some criticisms mentioned above were also directed at Verdi in the 1850s, and later at Wagner. London audiences, accustomed to Rossinian long-breathed lyrical melodies and English ballads initially found Meyerbeer's motivic approach and use of *ligne brisée* disjointed, and his more naturalistic integration of music and drama unsettling. Facilitated by Lind's performances and the queen's support, audience and critical adjustment were inevitable as expectations changed.

Despite his West End successes, wider dissemination of Meyerbeer's operas was comparatively slow. Comparatively small English-language touring troupes could not stretch to large choruses and orchestras so Meyerbeer's works were staged only occasionally outside London; acquaintance was typically via concert performances of extracted vocal items, circulation of vocal scores, and dance arrangements, such as Louis Jullien's quadrilles on themes from *Les Huguenots* and *L'étoile du nord*.

In London, Meyerbeer's consistency – he had no failures after 1847 – was an important factor in his success. Others were less fortunate: Halévy, Gounod and Berlioz (see below) all suffered major setbacks. For Halévy, the lukewarm reception of *La tempesta* was a critical blow to his British prospects and exemplifies the perils of excessive expectations.

By 1850, four of Halévy's works had been seen in London (*La reine de Chypre*, *Les mousquetaires de la reine*, and *La juive* (discussed above) and *Le val d'Andorre* (below)) but all experienced mixed receptions. Such was the importance attached to *La tempesta* (**1850**-3), however, that only unanimous acclaim would do. Lumley's decision to commission Halévy was highly unusual as London managers normally used evidence of continental (and especially Parisian) success to justify producing new works in the West End. But Lumley, having previously commissioned *I masnadieri*, was under pressure to respond to competition from Covent Garden; commissioning Halévy and Scribe, both at their Parisian peak, was a big gamble but with a huge potential pay-off. A complication was the well-known fact that Lumley had previously approached Mendelssohn, British idolisation of whom was then at its peak, such that even hypothetical projects aroused great interest. Halévy and Scribe came to London to supervise the final rehearsals while Lumley's publicity machine went into overdrive. Although initially acclaimed, *La tempesta* failed to survive the heightened expectations and scrutiny (see Figure 2.3).[97] Scribe's libretto attracted intense examination, focusing on his adaptation of Shakespeare's play. Speculation as to what Mendelssohn might have done also occupied significant press space. The consensus was that, although Halévy had done well, the opera was not a hit. *The Times* opined that 'Our impression of the whole work is ... so favourable ... that we should feel inclined to rank *La tempesta* higher than any previous effort of its composer', and praised music for Caliban, Ariel and Miranda, but criticised passages for Sycorax, and the use of progressive tonality in some numbers.[98] The *Examiner* damned the opera with faint praise: after referencing Prospero's famous lines ('The cloud capp'd towers ...'), the journal continued: 'M Halévy has given us no such music as this, and M Scribe no such words ... yet both the words and the music of this new opera ... are greatly beyond the average of such compositions'.[99] Although repeated regularly through the season, *La tempesta* was never revived. Lumley himself blamed the work's ultimate failure on its structure, each act being weaker than its predecessor, and on its most memorable melody being the quotation of Arne's 'Where the bee sucks'.[100]

Undoubtedly Halévy was unlucky when compared to Meyerbeer; the latter's successful establishment arose partially from fortuitous circumstance whereas, for Halévy, situations never came together and, after 1850, he was viewed as too great a risk.[101] The unparalleled 'hype' surrounding *La tempesta* was unhelpful and combined with a recurrent perception that his music, while immaculately crafted, lacked inspiration; Meyerbeer, meanwhile, despite long-standing resistance by some critics, eventually received sufficient support to experience a turning point, avoid the trap of failure, and remain well-regarded long after his death.

Opéra comique: St James's Theatre, 1849–50

Almost concurrent with Meyerbeer's success at the Italian opera came the sustained popularity of *opéra comique* at the St James's Theatre. Although not the first attempt to present faithful versions of this repertory, these seasons further heightened its aesthetic and commercial value.

The St James's, situated in the West End's most aristocratic quarter, was, by 1849, widely known as London's 'French theatre', due to the programming policy of its lessee, John Mitchell. Mitchell is an exemplary 'agent' of cultural exchange: he maintained homes and professional practices in London and Paris, and regularly brought popular Parisian works and performers to London. He managed the St James's from 1842 to 1854; the presentation of French plays in the original language and an eclectic selection of

SCENE FROM MAJESTY'S NEW OPERA OF "LA TEMPESTA," AT HER MAJESTY'S THEATRE.

THE THEATRES.

HER MAJESTY'S.—"LA TEMPESTA."

"La Tempesta," given for the first time on Saturday, forms a new epoch in lyrical art. Since the days of the great impresario Barbaja, when composers and artists of genius were as numerous as they are now rare, the lyrical stage has yearly become more needy in its repertoire. With the exception of that extravagant composer, Verdi, the Italian maestri have disappeared. On account of the extreme rarity of a

complete *troupe* of first-rate talent, and of the necessity of concealing vocal mediocrity, and in consequence of the tendency of an age in real life, itself however essentially dramatic, increased plot, action, and intensity of interest have been required; so that Da Ponte or Metastasio himself would not satisfy the exigencies to the present day of audiences in great European capitals; and Rossini would expose himself to a very critical measure of abolition if he were to give to another opera with a libretto like those with which he achieved some of the greatest of his first successes. In spite of these circumstances, and of England being the country in all the world that spends most money on lyrical music

SIGNOR LABLACHE AS "CALIBAN."

M. SCRIBE.

MADAME SONTAG AS "MIRANDA."

Fig 2.3 Halévy's *La tempesta* (*Illustrated London News*, 15 June 1850, p. 425)

French artistes including actors, magicians and dancers, became his trademark.[102] A permanent French troupe was established and supplemented by Paris-based stars, most notably 'Mademoiselle Rachel' (Félix), who appeared in 1846 and 1847. Mitchell also possessed an *entrée* to the royal family, and the queen attended regularly, conferring additional status and respectability. Once committed, Mitchell presented *opéra comique* with gusto.[103] A complete troupe, led by mezzo-soprano Arsène Charton-Demeur,[104] was installed, alternating with spoken drama and other entertainments. The first season opened on 15 January 1849 and, though originally intended to finish in late March, was extended to 20 June; twenty operas were presented. Most had already appeared in English adaptations and some, such as *Le domino noir* and *La dame blanche*, featured in the 1846 Brussels season; new works included Auber's *Zanetta* (**1849**-7) and *Actéon* (**1849**-9), and Boisselot's *Ne touchez pas à la reine* (**1849**-10), plus revivals of less familiar operas, including Grétry's *Richard, Coeur-de-lion*.

The evolution of critical opinion since 1830 is exemplified in the *Spectator*'s opening night review. *Opéra comique* was deemed both valuable and entertaining, best viewed in its authentic guise, the attitude previously applied to 'grand opera' (albeit performed in Italian) now firmly extended to *opéra comique*:

> A contemptuous opinion of French music has been a vulgar error, akin to the notion that the French live on frogs and wear wooden shoes, long prevalent in the mind of John Bull, but rapidly yielding to the influence of better acquaintance with his neighbours. Their musical stage ... is at this day more fertile in great works than that of any other country whatever.
>
> ... It is true that many favourite pieces of Grétry, Boïeldieu, Adam and Auber have been produced in vernacular versions in ... England, but it has been at the expense of all their native bloom and freshness. Full of the dramatic lightness and grace of French comedy, marked with the best features of the national music ... these pieces can no longer be recognised in the slovenly versions exhibited at our pretended musical theatres; and those who have formed an idea of the French Comic Opera from what they may have seen at the English Operahouse or the Princess's Theatre have now for the first time an opportunity of knowing what it really is.[105]

Even allowing for pro-Mitchell partisanship, such critical enthusiasm is striking although, for the St James's fashionable Francophile audience, it would have been neither exceptional nor unfamiliar.

Mitchell's season was received predominantly positively. Davison's enthusiasm for Auber (see above) remained in evidence: of *L'ambassadrice* (**1838**-2) he wrote:

> That Auber has written finer music, and that Scribe has composed dramas of a higher order, cannot be denied; but never have the gifted

collaborateurs more successfully exerted their combined talents ... The plot is interesting and artfully developed, while the dialogue is animated, witty and diverting; the music is light and effervescent ... [I]t is precisely what it should be, as charming as irresistible, and as ephemeral as the story and the life which it illustrates.[106]

The *Observer's* review of Boïeldieu's *La dame blanche* stressed the performance's completeness, again highlighting the importance now placed on fidelity in lighter works. The Act II finale, an extended number containing dramatic action and plot advancement, was singled out as 'a masterpiece of musical and dramatic treatment – it is perfectly graphic, the feelings of the characters are so marvellously individualised';[107] such remarks demonstrate how British taste, previously orientated towards passive sung items and active dialogue, was embracing dramatically progressive extended numbers. Despite its age, *Richard, Coeur-de-lion* was also well received: according to the *Spectator* 'the whole piece has an air of freshness, delightful to ears blasé with the commonplaces of modern opera'.[108]

A follow-up season (7 January to 23 March 1850) was followed by a provincial tour (see below). Mitchell introduced more works, either new entirely (*Le val d'Andorre* (Halévy, **1850**-1); *Le maçon* (Auber, **1850**-2); *Le caïd* (Thomas, **1850**-4); *Le roi d'Yvetot* (Adam, **1850**-5)) or played in French for the first time (including *Zampa* (Hérold, **1833**-3) and *Le postillon de Lonjumeau*). Of these, *Zampa* was most successful; Adam's music was generally thought too slight, even for *opéra comique*, and Halévy's too intellectual.[109] Davison thought the season creditable but sometimes under-rehearsed; continuing to emphasise fidelity, he criticised one-act curtain-raiser versions of *Le maître de chapelle* and *La dame blanche*.[110]

Although critical of Halévy, the *Spectator's* review of *Le val d'Andorre* opens with a striking appraisal of contemporaneous opera, rating France most highly. Italian opera, the writer argued, meant Verdi, of whom 'even his own countrymen are getting tired', while in Germany 'there is not a single dramatic composer of the smallest reputation'.[111] He continued:

Of our own musical stage it is unnecessary to speak ... Compare this decay and poverty with the condition of France, where, at this time, Meyerbeer, Auber, Halévy, Adolphe Adam, besides others of eminent talent ... are daily enriching *two* great lyrical theatres with masterpieces which make their way through Europe.

Their success was attributed to the equal treatment of music and poetry and requiring both to 'be subservient to dramatic propriety and truth'. While the *extent* of French opera's elevation here may be atypical, the article encapsulates the positive transformation of British critics' views of French theatre music over the previous twenty years.

Mitchell mounted no further seasons of *opéra comique* before retiring in 1854, but the combined successes of Meyerbeer at the Italian operas and various all-French seasons between 1845 and 1850 rendered French opera an integral part of London repertory. The following years, up to *Faust*'s premiere in 1863, were ones of consolidation. The flow of new works slowed, and managers largely focused on established works; Mitchell had no immediate successor, though short French seasons were given in 1858–59 and 1860.[112] In English adaptations, French opera also remained popular with middlebrow audiences. When the Pyne-Harrison Company and Royal English Opera were active at Covent Garden (1858–66), French works formed a significant part of their repertories; over eight seasons the two companies gave 61 performances of *Dinorah*, 55 of Massé's *Les noces de Jeannette* (**1860**-3), 35 of *L'Africaine*, 31 of *Le domino noir*, plus *Les diamants de la couronne*, *Fra Diavolo*, *Masaniello* and Gounod's *Le médécin malgré lui* (**1865**-2).

Beyond West End opera: concert music and the provinces

Throughout this period, most new French music was first heard in West End theatres; success in top-end establishments provided the cachet that encouraged performances elsewhere. The methods of dissemination and venues in which this music was performed were diverse, and its reach extensive, passing far beyond the *beau monde*, although impact was often superficial and fragmented. This section focuses upon selected concert music and theatrical works performed outside London; Berlioz is examined separately.

Following its late eighteenth-century expansion, William Weber argues that London concert-giving declined in the early 1800s before expanding again, by at least 300% between 1826/27 and 1845/46, a process principally facilitated by the upper middle class, who also increasingly regulated repertory and taste.[113] Later, 'the distinction between gentry and professional classes became less important, at least in regard to cultural experience ... with the end result being a reconstituted common elite, the bourgeoisie, by the end of the century'.[114] Concerts, like opera, were stratified by their attendees, and also by repertory choice.[115] At the top, both socially and musically, were orchestral and chamber/salon concerts, whose programmes increasingly centred on a corpus of German 'masterpieces', but which were typically accompanied by a diverse range of instrumental and vocal solos, including Italian and French opera extracts.[116] Initially organised mainly by private members' societies with rigorous admission policies, this category broadened, especially from the 1850s, to include public concerts that anyone who could afford a ticket could attend. In the middle were public 'selection' or 'miscellany' concerts and 'promenades', the latter group led by conductors such as Louis Jullien. Programmes comprised extracts from the same German corpus (for example, single movements from symphonies) and French and Italian operas, but also virtuosic instrumental solos, English vocal works (glees and ballads), and large amounts of dance music, especially quadrilles and waltzes; these were often visually as well as musically spectacular. Least prestigious were cheap concerts and recitals aimed at the lower middle and working classes, given in such places as pleasure gardens, music halls, Mechanics' Institutes and town halls; programmes in the first two types of venues emphasised the 'entertainment' angle still further by focusing more on dance and vocal music; in the latter two, a doctrine of 'moral improvement' was often apparent, demonstrated by the performance of more 'serious' items, albeit in modified versions. 'Benefit' concerts, which typically comprised varied selections of solos and items for small ensembles, operated at various social levels, depending on the reputation of the organising artiste; these were steadily superseded from the 1850s by the solo recital, with pianists leading the way. Amateur choral societies, whose members were often united by shared religious or political ideals, could straddle class boundaries.[117]

In 1830, French music featured only occasionally in high-end concert programmes. As noted in Chapter 1, French music had, in Britain, been entirely excluded from the emerging corpus of masterpieces, and its representation in high-end concerts was therefore extremely limited. According to the *Harmonicon*, no French repertory at all was heard at the Antient Music concerts, whose programmes were dominated by Handel; an innovation that year was the introduction of Mozart. At the Philharmonic Society, the only French pieces performed were a violin concerto by the Franco-Belgian Charles de Bériot (also soloist), a bassoon concerto by Pierre Crémont and chamber music by George Onslow; no French vocal music was performed.[118] Aimed at elite London's music enthusiasts, the *Harmonicon*'s reviews of middle-brow concerts are less detailed, but there is little reason to suppose that such programmes were substantially different regarding their repertory's national origins. Highbrow concerts outside London appear similar: three provincial festivals took place in 1830; the overture to *La muette de Portici* was heard at Worcester, while John Braham appeared in Liverpool and Norwich singing an aria from *Fra Diavolo*; de Bériot also performed at Liverpool, again as a soloist in one of his own concertos. Otherwise, French music was absent.

Subsequently, French music appeared more often, though still as a small proportion of the whole. Concerts of 'ancient music', sacred choral works and high-end chamber recitals still routinely excluded French works but others, ranging from the Philharmonic to Jullien's 'Promenade' and 'Monster' concerts, typically included short vocal items, including standalone songs, and opera and oratorio extracts; as French opera became popular in theatres, extracts were heard more regularly in concerts. Auber and Meyerbeer were best represented, the latter achieving popularity even before his firm establishment in West End theatres. Opera overtures, most frequently by Auber, but also Hérold and Boïeldieu, might open or close a concert. Taking 1853 as a sample, items performed around the country include the overture of Auber's *Le lac des fées* and an orchestral selection from *Robert le diable* at London's Amateur Musical Society; the overture to *Masaniello* and an aria from *Les diamants de la couronne* at the Bradford Festival; the overtures to *Zampa* and *Masaniello* at the Gloucester Festival; and an aria from *Robert* and the overture to *Gustave III* at the Leeds Musical Union.[119] In 1860, the Philharmonic's concerts included an overture by Hérold, two arias by Meyerbeer and one by Auber, and the New Philharmonic almost the same amount, replacing Hérold with Auber and adding an aria by Adam.[120] In the same season, 'Ombre légère' from *Dinorah* was included in at least seven high- and middlebrow concerts in London, alongside other arias by Meyerbeer, Adam and Auber. In Manchester, Charles Hallé, whose regular concert series started in 1858, took a similar approach. Other performances can be found by browsing almost any issue of the specialist music journals or daily newspapers; in all cases, though, German and Italian music dominated, while overtures were the most substantial French items. Modes of performance varied: at large-scale high- and middlebrow concerts, complete orchestral works were performed; in more modest events, especially outside big towns, arrangements – for military band through to solo piano or organ – were popular.

Adaptations also acted as vehicles for dissemination. Jullien regularly produced dance quadrilles on opera melodies, such as *Zampa* (1844), *Masaniello* and *Le prophète* (both 1850), and *L'étoile du nord* (1855). Professional soloists regularly created, performed and published their own 'fantasias': representative examples include violinist Henry Blagrove's fantasia based on *Les Huguenots*,[121] George Osborne's 'ingenious and very showy' piano duet on themes from *L'étoile du nord*, and an anonymous duet for harmonium and piano on themes from *Le prophète*.[122] Piano arrangements for domestic use were also important: complete opera vocal scores were increasingly available, but more widespread were individual arias with English words, while solo piano arrangements of quadrilles were ubiquitous. Almost entirely, though, while concerts and domestic music-making expanded knowledge of select French repertory, initial presentation was in West End theatres. This is true even of Félicien David's *Le désert*, the only piece of large-scale concert music performed in Britain prior to 1863 (Berlioz excepted, see below), spectacularly premiered by Lumley (**1845**-1). *Le désert* was a one-off; premiered in Paris in December 1844, it had transformed David's reputation and, due to this success and its novel format (a combination of cantata and programme symphony, with short sections of spoken narrative), the London performance received extensive coverage, although reactions were diverse, varying from a 'monstrosity' in the *Musical World* to a 'really great work' in the *Examiner*.[123] As with music by Meyerbeer and Berlioz, *Le désert* was viewed primarily a work of 'effect' rather than substance, but its evocative portrayal of the exotic led to short-term notoriety, though little in the way of an after-life.[124]

Outside London, dissemination of opera via staged performances was erratic but discernible patterns emerge in the 1850s. Provincial audiences, especially in larger towns, might see new works within months of their London premiere, but could wait years; *Robert le diable* was given in Dublin in June 1832 but *Les Huguenots* did not appear until 1857 (see below). Such inconsistency arose from the flexible and unpredictable nature of theatre organisation. The resident 'stock companies' of provincial venues, (semi-)permanent groups of repertory actors who played theatrical material ranging from Shakespeare to burlesque and melodrama to opera, rarely possessed professionally trained singers, while a typical evening show comprised a principal piece (e.g. opera or melodrama), supplemented by shorter items such as recitations, songs, dances, and farces or burlesques. West End 'stars', including opera singers, toured regularly, brought the latest London successes with them and took leading roles, while residents moved down to supporting parts. Visitors were often engaged at short notice and regularly revised their engagements with little warning. Consequently, it is not unusual to find significant disparities between the first appearances of new operas in different towns.

An exhaustive account of this activity is prevented by omissions and errors in surviving records. Although the provincial press expanded rapidly after 1850, thanks to improved communication technology, and reductions and then elimination in 1855 of stamp duty, coverage remained selective; in particular, entertainment reports focus on events of interest to the literate population. Theatre playbill collections, though of great value, are regularly incomplete, and sometimes inaccurate, with, for example, first performances sometimes erroneously claimed either for marketing purposes or through simple error.

Masaniello was one of the first French operas to reach provincial theatres; surviving playbills and reviews document performances in Bath (January 1831), Leeds (May 1831) and Birmingham (May 1832).[125] Press coverage is sometimes uninformative: of the Bath performance, starring John Braham, the local reviewer wrote, 'Of the merits of the opera *as an* opera we shall say nothing – its character is too well known to need any remark from us' but noted that it was produced with a level of splendour 'which we should not have thought attainable in a provincial theatre'.[126] The first Leeds performance was sufficiently successful to justify a week-long run; this three-act version was presented 'with the splendid overture and all the original music ... the orchestral parts arranged by Mr Aldridge of the Theatre Royal, Liverpool'.[127] In Birmingham, *Masaniello* was given at least seven performances as a two-act afterpiece and reappeared in October.

Extensive adaptation was standard practice, though declining in extent throughout the century; performances were almost exclusively in English. When *Robert le diable* was performed in Dublin by visiting singers Joseph and Mary Ann Wood in June 1832, the amendments, made 'expressly for the Dublin theatre by Mr Lacy' were lauded; noting earlier London performances, the *Freeman's Journal* commented:

[W]e are inclined to believe it does not lose by the new investment, either in beauty, musical excellence or dramatic effect. *Here* we have not only a beautiful opera but a charming melo-drame ... There are in it, some exquisite musical compositions – partly by Meyerbeer and partly by Rossini – a gratifying circumstance which gives the public an opportunity of comparing the respective merits of each composer.[128]

Despite this writer's enthusiasm, however, *Robert* does not appear to have been widely performed outside London.

Fra Diavolo, by contrast, was extremely successful, reaching Dublin and Edinburgh in 1833, and Leeds and Birmingham in 1835.[129] The *Caledonian Mercury* thought little of the scenario, stating that 'it does not appear to rise above mediocrity', but was greatly enthused by the music:

> The Overture is a production worthy of its highly talented author. Although not possessing the energy and fire of that to *Der Freyschutz* or *Don Giovanni* it is exceedingly beautiful, from the pleasing character of the melodies introduced. Indeed, this is the great characteristic of all Auber's music, which abounds with the most rich, delightful and flowing melodies, varying in expression from grave to gay.

Fra Diavolo's popularity is attested by regular revivals; it became a stock opera for several touring singers, and popular with more modest touring companies.[130]

From the 1850s, the expanding rail system facilitated the formation of dedicated touring companies. Initially comprising only principal artistes, as the practice developed and theatres were syndicated, auxiliaries were added, including chorus, orchestra and stage management; resident stock companies were disbanded.[131] London's Italian troupes undertook limited tours in the 1850s and '60s (partly prompted by the Covent Garden fire in 1856), which occasionally included French works: they introduced *Les Huguenots* to Bristol (1853), Dublin (1857) and Birmingham (1870).[132] The *Bristol Mercury* reckoned the opera was a challenging choice for a city that only rarely hosted Italian companies, and echoed criticisms of Meyerbeer made in London: 'It is deficient of that leading melody which runs through all Bellini's and most of Donizetti's operas ... [I]t is also less easily grasped by the audience, who require to hear it more than once to clearly comprehend its meaning'. Although somewhat patronising, this is a fair point insofar as provincial audiences were primarily dependent on vocal scores and extracts performed in concerts for their knowledge of Meyerbeer.

The only known instance up to 1863 of French language performance outside London is John Mitchell's brief provincial tour in spring 1850, following his second St James's season (see above). His company was particularly well received in Liverpool, and returned on three separate occasions, appearing also in Birmingham, Manchester, Dublin and Belfast. The first review by the *Musical World*'s Liverpool correspondent is telling (though perhaps exaggerated) with reference to provincial performance standards and the local audience's appreciation of the works' humour:

> The performance [of *Le domino noir*] was a complete triumph, the audience being perfectly delighted with the excellence of the acting, singing and music, so totally different to what they had previously been accustomed

to. Formerly operas were given with, at most, three good singers, and a band, chorus and subordinates, who were neither acquainted with the language nor the music, and whose desperate efforts to please, only made their musical and artistic poverty the more conspicuous ...

[In *Les diamants de la couronne*, Chateaufort] and Buguet provoked all the laughter of the evening – a luxury in which the audience indulged frequently, a great compliment to the artistes for, of course, in a provincial town, the number of the audience who understand French is comparatively few.[133]

In Manchester, the critic noted a 'fairly filled pit, and a full dress circle' but the almost empty upper circle and galleries; of those present, 'a good proportion must have understood French well, to enjoy the points in the dialogue as evidently as they did'.[134] In Dublin, the *Freeman's Journal* claimed the city's own actors and musicians could have done as well and that the visitors' abilities were exaggerated; overall, the audience's pleasure 'was not of the thrilling and exciting character which wearied fashion looks for, and which quiet good taste does not disdain'.[135] Nevertheless, *Saunders's Newsletter* claimed that Mitchell extended his stay, but also noted the entertainment's rarefied appeal:

[I]t evinces that there is a taste in Dublin to appreciate a style of performance, the perfect enjoyment of which must of necessity be confined to the educated circles ... [The company is] a perfect transport from the French to the British stage, such as none who have not visited the Parisian theatres can form a just idea of.[136]

Overall, Mitchell's tour's success appears limited. Works containing extensive dialogue must have proved challenging (no reviews mention the provision of translations) and relied on visual humour; many non-French speakers probably stayed away. In English adaptations, though, French *opéras comiques* proved popular and continued to be so; the subsequent immense popularity of *opéra bouffe* built on this foundation.

The singular case of Berlioz 1840–62

Berlioz confounded British critics more than any other nineteenth-century French composer. Until 1848, little of his music was known but interest rose rapidly when he was engaged by Jullien that year to conduct concerts at Drury Lane and was rekindled when he conducted the New Philharmonic Society in 1852. The failure of *Benvenuto Cellini* in 1853 undermined his reputation, which only recovered in the late 1870s.

Berlioz was not unknown to *cognoscenti*; reports of Parisian performances had featured regularly in the *Musical World* from its launch in 1836; it reproduced a long review of the premiere of *Benvenuto Cellini* and, alongside *The Times*, reported the first performance of *La damnation de Faust*.[137] There were also occasional performances in London: the Societa Armonica gave the overtures *Les francs-juges* and *Waverley* (**1840**-2 and **1840**-3), though the *Musical World* viewed the latter as 'an unqualified failure ... [A]s a work of art, abstractedly, it never reaches the condition of beautiful, while it is frequently extravagant and unpleasing to the last degree'.[138] The overture to *Benvenuto Cellini* (**1841**-1) at the Philharmonic – a bold choice by a staid body – fared little better. The work was excoriated by the *Spectator*: '[I]n Berlioz there is nothing unintelligible – there is nothing difficult: to write uncouth passages, to string together unconnected and strange phrases, and, above all, to make a hideous din, requires neither genius nor skill'.[139]

When Berlioz visited London in 1848 and conducted two concerts of his own music (Drury Lane, 7 February; Hanover Square, 29 June), critical opinion was more sympathetic. His demeanour – the *Musical World* noted that he made a 'highly favourable impression', due to his 'polished and courteous manners'[140] – doubtless smoothed the way.[140] The first programme included *Carnaval romain*, *Harold en Italie*, extracts from *Faust*, *Symphonie funèbre* and *Grande messe des morts*, and short vocal items (**1848**-1 to **1848**-5); the second was largely a repeat, with changes to some of the shorter pieces.

Initial reactions were uncertain: many reviewers relied on formulae similar to Davison's comment on *Harold*: '[it] is a work of too large design and pretensions too much beyond the ordinary limits to be analysed in the few lines our crowded columns will permit'.[141] Most were reluctant to dismiss Berlioz out of hand and his stature and ability were recognised consistently; nor did they want to be thought reflexive reactionaries, especially following the Drury Lane audience's enthusiastic response. The general consensus was that Berlioz was a master of orchestration and 'effect' (like Meyerbeer) but a weak melodist with an eccentric approach to form, reflecting British admiration of *cantilena*, the transparent use of recognised structures and rigorous motivic development and connection. The *Observer* argued that:

> No great musician was ... ever understood at once ... It cannot be doubted, however, that Berlioz is a most imaginative composer, that his mind is richly stored with new and striking ideas; that he is a consummate master of all the resources of his art; that he has carried its descriptive powers further, probably, than they have ever been carried before; Beethoven always excepted.[142]

Chorley concurred regarding the 'admirable sonority of [the] orchestral effects' and deemed Berlioz 'an original colourist of the very first order',[143] but criticised his approach to structure and harmony: '[He] seems to work by reiteration and interjection, rather than by episode and development harmoniously combined with the principal topic:—his management of modulation ... is eccentric rather than genial'. Chorley found *Harold* 'attractively picturesque in colour, agreeable (rather than satisfactory or symmetrical) in melody, but disappointing in construction', and inferior to Beethoven's

'Pastoral' Symphony; despite normally supporting Meyerbeer, he argued that both he and Berlioz put 'dexterous artifices' before 'mastery of form'. A more consolidated view emerged after the second concert: Berlioz was accepted as a great composer despite or perhaps because of his flouting of convention. In *The Times* the normally conservative Davison argued, 'To this impatience of restraint may be traced all the faults of M Berlioz ... but to this must be traced also that daring originality which places him apart from all composers'; of *Harold* he stated: 'There is a world of poetry in this work which, despite its inexplicable design, places it in the highest rank of imaginative music'.[144]

Despite the concerts' success, Berlioz's work was not taken up: technical difficulty and resource requirements were inhibiting, but the strong association of his music with his personal appearances may also have proved discouraging. Consequently, Berlioz's music fell largely into abeyance until the New Philharmonic Society concerts, when his works were integrated into mixed programmes; Part I of *Roméo et Juliette* was the main new work (**1852**-1); *Les francs-juges* and extracts from *Faust* also appeared (28 May and 9 June). Although Davison still found Berlioz's music challenging, he had been entirely won over; his reviews of *Roméo et Juliette* are glowing.[145] The *Critic* was also enthusiastic, calling the music 'wild, passionate, and perfectly original in its piquancy of treatment ... The ideas are worked out in a thoroughly dramatic manner, and there runs throughout the whole an unfailing vein of imagination, sometimes bright and sparkling, and again plaintively and passionately sombre'.[146] In the final concert, *Faust* followed the Ninth Symphony and Berlioz was popularly and critically acclaimed; the *Leader* declared that the performance 'fairly transported the immense audience to an enthusiasm rarely known in England',[147] while even Chorley allowed that sections of *Faust* were 'deliciously voluptuous'; Davison was again unstinting in his praise.[148]

Berlioz had every reason to be positive about his London experiences,[149] and returned for the British premiere of *Benvenuto Cellini* (**1853**-1), only to be disappointed: the reception was largely hostile, and, at Berlioz's request, the opera was immediately withdrawn.[150] Several reviews mention a partisan section of the audience determined to derail the opera; even the queen's presence failed to deter their barracking.[151] The *Morning Post* blamed an 'extremely suspicious' clique; the *Spectator*, though, opined that the performance was 'fairly and dispassionately judged by an immense audience'.[152] The critics focused principally on the scenario, finding it slight and absurd; the *Spectator* asserted that 'the rest is mere *remplissage*, got up for the sake of spectacle', while Davison asserted that 'the authors have overlooked almost every opportunity for effect, spinning out scenes destitute of action to an intolerable length, and failing to invest any of the personages with the smallest degree of interest'.[153] Like others, he wondered why Berlioz, known for his literary interests, had accepted the libretto. Regarding the music, opinions diverged. Davison thought it typical of Berlioz's approach and attributed the opera's failure to audience conservativism:

Granting that there are many things to offend the prejudices of those who look exclusively to the accepted models of dramatic musical composition, that there is much that sounds prolix and monotonous, that the voices are at times injudiciously taxed ... we find, on the other hand, enough of the pleasing, original and effective to counterbalance these drawbacks.

The *Spectator* concurred, but blamed Berlioz:

[O]pera is a popular entertainment ... It must contain so much that gives immediate delight, that the public will learn by degrees to appreciate beauties which at first they do not perceive ... [Berlioz's] orchestral pieces ... are so rich and glowing in their colours, so gorgeous and picturesque, that they are listened to with increasing pleasure ... In respect to melody, however, we cannot help thinking that there must be some radical defect in Berlioz's organisation ... We cannot otherwise account for the total absence of grace, smoothness and flow in his vocal pieces. They are destitute of rhythm, and their harsh unvocal intervals ... give the hearer nothing but pain.

For Chorley, Berlioz was too 'self-willed'; his undoubted skills could not 'make amends with a general audience for the disdain of known rules and for the mystification of form'.[154]

The stark difference between the reception of Berlioz's concert music and *Benvenuto Cellini* is striking. Even allowing for a hostile clique, it seems likely that different audience profiles, with divergent 'horizons of expectations', were a significant factor. The concert audiences were more likely to be dominated by genuinely interested parties; the recently established New Philharmonic presented itself as a dynamic, adventurous alternative to the staid (old) Philharmonic, while Covent Garden had a significant constituency whose attendance was governed by social ritual and was less educated or catholic in its musical tastes. It had, after all, taken over fifteen years for Meyerbeer to be accepted, and only after a firm 'push' by Jenny Lind; Verdi dealt simultaneously with similar attitudes.

The consequences for Berlioz's reputation were significant. He conducted the New Philharmonic again in 1855 (in the same season that Wagner conducted the 'old' Philharmonic), but his music was then largely disregarded in Britain until the late 1870s (see Chapters 3 and 4). Although the failure of *Benvenuto Cellini* was damaging, the orchestral works' success suggests there would have been an audience for Berlioz's concert music; at the time, however, his music's reputation was partly tied to his own urbane conduct and he lacked British advocates, while its technical challenges were a disincentive in a country whose orchestras undertook minimal rehearsals. Two short-term exceptions were Manns at the Crystal Palace and Hallé in Manchester, who started performing smaller works almost as soon as they were in position in

1855 and 1858 respectively.[155] Both men, though, focused strongly on their 'home ground' and their interest in Berlioz had only a limited effect elsewhere.

One notable aspect of Berlioz's early reception is absence of references to nationality. Whilst Auber, Adam and even Meyerbeer were presented in relation to France or Paris, Berlioz largely transcended this. Unable to place him in a 'national school', the favourite comparator was Beethoven; anxious not to miss foreseeing that Berlioz might, like Beethoven, be regarded later as an iconoclastic genius, many writers hedged, suggesting that Berlioz's music might be 'too advanced' for contemporaneous ears. Parallels can also be seen with Meyerbeer, whose fondness for orchestral 'effect' and intricacy were also thought to come at the expense of elegant melodies and the conventions of musical structure. In this first phase, however, Berlioz was presented as neither a characteristic nor a representative French composer.

Conclusion

Improved diplomatic relations and an unprecedentedly long period of peace undoubtedly facilitated more positive perceptions of France but were less important than the tangible availability of French goods and easier access, especially to Paris. In generalised terms, beyond the *beau monde*, often virulent Georgian Francophobia softened to less aggressive chauvinism and grudging acknowledgement that the French had some positive attributes: British views of French 'Otherness' mutated and were steadily redefined.

Dominated by theatrical activity in the West End, the performance of French music increased rapidly from 1830 but its dissemination was uneven: in central London, French operas became a mainstay, extending beyond *beau monde* audiences that dominated the leading opera houses; in adaptation, with wide variations in fidelity, *opéras comiques* reached wider though still comparatively affluent audiences. It nevertheless took many years and some extra-musical prompts to establish Meyerbeer, while both Berlioz and Halévy suffered at the hands of London's quixotic opera audiences. While in theatres, opera repertory was driven principally by fashion, in concert halls, French music had to compete with an expanding and consolidating body of 'masterpieces', a body from which it had been and continued to be excluded. While comprising only a small proportion of concert repertory and being overwhelmingly operatic in origin, French music nevertheless established a foothold; German and Italian works still dominated, however, with British music a poor third and French a distant fourth. Beyond the West End and fashionable season, the dissemination of all French music was slight and highly erratic. Adapted operas appeared in larger provincial theatres but, beyond these and extracts occasionally performed in concerts, encounters with French works were likely to come via the mediated modes of dance arrangements, opera scores and piano versions of popular melodies, giving only a partial sense of the music's original function and context. Nevertheless, by 1860, knowledge of French music was certainly common among London's regular theatre- and concertgoers, and filtering out to a significant extent beyond the *beau monde* and cultured middle class.

Critical evaluations also became more open, especially in relation to opera. Suspicion and a belief in aesthetic inferiority were gradually replaced by acknowledgements of positive qualities; critics increasingly called for 'faithful' productions of operas, according them higher aesthetic value. Some writers were better disposed than others: Chorley and Gruneisen were enthusiastic supporters of Meyerbeer; more surprisingly, given his innate conservatism, Davison was also gradually won over. When David's *Le désert* was first performed in London, Davison wrote that

> For our own parts we always entertain a strong suspicion of any work of art that travels over to England with a French reputation. In our eyes it could hardly present a more equivocal diploma of merit. The temper of our volatile neighbours is so easily inflamed that their judgement is often destroyed by a kind of natural combustion. In music especially, we arraign their taste as vicious.[156]

Yet Davison enthused about Auber and was swept away by Berlioz; in 1859, he wrote of *Dinorah* that 'No opera … is more replete with tune … [It] will take its place among the most consummate achievements of its composer's genius'.[157] Critical appreciation of French music and acknowledgement that France was a 'musical nation' had increased enormously.

Considering French culture overall, it is in respect of music that British views were most radically transformed, moving from dismissiveness to widespread appreciation in around 30 years. The primary cause was the popularity of *opéra comique*, which largely accorded with British conceptions of Frenchness; common adjectives in reviews include 'gay', 'light', and 'sparkling', fitting with established notions of French wit and sophistication, albeit tinged with shallowness and frivolity. The arrival of Gounod's *Faust* in 1863 provided another push towards acceptance, a trend which continued through the rest of the century; as French composers wrote concert music more regularly, so its reach in Britain also broadened. Either ignored or derided in 1820, by 1900 French music was virtually indispensable.

Notes

1 Exemplified by the apocryphal exchange between a British naval officer ('You French fight for money, while we British fight for honour'), and the corsair Robert Surcouf ('Each of us fights for what he lacks the most') (see Robert and Isabelle Tombs, *That Sweet Enemy* (London, 2006), p. 262). Grudging French admiration of foolhardy British valour is encapsulated by General Pierre Bosquet's comment upon the Charge of the Light Brigade: 'C'est magnifique, mais ce n'est pas la guerre'.

2 Nicholas Dames, 'Britain and Europe', in Kate Flint (ed.), *The Cambridge History of Victorian Literature* (Cambridge, 2012), pp. 628–9.

3 William Thackeray, *Vanity Fair* (Harmondsworth, 1968), p. 130.

4 Elizabeth Gaskell, *Cranford* (London, 1904), p. 144; that Signor Brunoni is obviously Italian is both comic and telling.

5 Ceri Crossley and Ian Small (eds), *Studies in Anglo-French Cultural Relations* (London & Basingstoke, 1988), p. 11.

6 Valerie Mars, 'Experiencing French Cookery in Nineteenth-century London', in Debra Kelly and Martyn Cornick (eds), *A History of the French in London: Liberty, Equality, Opportunity* (London, 2013), p. 227.

7 *Advice to a Young Gentleman, on Entering Society* (2nd ed, London, 1839), p. 27.

8 Benjamin Disraeli, *Coningsby* (2nd ed, 3 vols, London, 1844), vol. 2, p. 102.

9 Mary Berry, *Extracts of the Journals and Correspondence of Miss Berry* (3 vols, London, 1865–66), vol. 1, p. xxxviii.

10 See Michèle Cohen, *Fashioning Masculinity: National Identity and Language in the Eighteenth Century* (London, 1996).

11 See Peter Thorold, *The British in France: Visitors and Residents since the Revolution* (London, 2008), pp. 92–5.

12 Whitney Walton, *France at the Crystal Palace: Bourgeois Taste and Artisan Manufacture in the Nineteenth Century* (Berkeley, 1992).

13 Walton, p. 27.

14 Walton, p. 222.

15 Walton, p. 225.

16 Dames, pp. 623–4.

17 Before the establishment of the Royal Italian Opera at Covent Garden in 1847, the King's Theatre dominated and was socially most exalted; Frederick Gye's success at Covent Garden gradually shifted perceptions in its favour. For opera, Drury Lane was generally the least popular.

18 At least three of Auber's operas were produced in London before 1830: *La neige* (Covent Garden, 1824), *Léocardie* (Drury Lane, 1825), and *La muette de Portici* (see below). Operas by Boïeldieu also appeared: *Le calife de Bagdad* (Haymarket, 1809), *Jean de Paris* (Covent Garden, 1814), *Le petit chaperon rouge* (Covent Garden, 1818), *La dame blanche* (Drury Lane, 1826) and *Les deux nuits* (**1829**-2).

19 Christina Fuhrmann, *Foreign Opera at the London Playhouses: From Mozart to Bellini* (Cambridge, 2015), p. 1. Complete orchestral scores and libretti were rarely available; adaptation was not only desirable but unavoidable.

20 Regarding Bishop's amendments to Boïeldieu's *Jean de Paris*, Fuhrmann notes that British audiences preferred reflective sung items with plot development placed mainly in spoken text; for French works, whose ensembles were often kinetic and lengthy, this meant considerable abbreviation or omission altogether. French operas generally lacked ballads, so these would be specially composed or borrowed (Fuhrmann, pp. 26–7).

21 The 1842 Copyright Act introduced limited rights for composers and librettists, but they were difficult to enforce.

22 This name was invariably used in Britain and is used hereafter.

23 *Times*, 5 May 1829, p. 3.

24 *MP*, 6 May 1829, p. 3.

25 *Spectator*, 9 May 1829, p. 297.

26 See Fuhrmann, pp. 2 and 190. On London productions of *Masaniello* specific-
    ally, see pp. 148–52. Fuhrmann concludes that, although critical opinion varied,
    Auber's music was considered sufficiently interesting and skilled for French opera
    to be taken seriously.

27 *LGa*, 5 February 1831, p. 91.

28 *Spectator*, 5 February 1831, p. 135; *The Times* (2 February, p. 3) was more positive.

29 *Tatler*, 4 November 1831, p. 431.

30 *Standard*, 4 November 1831, p. 3.

31 *Times*, 4 November 1831, p. 2; *MP*, same date, p. 3.

32 Extract from private journal, quoted in Alfred Bunn, *The Stage: Both Before and
    Behind the Curtain* (3 vols, London, 1840), vol. 1, p. 131. Bunn also saw *Robert le
    diable*, Hérold's *Le pré aux clercs* (**1833**-4) and Halévy's *La tentation*. He disliked
    the last intensely, writing that it was 'the worst piece with the worst music and the
    worst dancing imaginable, but the *mise en scène* is very fine' (p. 128).

33 Bunn, p. 138.

34 Fuhrmann, p. 186.

35 *TO*, 14 November 1833, pp. 1–2.

36 *MC*, 14 November 1833, p. 3

37 *Spectator*, 16 November 1833, p. 1074.

38 *Times*, 14 November 1833, p. 2.

39 Fuhrmann, p. 183.

40 See *Caledonian Mercury*, 12 February 1835, p. 2, and Playbills Collection at BL,
    shelfmark mic.c.13137/playbills.

41 *Times*, 2 April 1851, p. 5.

42 Meyerbeer's Italian operas, *Il crociato in Egitto* and *Margherita d'Anjou*, were
    performed in London in 1825 and 1828 respectively, but neither made a substan-
    tive impression.

43 See Joanne Cormac, 'From Satirical Piece to Commercial Product: The Mid-
    Victorian Opera Burlesque and its Bourgeois Audience', *Journal of the Royal
    Musical Association*, **142** (2017), 69–108.

44 See Robert Bledsoe, *Henry Fothergill Chorley, Victorian Journalist* (Aldershot,
    1998), p. 52; *Harmonicon*, 1 May 1832, pp. 119–20 and 1 June, p. 138; 1 July,
    pp. 155–6.

45 *Harmonicon*, 1 February 1832, p. 47.

46 *Harmonicon*, 1 March 1832, pp. 69–70, and Fuhrmann, p. 162.

47 *Harmonicon*, 1 April 1832, p. 87. This is definitely the case for Bishop's score for
    Drury Lane, which has survived (Fuhrmann, p. 163).

48 *Tatler*, 14 June 1832, pp. 247–8.

49 *LGu*, 30 June 1832, p. 206.

50 *Athenaeum*, 16 June 1832, p. 388; see also *Observer*, 18 June, p. 3; *Harmonicon*, 1
    July, pp. 159–60.

51 Fuhrmann, p. 160.

52 Fuhrmann, p. 169.

53 *Spectator*, 16 June 1832, p. 562.

54 *CM*, 1 July 1832, p. 41.

55 *Harmonicon*, 1 July 1832, p. 160.

56 The same company revived *Robert* at Drury Lane in 1841 and Covent Garden
    in 1842; this version was not received well, mainly due to poor performance (see
    Athenaeum, 26 June 1841, p. 494, *Examiner*, same date, p. 406).

57 *Athenaeum*, 25 June 1842, p. 542.

58 *MW*, 23 June 1842, p. 198.

59 *MP*, 21 June 1842, p. 5 (reproduced with minor amendments in *Era*, 26 June, pp. 5–6).

60 *Spectator*, 25 June 1842, p. 615.

61 *Times*, 21 June 1842, p. 6 (reproduced with minor amendments in *Observer*, 26 June, p. 4).

62 *Spectator*, 25 June 1842, p. 615.

63 *MC*, 4 July 1842, p. 6.

64 *MW*, 23 June 1842, p. 198.

65 Including: *Guillaume Tell*; *La favorite*; *Les diamants de la couronne* (**1844**-1); *La muette de Portici*; *La dame blanche*; *Robert le diable*; *Les Huguenots*; and *Le postillon de Lonjumeau* (Adam; **1837**-1).

66 Possibly due to inadequate publicity: see *Examiner*, 14 June 1845, p. 373.

67 Victoria allegedly refused to visit Covent Garden due to its associations with the Anti-Corn Law League; relocation to Drury Lane was engineered to facilitate her presence (*Times*, 5 July 1845, p. 5).

68 *Spectator*, 7 June 1845, p. 539.

69 *Critic*, 21 June 1845, p. 165.

70 *Athenaeum*, 21 June 1845, p. 621; Chorley argued later, though, that the company was too small to represent adequately crowd scenes in Meyerbeer and Halévy's operas (12 July, p. 696).

71 *Times*, 19 June 1845, p. 5.

72 *MW*, 31 July 1845, pp. 362–3; see also *Times*, 1 July, p. 5.

73 *Observer*, 13 July 1845, p. 2. The writer noted that '[Halévy] is a Jew by birth and by faith, and therefore is of no country', suggesting antisemitic bias.

74 *Times*, 8 July 1845, p. 5.

75 *Times*, 12 June 1845, p. 4.

76 *Athenaeum*, 12 July 1845, p. 697.

77 See *Spectator*, 18 July 1846, p. 692; *MW*, 25 July, p. 345; *Connoisseur*, 1 August, p. 164; *Observer*, 9 August, p. 9.

78 *Times*, 30 July 1846, p. 8; see also *MW*, 1 August, p. 359. Both reviews are probably by Davison; already editor of *MW*, he joined *The Times* in 1846.

79 See *Athenaeum*, 8 August 1846, p. 820; *Observer*, 9 August, p. 6.

80 *Spectator*, 22 August 1846, p. 804.

81 Played in Italian, in four acts; see *Times*, 5 May 1847, p. 5. Meyerbeer had supported Lind previously; her choice of Alice was probably reciprocal.

82 Journal, 4 May 1847 (www.queenvictoriasjournals.org, accessed 19 January 2018). Victoria had a consistently good view of Meyerbeer and enjoyed all his operas.

83 *Athenaeum*, 22 July 1848, p. 732, of the performance on 20 July; the first two acts were joined and shortened; omissions were also made in the third and fifth acts.

84 *Athenaeum*, 29 July 1848, p. 754.

85 *Observer*, 23 July 1848, p. 3.

86 *MW*, 29 July 1848, p. 485.

87 See *MW*, 28 April 1849, pp. 257–9; *Athenaeum*, 21 April, pp. 416–8; *Examiner*, 24 April, pp. 261–2.

88 *MW*, 28 July 1849, p. 467; Acts I and II were merged and shortened.

89 Excluding the Lyceum seasons of 1856 and 1857, when Covent Garden was being rebuilt, but including the 'Coalition' seasons with James Mapleson in 1869 and 1870. The second and third placed operas were *Il barbiere di Siviglia* (121) and *Faust* (109).

90   More frequent performances of *L'étoile du nord* may have been inhibited by the destruction of relevant materials in the 1856 fire; it was not revived until 1864. *Dinorah* was the name accorded to the Italian version of *Le pardon de Ploërmel*.

91   Edward Smith produced a pre-emptive English version of *L'étoile* in a season of 'Italian operas at popular prices'. Critics regarded Smith as an upstart and *L'étoile*, allegedly given against Meyerbeer's wishes, was widely criticised but popular; Smith's performances reached a different audience to Covent Garden's. See *Times*, 1 March 1855, p. 6; *Critic*, 1 March, p. 124; *Athenaeum*, 3 March, p. 272; *Examiner*, 3 March, p. 134; *MW*, 3 March, p. 139.

92   *MW*, 30 June 1855, p. 417, and 7 July, p. 435

93   *MW*, 21 July 1855, p. 470.

94   *Observer*, 31 July 1859, p. 3.

95   *Examiner*, 30 July 1859, p. 485.

96   *MW*, 30 July 1859, p. 488.

97   *MW*'s own review covered over four pages and six more were devoted to dissecting others (15 June 1850, pp. 365–73, and 29 June, pp. 399–401).

98   *Times*, 10 June 1850, p. 5.

99   *Examiner*, 15 June 1850, p. 364.

100   Benjamin Lumley, *Reminiscences of the Opera* (London, 1864), pp. 276–82.

101   *La juive* was produced at Covent Garden in 1850 and 1852, and once in 1893. It was Halévy's only opera performed outside London before 1914, being given by Carl Rosa's troupe in 1888–89 and the Moody-Manners Company in 1906; in both cases it was a curio more than a success.

102   See Barry Duncan, *The St James's Theatre: Its Strange and Complete History 1835–1957* (London, 1964), pp. 60–83.

103   Previewing the 1849 season, *MW* wryly noted that, as Paris's eminent actors had all already been seen, the 'new speculation may easily be accounted for … There [is] nothing left for Mr Mitchell in his search after novelty but to call in music to his aid' (28 December 1848, p. 817).

104   Always referred to 'Mademoiselle Charton', she appeared with the Brussels company in 1846 (see above).

105   *Spectator*, 20 January 1849, p. 57.

106   *Times*, 29 January 1849, p. 8; see also *Times*, 16 January, p. 8, regarding *Le domino noir*.

107   *Observer*, 4 February 1849, p. 3.

108   *Spectator*, 3 March 1849, p. 202; see also *Times*, 28 February, p. 5, which noted the omission of several numbers.

109   For *Le postillon de Lonjumeau* see *Times*, 21 February 1850, p. 8; for *Le val d'Andorre* see *Spectator*, 12 January, p. 34.

110   *Times*, 25 March 1850, p. 8.

111   As note 109.

112   The St James's hosted an *ad hoc* troupe managed by flautist Jean Remusat for several weeks from 27 December 1858, which received mixed reviews (see *MW*, 1 January 1859, p. 10; *Times*, 7 January, p. 5, and 1 February, p. 6); the only new work presented was Adam's *Le toréador* (**1859**-1). A season opened at the Lyceum on 9 May 1860 but failed after three weeks (see *MP*, 10 May 1860, p. 5, and *Examiner*, 2 June, p. 342).

113   See William Weber, *Music and the Middle Class: The Social Structure of Concert Life in London, Paris and Vienna between 1830 and 1848* (2nd ed, Aldershot,

2004). The idea that the period 1795 to 1813 (the end of Haydn's residency to the foundation of the Philharmonic Society) represented a nadir in London concert culture has been challenged by Ian Taylor: see *Music in London and the Myth of Decline: From Haydn to the Philharmonic* (Cambridge, 2010).

114 Weber, *Music and the Middle Class*, p. xiv.

115 For further discussion, see William Weber, *The Great Transformation of Musical Taste: Concert Programming from Haydn to Brahms* (Cambridge, 2008), especially pp. 134–9; 184–90; and 216–19.

116 For focused discussion on two of the most prominent institutions of this period, see Cyril Ehrlich, *First Philharmonic: A History of the Royal Philharmonic Society* (Oxford, 1995), and Christina Bashford, *The Pursuit of High Culture: John Ella and Chamber Music in Victorian London* (Woodbridge, 2007).

117 For example, London's Sacred Harmonic Society, founded in 1832; it performed almost exclusively Protestant religious music, according with the policies of Exeter Hall's non-conformist management, where it performed from 1836 onwards.

118 Onslow (1784–1853) had English and French parents but lived mostly in France; his ancestry and social networks encapsulate eighteenth-century aristocratic cosmopolitanism. He was elected an honorary fellow of the Philharmonic Society in 1831, for which he composed his Second Symphony.

119 See *MW*, 12 March 1853, p. 156; 10 September, p. 577; 17 September, p. 592; 24 September, p. 605.

120 See *MW*, 31 March 1860, p. 201; 12 May, p. 297; 19 May, p. 314; 26 May, p. 331; 9 June, p. 366; 23 June, p. 393.

121 *MW*, 11 June 1840, p. 368.

122 *MW*, 18 June 1860, p. 377.

123 *MW*, 3 April 1845, p. 163; *Examiner*, 29 March, p. 197; see also *Times*, 28 March, p. 4; *LGa*, 29 March, p. 203; *Spectator*, same date, p. 306; *Observer*, 30 March, p. 2.

124 As a typical instance of 'middlebrow' entertainment, and exemplifying Victorian adaptation practice, it was performed at Drury Lane in a 'Grand Oriental Spectacle', with a superimposed narrative and featuring 'Mr Hughes's collection of elephants, camels, horses, ponies and bipeds' (*DN*, 6 April 1847, p. 4). Unadorned concert performances were given in London (*DN*, 27 October 1853, p.2); Manchester (*Manchester Times*, 20 November 1852, p. 5; 23 October 1858, p. 4); and Dublin (*FJ*, 2 February 1856, p. 3; 30 May 1857, p. 3). It was later revived in Birmingham (*MT*, 1 May 1897, p. 320).

125 *Bath Chronicle*, 13 January 1831, p. 3 (performance on 6 January). For the Leeds production see playbill for 31 May 1831 (www.leodis.net/playbills, accessed 31 January 2018). Subsequent performances, almost certainly not isolated, took place in August 1831, October 1837, October 1838 ('compressed into two acts'), and May 1839. For the Birmingham production, see Theatre Royal playbill for 14 May 1832 and later that month at BL, shelfmark mic.c.13137/playbills.

126 The writer censured a ballet-dancer's unduly short petticoats, advising her to 'add a little to the longitude of those essential portions of the female attire … and add considerably to the proprieties of the stage'.

127 Unusually, these performances appear only to have involved the stock company; they were supplemented by 'a new musical interlude entitled *French Washerwomen* … [and] the new laughable Eastern entertainment called *The Two Bears*'.

128 *FJ*, 5 June 1832, p. 2. The Woods played the two leading roles, Isabelle and Robert, in the Drury Lane production discussed above.

129 *FJ*, 2 July 1833, p. 3; *Caledonian Mercury*, 19 October, p. 3; Birmingham Theatre Royal playbill 5 January 1835 (Playbills Collection, LoB); Leeds Theatre playbill, 5 May 1835 (www.leodis.net/playbills). Except in Edinburgh, Diavolo and Zerlina were played by Joseph and Mary Ann Wood respectively.

130 In Birmingham, for example, performances can be traced by seven companies in twenty-one years between 1839 and 1907.

131 With reference to Dublin, see Paul Rodmell, '"The Italians are Coming": Opera in mid-Victorian Dublin' in Rachel Cowgill and Julian Rushton (eds), *Europe, Empire and Spectacle in Nineteenth Century British Music* (Aldershot, 2006), pp. 97–112.

132 See *Bristol Mercury*, 17 December 1853, p. 4 (performance on 14 December); *FJ*, 5 October 1857, p. 3 (performance on 1 October); *BDP*, 31 October 1870, p. 7 (performance on 29 October). *Le prophète* was also brought to Dublin on 6 September 1856 (see R C Levey, *Annals of the Theatre Royal, Dublin* (Dublin, 1880), p. 167).

133 *MW*, 20 April 1850, pp. 245–6.

134 *MW*, 18 May 1850, pp. 307–8. The writer stated that 'there is scarcely a bit in the whole of the *Crown Diamonds* which dwells in memory', earning the editorial rebuke, 'when he is more familiar with Auber's music, he will retract these hurried opinions'.

135 *FJ*, 23 April 1850, p. 3.

136 *SN*, 27 April 1850, p. 2.

137 *MW*, 20 September 1838, pp. 35–7 (from *Galignani's Messenger*); *MW*, 19 December 1846, p. 657; *Times*, 23 December, p. 7.

138 *MW*, 30 June 1840, p. 345. The reviewer nonetheless devoted almost 500 words to the work, whilst most other items were allocated one or two short sentences. He even suggested the parts had been incorrectly copied (unaware, presumably, of Berlioz's direction on the subject in the 'Marche au supplice' of the *Symphonie fantastique*).

139 *Spectator*, 20 March 1841, p. 279; *Examiner*, 21 March, p. 181; for a somewhat less hostile view, see *Times*, 16 March, p. 6.

140 *MW*, 12 February 1848, p. 97.

141 *Times*, 8 February 1848, p. 6.

142 *Observer*, 13 February 1848, p. 6.

143 *Athenaeum*, 12 February 1848, p. 170.

144 *Times*, 30 June 1848, p. 8. Davison's positivity was a *volte face*; he had previously written that Berlioz was '*la jeune France* run to seed – a very nightmare of music' (*MW*, 27 March 1845, p. 145).

145 *Times*, 25 March 1852, p. 5 (reproduced in *MW*, 27 March, pp. 202–4), and 29 April, p. 5.

146 *Critic*, 1 April 1852, p. 187.

147 *Leader*, 12 June 1852, p. 570.

148 *Athenaeum*, 12 June 1852, p. 658; *Times*, 10 June, p. 8 (reproduced in *MW*, 12 June, pp. 370–1).

149 See David Cairns, *Berlioz* (2 vols, London, 1999).

150 Cairns, vol. 2, p. 510, and Harold Rosenthal, *Two Centuries of Opera at Covent Garden* (London, 1958), pp. 102–3.

151 Victoria referred to *Cellini* as 'one of the most unattractive & absurd Operas, I suppose anyone could ever have composed ... The 2 1ʳˢᵗ acts kept us in fits of laughter, owing to their extreme foolishness' (Journal, 25 June 1853; see note 82).

152 *MP* quoted in *MW*, 2 July 1853, p. 416; *Spectator*, same date, p. 631.

153 *Times*, 27 June 1853, p. 5.

154 *Athenaeum*, 2 July 1853, p. 804.

155 Manns's early performances include 'Marche Hongroise' from *Faust* (1856), and *Le carnaval romain* and *Les francs-juges* (1857 and 1859); see Michael Musgrave, *The Musical Life of the Crystal Palace* (Cambridge, 1995), p. 104, and Chapters 3 and 4. Hallé gave 'Les sylphes' (*Faust*) seven times in his first two seasons, *Le carnaval romain* (1858) and *Les francs-juges* (1860).

156 *MW*, 27 March 1845, p. 145.

157 *MW*, 30 July 1859, p. 488.

3   From *Faust* to *Carmen*, 1863–78

The period 1863–78 is bookended by the London premieres of the two most popular nineteenth-century operas: Gounod's *Faust* and Bizet's *Carmen*. Their successes were unusually long-lasting: *Faust* appeared regularly at Covent Garden until the mid-1920s, while *Carmen*'s popularity remains undiminished. Although admiration of Gounod was ultimately time-limited, his impact in Victorian Britain was substantial and remains under-appreciated; his residency in London (1870–74) enabled him, like Mendelssohn, to network and better understand British musical taste. Bizet's success was inevitably different: almost unknown in Britain when he died in 1875, his posthumous reputation is dominated by *Carmen*.

Other new works, mainly *opéras comiques*, appeared in the West End, some being taken up by touring companies, but they reinforced rather than redefined perceptions of French music. Far greater impact was made by Offenbach's *opéras bouffes*. These works inaugurated a sustained British interest in this new, light-hearted genre, and facilitated a British counterpart, most prominently represented by the 'Savoy Operas' of Gilbert & Sullivan, which superseded mid-century burlesque.

While French music occupied an increasingly important place in British musical culture, until 1880 it remained mainly confined to the theatre: some modest successes of Gounod excepted, concert music made little impact, although it was in this period that French organ music started to become known. In parallel, Britain's political and cultural relationships with France were unavoidably redefined by the Franco-Prussian War, the collapse of the Second Empire and the establishment of the Third Republic.

Franco-British political and cultural relations 1863–78

Pragmatic alliances in Crimea and China, and the Cobden–Chevalier Treaty, created a greater sense of cordial stability in Franco-British political relations. While mutual (sometimes grudging) respect is perhaps a better summary than close friendship, a sense that Britain and France (even under Napoléon III) comprised Europe's most enlightened, liberal and advanced nations was sustained. British politicians wanted to maintain the European balance of power, requiring a stable and temperate France. Napoléon's diplomatic manoeuvres were scrutinised for signs of expansionism that might threaten British interests, while disagreements over the American Civil War, the Schleswig-Holstein Question and Italian unification were carefully managed and contained. Worldly British politicians noticed Prussia's growing ambition and confidence under its minister president, Otto von Bismarck, appointed in 1862, increasing belief that French strength was essential for European stability.

Meanwhile, French economic progress could scarcely fail to provoke admiration and some wariness. British views of France were defined primarily by knowledge of Paris, and visitors in the 1850s and '60s were confronted by the massive slum clearance and building programme managed by Georges-Eugène Haussmann. Projects included the creation of Place du Château d'Eau (now Place de la République) and roads radiating from it, new roads easing access to the Gare Saint-Lazare and Gare du Nord (itself completely rebuilt, and reopened in 1866), new parks in the Bois de Boulogne and Vincennes, and, inspired by Crystal Palace, the reconstruction of the central market (Les Halles) in iron and glass. The obliteration of substantial parts of old Paris, replaced by wide boulevards with buildings of uniform height and cream-coloured facades, cannot have failed to strike visitors. Although such schemes were inspired by London,[1] the British capital could hardly compete.

Concurrent with physical transformation came economic growth. Paris's expanding population facilitated small manufacturing enterprises producing bespoke goods for the bourgeoisie. Cafés and restaurants prospered, cementing the city's reputation for good living, while its status as a retail centre was augmented by the world's first 'department stores', including Bon Marché (1852, rehoused in 1869 in a massive building designed by Gustave Eiffel), Grand Magasin du Louvre (1855), Printemps (1865), and La Samaritaine (1870). These were supported by Paris's growing importance as a financial centre, attested by the establishment of the banks Crédit Lyonnais (1863) and Société Générale (1864).

In Britain, wide-ranging press coverage and literature cemented Paris's reputation as Europe's cultural and consumer centre. Charles Dickens included fulsome comments in *Household Words* (1850–59) and *All the Year Round* (1859–95), which both aimed at middle-class readers. Even before Haussmann's renovations started, Dickens described his excitement at reaching Paris in just twelve hours and delight in

> the crowds in the streets, the lights in the shops and balconies, the elegance, variety, and beauty of their decorations, the number of the theatres, the brilliant cafés with their windows thrown up high and their vivacious groups at little tables on the pavement.[2]

A direct reference to the improvements came in 1864: '[I]t's town and country both in one, and carved stone and long streets of high houses and gardens and fountains and statues and trees and gold'.[3] Reversing Georgian attitudes, W H Wills contrasted France's centralised government with London's hotch-potch administration, which meant that London would 'go on talking for and against improvement, for another half-century' while Paris steamed ahead.[4]

The emblematic climax of Napoléon's commercial and cultural agenda came in the 1867 Exposition Universelle. Easily surpassing recent equivalents, including the Great Exhibition, the 1867 event included not only technological and commercial innovations but also popular entertainments in a large park of national pavilions and curios. While France dominated, Britain was the second most prominent exhibitor, in a display of both commercial rivalry and combined economic strength. The *Saturday Review* was overawed: 'Its only fault or difficulty is that is too glorious, too sublime, too magnificent. We are affronted at our own insignificance'.[5] It deemed the Exhibition a warning for Britain:

> The year 1867 has done much towards establishing the boast that Paris is the capital of the world; and Paris certainly never behaved better, nor looked better, nor made more money ... [T]here was one impression from which no Englishman could escape; and it was that in many of the arts of life, and in all that makes up civilisation, we are not quite so excellent, and not so completely the salt of the earth, as we are apt to think.

Barely three years later, this edifice collapsed. Prussia's defeat of France came as a surprise to almost all spectators who assumed, even if forewarned by victories over Denmark (1864) and Austria (1866), that France's military prowess was of a different order. The French army's rapid capitulation and Napoléon's capture only increased amazement. The refusal of French politicians and parts of the populace to concede led to the German army's besieging Paris, the Empire's collapse, the Paris Commune and the tentative establishment of the Third Republic, all within a year. Britain remained steadfastly neutral, offering (unless either side invaded neutral Belgium) only mediation. Public opinion initially mainly favoured Prussia, viewing France, the traditional antagonist, as aggressor, although a minority, especially within the *beau monde*, supported France. As French humiliation became total, however, opinion shifted. Picturesque accounts of the exodus from Paris personalised and reified events for otherwise detached readers.[6] A new flow of refugees came to Britain: Empress Eugénie arrived in September 1870 and Napoléon himself in March 1871;[7] Gounod, Saint-Saëns and the painters Monet, Tissot, Pissaro and Sisley all relocated.[8]

The liberal *Fortnightly Review* sympathised with France; its regular contributor Frederic Harrison argued that Bismarck had an ulterior motive: 'Can we doubt that the real object of Germany is the dismemberment of France?'[9] Her defeat would destabilise the balance of power, a major threat when 'France and England [have] stood out as the guarantees in the long run of progress and of right'.[10] The *Musical World* stressed the calamitous cultural consequences of a prolonged siege:

> The very thought of the Louvre, the Imperial Library, and the Picture Galleries exposed to a bombardment, makes one's blood creep. We are so accustomed to think of Paris as the capital of luxury and pleasure, that we are apt to forget that it is the metropolis of letters and art – the very cynosure of civilisation ... To destroy the contents of Paris would be to tear out of the great book of humanity half of its noblest pages.[11]

The author even suggested that Parisians might destroy their own city, as Muscovites had done in 1812, rather than surrender.

Writing in February or March 1871, Edward Dicey presented a pessimistic picture:

> [T]he life has somehow gone out of Paris. It is not only that the streets are half empty, that carriages have well-nigh disappeared, that the shop-windows are bare of wares, that trade is obviously at a stand-still, that house after house is shut up, that there is no building going on ... [E]ven when order is restored under a settled government, I question whether the recovery of Paris will be a very rapid, or even a very thorough one.[12]

He was wrong. Despite the self-inflicted damage in May during 'la semaine sanglante', which brought the Commune to a traumatic end, and subsequent challenges, the new French government paid its war debt to Germany, whose troops gradually withdrew, and the city authorities started to rebuild: *belle époque* Paris quickly regained its reputation for *joie de vivre*, exemplified in such paintings as Renoir's 'Bal du moulin de la Galette' (1876) and Béraud's 'Une soirée' (1878). Nevertheless, France was politically and financially diminished. Presidents Thiers and MacMahon focused on domestic issues, leaving little time for foreign ventures that might antagonise others, Britain included; not until the 1880s did Franco-British relations come under serious strain, due to competing ambitions in Africa.

In cultural terms, proof of Paris's phoenix-like rebirth came with the Palais Garnier's completion in 1875.[13] Its opening was hailed as evidence of Paris's return and was covered extensively by the British press. Sheer size and chutzpah compelled a sense of awe; Chorley declared that 'the grand staircase will be the wonder of the world' but felt the auditorium was 'overdone ... the gilding is dazzling and bewildering, and the eye seeks for relief'.[14] Conclusive evidence of rejuvenation came in 1878 with the third Exposition Universelle. Deliberately conceived as a celebration of recovery, it was the biggest yet. *The Times* marvelled at the achievement:

> When France, in 1867, showed on the famous Champ de Mars a new world of industrial competition, surpassing for beauty, picturesqueness

and variety, all previous Exhibitions of the kind, the most perverse prophet of ill could not have imagined such a blow as only three years after she brought on herself ... [A]s little could it be imagined that in eight years more, France would surpass herself in the triumphs of peace, and look as if she had not lost a drop of blood or a piece of coin since her last exhibition.[15]

Britain was again a major exhibitor and a delegation, headed by the Prince of Wales, attended the official opening. A lifelong Francophile, Edward declared that

I am glad ... to think [that] we should have met here this evening in a country and in a city which have always received Englishmen with hospitality, and that though, not many years ago, there was a time when we were not so friendly as we are now, still that time is past and forgotten. The jealousy which was the cause of animosity has now, I feel sure, ceased for ever, and I am convinced that the *entente cordiale* which exists between this country and our own is one not likely to change.[16]

His sentiments were echoed in the press; Franco-British relations were arguably more cordial than ever before.

For increasing numbers of British people, France was, despite obvious differences, a nation whose values and culture complemented their own. A *Times* editorial in May 1878 romanticises lower middle-class Londoners, but its positive tone is noteworthy:

The friendship between the nations is now so close that we are entitled to believe that it would be impossible to stir up the ignorant jealousies and antipathies that so long made each regard the other as its natural enemy. There has been much visiting and going to and fro and this has been due in a large measure to these successive exhibitions. A young man, shopman or clerk, who has a week's holiday, is induced to go to Paris to see the Exhibition, and he finds the education of a new world so interesting that he repeats his visit again and again, and his friends follow his example. Those who know the popular sentiments of the inhabitants of London say that one of the strongest of them is sympathy with the French people.[17]

Some months later, the paper returned to the subject:

France is the country and Paris is the capital in which men feel most at home when they quit their native land. Intensely national as France is, its nationality is not exclusive ... It is cosmopolitan almost to a fault ... Hence French literature ... and French art ... is the common possession of Europe ... The French drama supplies the stages of Europe; French fiction is the literary recreation of the whole civilised world ... [W]e are glad to think that the friendship between England and France is one of long standing and of solid foundation. It has been knit the closer by the interchange of compliments, courtesies, and hospitalities during the present year ... [W]e must all hope it will never cease.[18]

The ascendancy of Gounod

Gounod's impact on Victorian musical culture has been under-appreciated. Its intensity was great, though ultimately neither sustained nor highly regarded; the pioneers of the 'British Musical Renaissance' thought Gounod's music vapid and sentimental, and wanted to smother it. In compositional terms, the success of Parry, Stanford and other teachers was almost comprehensive, aided, from the 1880s, by British enthusiasm for Brahms and Wagner; amongst concertgoers, though, Gounod remained immensely popular. Subsequently, having fallen comprehensively out of favour, Gounod's role has been largely ignored, even during the post-1980 resurgence of interest in nineteenth-century British music.

British knowledge of Gounod's music started building from around 1850. In that year, Chorley referred to 'one to whose compositions we are looking forward with such cordial expectation',[19] but it was probably John Hullah who introduced his music at St Martin's Hall on 15 January 1851, including the Sanctus and Benedictus from an unnamed Mass, 'Libera me' from the early Requiem (1843), and a 'dramatic scena', 'Peter the Hermit'.[20] Chorley wrote positively: the 'Libera me' was 'severe, dignified and solemn', the encored Sanctus 'original and beautiful ... [W]e recollect no melody sweeter or simpler ... or loftier in its tone'.[21] Davison took the opposite position: the Sanctus was 'common and theatrical, not to say vapid' and the 'Libera me' 'no more nor less than a collection of chords, progressions and modulations'; Davison viewed Gounod's orchestration as 'singularly monotonous and tame'.[22]

There was clear *schadenfreude* when *Sapho* (**1851**-4) flopped at Covent Garden, barely four months after its Paris premiere. Davison accused Gounod of securing performances through personal connection rather than objective merit and complained of 'want of melody, indecision of style, ineffective treatment of voices, inexperience in the use of instruments, accompanied by an affectation of originality'.[23] Chorley later blamed *Sapho*'s failure on audience conservatism, and 'the wrath and ridicule outpoured by most of the censors of the press', and argued that it was 'the best *first* opera ever written by a composer – Beethoven's *Fidelio* always excepted'.[24]

Progress was slow. Hullah remained an advocate, introducing the original version of *Ave Maria*, the arrangement of Bach's C Major Prelude (**1853**-2), which drew the rebuke: 'the forced alliance in which the greatest of contrapuntists is made to play second to M Gounod appeared to us simply ridiculous'.[25] The two early symphonies (appearing in reverse order, **1856**-1 and **1857**-4) did slightly better. The *Musical World* described the Second as 'cleverly instrumented [with] some brilliant passages and occasional power;

but a want of originality everywhere is apparent',[26] but others were more generous, especially regarding the last three movements; Chorley was again fulsome.[27] Regarding the First, the *Musical World* moved further, finding it 'fresh, easy and melodious throughout'.[28] The classicism of both works, recalling Mozart, Schubert and Beethoven, played well, though it led also to charges of regression. Hullah's performance of the *Messe solennelle à Sainte-Cécile* (**1860**-1) also gained mixed reviews; the *Morning Chronicle* opined that the Mass 'can never find favour with musicians. It is certainly ... well and clearly written ... [T]he themes, however, are almost invariably commonplace, and a want of invention, not to say inspiration, is apparent from first to last'.[29]

These early works' equivocal reception makes the runaway success of *Faust* especially surprising. British interest came early but inconsistently. Frank Chappell bought publishing rights in 1860 and issued a piano solo version shortly afterwards,[30] while, in the unlikely venue of the Canterbury Music Hall, Lambeth, a selection from the opera was performed for several weeks from 28 April 1860. This attracted little press interest; the Canterbury did not have sufficient social cachet, though both the *Era* and *Morning Chronicle* lauded the enterprise while questioning the merits of the music.[31] The 'Air des bijoux' started to feature occasionally in London concerts.

Despite successful performances in Paris, provincial France, Germany and Italy,[32] nothing further happened in Britain until 1863. At Covent Garden, Frederick Gye, uninterested, omitted *Faust* from his prospectus, leaving the field free for James Mapleson at Her Majesty's (**1863**-1) (see Figure 3.1).[33] Stunned by Mapleson's success, Gye engaged in a furious game of catch-up, producing his own version within three weeks. This *volte face*, the ensuing competition (echoing the practices of the 1830s) and comparison of productions augmented publicity and fuelled *Faust*'s reputation; there were twenty performances at Her Majesty's and eleven at Covent Garden that season.[34]

Critical reaction was somewhat at variance with evident public enthusiasm. Chorley, now personally acquainted with Gounod, was enthusiastic and declared that '*Faust* is the work of an original, vigorous genius – and by many degrees the best among modern operas';[35] he reserved his criticism for the performers and was unusual in finding Tietjens miscast as Marguerite. Even Davison acknowledged the opera's popular success:

> [I]f not remarkable for wealth of melodic invention, or for musical conception or contrivance of a very high order, [it] is full of merit, never, or very rarely, dull, and carried through triumphantly from first to last by a command of the resources of the orchestra which any modern composer might envy. That it has the elements of extraordinary success has been acknowledged; and that is will take its place among the most admired operas ... is more than probable.[36]

For the *Daily News* the (re-)conception of Goethe's well-known characters was a contributory factor, viewing Marguerite and Faust as manipulated

SCENE FROM THE NEW OPERA OF "FAUST," AT HER MAJESTY'S THEATRE.—SEE NEXT PAGE.

Fig 3.1 Gounod's *Faust*, Her Majesty's Theatre (*Illustrated London News*, 4 July 1863, p. 4)

victims who, in accordance with popular Victorian morality, still paid for their actions.[37] Regarding the music, the writer was more reserved:

> It is bold, powerful, and full of dramatic effect ... [but] while there is much that we listen to with admiration and delight, there are nevertheless things which do not please us ... The ear is assailed by dissonances unprepared and unresolved, sudden modulations and transitions into remote and unrelative [sic] keys, vague and equivocal chords, irregular rhythms, and other violations of the laws of harmony and melody – so that it is perplexed and confused if not positively offended. We confess our teeth have often been set on edge.

The *Observer* made a serious attempt to explain the work's popular success:

> It is difficult to say why the music of *Faust* pleases so thoroughly as it does at the first hearing ... Gounod's forms of melody are various, and not at all times pleasing, but in his warm and felicitous instrumentation ... there is an obvious and abiding charm ... Nor is the art of strongly and emphatically individualising the personages of the drama absent. The music given to the unfortunate Gretchen ...is singularly gentle and feminine, and typifies the spirit of one of the loveliest creations in the entire region of poetry ... The tenderness, too, of Faust, while pursuing his victim, has also its individuality; and so also the demoniacal *brusquerie* of Mephistopheles ... The ensembles are treated with signal dramatic effect: and the wild and reckless hilarity of the Kermesse, and the death of Valentine, may be mentioned as special examples of power in grouping complicated incidents and unceasing picturesqueness.[38]

Reviewers suggested various antecedents, Meyerbeer most frequently, but also Gluck, Rossini and Weber. Discussion of national attributes was largely lacking; like Berlioz, Gounod was not considered a representative or typical French composer. The *Illustrated London News* viewed Gounod's main characteristic as modernity, claiming that, 'though not a German, [Gounod] belongs nevertheless to the "Young Germany" of music, and may be classed in the same category as Berlioz, Liszt, and (above all) Wagner, whom in many respects he strongly resembles'.[39] Gounod's amalgam of styles facilitated *Faust*'s success: it appeared fresh, modern and varied, but with advantageously placed, effective and memorable numbers, which struck both aficionados and casual listeners. Prominent vocal melodies often using eight-bar periods, strong rhythmic drive derived from dance and military figures, varied genre references, and colourful, transparent orchestration balanced some complex dissonances, and passages of arioso and counterpoint. Effective characterisation and emotional expression, mentioned by almost all reviewers, particularly enhanced the work's appeal for British listeners.

Faust rapidly moved beyond the West End, thanks to Britain's expanding network of touring companies and Chappell's failure to register exclusive performing rights, meaning it could be performed without paying. Exceptionally, a new work with an excellent West End pedigree was freely available: managers took advantage, leaving Gounod out of pocket.[40] Mapleson gave *Faust* in Dublin (1 October 1863) and Manchester (16 December) while the *Era* noted performances by various companies using Chorley's English translation in Brighton, Leeds, Manchester, Birmingham, Dublin, Newcastle and Glasgow by the end of 1865. Further dissemination was achieved by selections and single items performed in concerts, by military bands at public functions, and a plethora of published arrangements.[41]

Faust's success secured Gounod's British reputation, resulting in sustained interest in his music. Subsequent operas, however, mostly failed to stand comparison. Mapleson's production of *Mireille* (**1864**-1), within four months of the Paris premiere, did not stand comparison; it was dropped shortly afterwards.[42] Curiously, Davison's view was largely positive; he thought the book poor and literary source obscure but the music 'happy and effective', containing 'a marked individuality of style', and the work overall 'genuine and charming'.[43]

With *Le médecin malgré lui* (**1865**-2) Gounod was unlucky: the Royal English Opera's production was well reviewed and its musical style, aligned with familiar *opéra comique*, should have had broad public appeal.[44] It received eighteen performances and was revived the following season, but the *Examiner*'s prediction that it would become one of the REO's stock operas was confounded by the company's bankruptcy less than a year later.[45] *La reine de Saba* (**1865**-4) was hampered by its transformation by H B Farnie into a secular cantata under the title *Irene* (an anagram of 'reine'!). The original's scriptural source rendered it unperformable on British stages due to censorship and unpalatable even as oratorio as it presented 'biblical characters in extremely secular action';[46] the removal of visual elements in concert performance left little more than a curio.[47]

Public and critical interest in *Roméo et Juliette* (**1867**-1) was greater and it became Gounod's second most successful opera in Britain. *Faust*'s popularity still counted significantly and Gye seized the opportunity to introduce *Roméo* within four months of its Paris premiere. Adelina Patti, then London's foremost soprano, played Juliette, greatly heightening excitement. Critics, though, felt that *Roméo* failed to surpass *Faust* in either innovation or memorability. Despite reviewers' raised sense of expertise when dealing with Shakespeare, Barbier and Carré's adaptation was well received, most writers judging that fundamental narrative and characterisation had survived sufficiently intact. Gounod, however, was criticised for some shallow characterisation; the *Pall Mall Gazette* opined that 'Juliet was something more than a very nice girl, and Romeo's passion for her was "more fierce and more inexorable far" than any sequence or combination of sounds invented by M Gounod could express',[48] while the *Standard* argued that Juliet's glittering waltz, 'Je veux vivre', was 'utterly unworthy of the character and the situation',[49] and the *Daily News* that the Act I ball scene was too 'suggestive of a modern Parisian ballroom'.[50] Chorley thought cuts had damaged the work's proportions and concluded: 'the predominance of monologue and recitative, mostly richly accompanied, presses on the patience';[51] Gounod had gone too close to Wagner for Chorley's liking. Despite audience excitement, critics were uncertain about the work's future; in the short and medium terms, the doubters were proved correct: the opera appeared only intermittently at Covent Garden until revived by Augustus Harris in 1889, when its fortunes changed (see Chapter 4).

Gounod was one of the first to leave Paris in 1870 and arrived in London with his family shortly after Napoléon's capture at Sedan on 1 September. His family returned home in May 1871 but Gounod, who had recently met the singer Georgina Weldon, with whom he had a long affair, remained in England until 1874.[52] Consequently, Gounod reoriented himself towards British musical tastes and started producing music in genres central to English [*sic*] culture: music for worship and more broadly based devotional songs for domestic use.

An early creation was *Gallia*, a short choral piece premiered at the South Kensington International Exhibition (**1871**-2). Circumstances could hardly have been more propitious: the Exhibition was a high-profile event in which music played a major role at the newly opened Albert Hall; new works by Pinsutti, Gounod, Hiller and Sullivan represented the hosts and Europe's three 'great musical nations'. The symbolism in *Gallia*, a setting of verses from *Lamentations*, was unmissable and thrown into sharper relief by Hiller's 'Grand March': one reviewer stated that

> While M Gounod told the sorrows of Paris in the fine biblical passage beginning 'How doth the city sit solitary that was full of people', Dr Hiller celebrated the triumph of Germany in a march as jubilant as M Gounod's anthem was despairing.[53]

There were few discordant notes; the *Musical World* even wondered if *Gallia* signalled that the French were abandoning 'the semi-theatrical wholly secular stuff which passes with our neighbours for sacred composition' and replacing it with music 'graver, more ennobled and more dignified'.[54] While the immediate circumstances provoked sympathy, *Gallia* received few subsequent performances; it was primarily a *pièce d'occasion*, whose operatic soprano solo rendered it impractical for the English church choirs to which it might otherwise have appealed.

During his remaining time in London, Gounod set about a series of self-promoting activities.[55] He was appointed conductor of the newly founded Royal Albert Hall Choral Society in late 1871 and conducted its first season.[56] The three concerts comprised mainly his own music and arrangements; the choir of almost 1,200 was inevitably unwieldy and reviews were generally moderate.[57] Gounod seems to have ingratiated himself with choir members, though, who participated in a 'Gounod Festival' at Crystal Palace on 27 July 1872,[58] but, shortly after, the choir was taken over by his friend and well-regarded choir director Joseph Barnby, while Gounod set up his own ensemble (comprising only 70 singers) which gave concerts at St James's Hall in spring 1873 and 1874.[59] Weldon appeared regularly as a soloist and almost certainly exploited her social connections for Gounod's benefit; audiences are regularly referred to as 'fashionable'. Some new works were introduced, including *Messe brève pour les morts* (**1873**-2) and *Funeral March of a Marionette* (**1873**-5).

In parallel, perhaps due to the influence of the notoriously litigious Weldon, Gounod publicly fell out with several British publishers, including Boosey, Novello and Chappell; disputatious correspondence regarding royalties, fees, promises made or broken, copyright and performing rights appeared regularly in the musical press.[60] Although Gounod and Weldon's affair remained the subject of gossip, some journals, notably the *Musical Standard*, lampooned Weldon and sneered at Gounod's activities (see note 59), while in January 1873 the *Musical World* published a thinly veiled attack, virtually accusing Gounod of desertion and Weldon of fomenting poor behaviour: 'The English public are intolerant of bores and M Gounod is in a fair way to be set down as the latest addition to the ranks of a questionable army'.[61] Finally, in June 1874, Gounod reconciled with his wife and returned to Paris. Beyond the circles of *cognoscenti* and chatterers, however, Gounod's time in London was perceived positively: upon leaving he was one of the French composers most familiar to amateur musicians and concert- and theatregoers, alongside Auber and Offenbach; his timely retreat doubtless helped to keep his public reputation intact.

Gounod's status was further enhanced by his popularity in English churches; he was the only nineteenth-century French composer accepted in this context. While his Catholic sacred music was unperformable in an Anglican environment,[62] the publication of English-language adaptations allowed supporters, such as Barnby and Stainer, to perform his works in liturgical services. Barnby's own edition of the 'St Cecilia' Mass was performed in 1866 at St Andrew's, Wells Street, where Barnby was choirmaster.[63] Further adaptations followed: of the first 50 of Novello's low-price 'Octavo' anthems, a series launched in the 1870s, eight are by Gounod, mainly taken from *Douze choeurs et une cantate*.[64] The first issued, 'O day of penitence', received a tolerably good review in the *Musical World*, which stated that Gounod's 'undoubted predilection and capacity for church music lead us to anticipate good results ... [and] in the present case expectation is gratified to some degree at least'.[65] While resident in London, Gounod also started to produce original settings of Anglican liturgical texts: the Te Deum for the Prince of Wales (note 57) was followed by a Benedictus, forming a complete Morning Service; an Evening Service followed. Works including the C major 'Ave verum corpus', 'Pater Noster' and *Messe brève pour les morts* (all 1873) were published in dual-language versions (the first as 'Hear my crying'). In the same year came several devotional songs for the domestic market, including 'Abraham's request' (published simultaneously as 'Prière d'Abraham') 'My beloved spake' (dedicated to Weldon, reissued in 1875 as 'Viens mon coeur'), 'Blessèd is the man' (Psalm 1, later published as 'Bienheureux') and, most successfully, the setting of Mrs Alexander's popular hymn 'There is a green hill far away'.[66] There is little evidence that Gounod altered his compositional style beyond ensuring that the music was performable by competent amateurs; rather, he influenced several English contemporaries (most notably Stainer, Barnby, Sullivan and Gaul).

Documenting the dissemination of this music is challenging, but surviving church music lists provide guidance and suggest that anthems in particular appeared regularly from the late 1860s, remaining popular until at least 1900; a representative example is given in Table 3.1. Stainer, who played for Gounod's choral concerts, was particularly supportive: Gounod's music was heard regularly at St Paul's Cathedral, where Stainer was organist, from early 1873, replacing much Restoration and eighteenth-century repertory.[67] Gounod was one of three modern composers, alongside Goss and Sullivan, commended by Stainer at the Church Congress at Brighton in 1874, who argued that 'there runs through his music a true Church feeling'.[68]

Gounod's entrepreneurship served him well and, when he left London, his British reputation was secure. Although he continued working on operas for Paris, he knew that in London, where his reputation still depended on *Faust*, theatre music was an unlikely source of income; nor was he established as a composer of oratorios or cantatas, fields of paramount importance to British musical culture. By focusing on liturgical music and devotional songs, Gounod charted a clear path to success that extended well beyond *Faust*; this reorientation was imposed but Gounod seized the opportunity without

Table 3.1 Selected works by Gounod performed in British cathedrals January to June 1874.

Date	Work	Cathedral
11 January	Blessed is He	Durham
18 January	Sing Praises	St Asaph
15 March	Send out thy light	Ely
22 March	Sing ye praise	Norwich
	I waited for the Lord	Norwich
29 March	All ye who weep	Llandaff
	Blessed is He	Norwich
4 April	Nicene Creed	Norwich
10 May	Send out thy light	Chester
27 June	Morning Service in C	St Paul's
	Evening Service in G	St Paul's

Source: 'Service Lists', published weekly in *MS*

compromising his musical style. He would later tackle the oratorio genre with *The Redemption* and *Mors et vita* (see Chapter 4).

'An evil sign of the times': Offenbach and *opéra bouffe*

The manner of Offenbach's establishment in Britain contrasts markedly with Gounod's. Focused on Paris, Offenbach showed only occasional active interest in Britain: success was achieved through the sheer vivacity and memorability of his music, which quickly entered popular consciousness.

The earliest British encounters with Offenbach were made by visitors to Paris's Exposition Universelle in 1855, which coincided with the opening of *Les Bouffes Parisiens*.[69] This spurred John Mitchell to emerge from retirement and engage Offenbach's company at the St James's Theatre (20 May to 14 July 1857). The *Leader*'s preview stated that the troupe 'perform the wildest, and most extravagant farces, interspersed with the gayest, the prettiest, and most *piquante* music', while cautioning that '[t]o enjoy their fun and frolic one must not only be thoroughly at home in the French language but … in Paris life, and manners and slang'.[70] According to Andrew Lamb, eleven of Offenbach's one-act shows were performed, plus eight others, including Mozart's *Der Schauspieldirektor*.[71] As escapist entertainment, the venture succeeded; the St James's upper-class audience, probably supported by the French community in nearby Soho, was well versed in Parisian culture, although the most popular work, *Les deux aveugles* (**1857**-1), was a primarily visual comedy about two 'blind' buskers competing on a Seine bridge.

Of Offenbach's music, the *Era* commented, 'the sparkling little ballads which ever and anon light up the dialogue with a sort of sunshiny effect, give great charm to the action', while the *Morning Chronicle* noted that 'in more than one place the [music] is deserving of higher praise than that of being merely amusing – it is really good', betraying its author's modest expectations.[72] Music journals generally felt the venture beneath them; 'sparkling' was readily used but otherwise Offenbach's music attracted little critical appraisal, with attention focused on plotting and actors, particularly the comedian Etienne Pradeau. As with the Brussels *opéra comique* seasons, the ensemble's professionalism was commended and used as a stick to beat local performers:

> If an English actor has a secondary or unimportant part to play, he often scamps it … A Frenchman never does this. If he only has to play a sentry, and not speak a word, he will devote all his energies to making himself look a natural and complete sentry, and not like a strange hybrid 'super'.[73]

The St James's status guaranteed press coverage and, despite competing against two grand opera seasons, attendance was good and the performances considered excellent specimens of their kind.

More works were introduced, initially with indifferent receptions but highly successfully after 1865.[74] The contemporaneous expansion of West End theatre provision enabled this process, as demand for novelties, especially those suitable for middlebrow audiences, increased rapidly.[75] Prior to 1868, the original St James's season excepted, Offenbach's works were given in English, with the need to retain the patronage, especially that of the middle class with moderate disposable incomes, resulting in productions that were heavily adapted, sanitised and shortened. *Le mariage aux lanternes* (**1860**-2) provoked only passing interest,[76] but a substantial selection from *Orphée aux enfers* ran at the Oxford Music Hall for several months in 1864, although it attracted little press attention.[77] Nevertheless, Laurence Senelick argues that these performances were Offenbach's 'break-through' moment, as he was now 'regarded by English managers as a source of whistleable melody', and particularly suited to music-hall performers.[78]

In James Planché's complete adaptation at Her Majesty's the following year, *Orphée* was the first of Offenbach's full-length works to appear in Britain (**1865**-5). Press interest was greater as both venue and adapter were well-regarded although, as a pantomime proxy, *Orpheus in the Haymarket* was still viewed as light entertainment. Halévy and Crémieux's *risqué* humour was toned down and Planché employed his standard 'burlesque' style but Offenbach's music was performed almost complete. Overall, the adaptation was anodyne, aimed at audiences eager to be entertained but neither shocked nor offended; Chorley approved, welcoming Planché's more chaste wit, compared to that of some competitors.[79] Though essential to the production's success, Offenbach's music received little direct attention; the handy epithet 'sparkling' appeared in *The Times*.[80]

From this point, interest grew rapidly; Offenbach's works were produced regularly and his music, according to Kurt Gänzl, was 'filched liberally by the compilers of burlesques to re-set again and again with fresh lyrics, and almost any theatre showing musical *pasticcio* included at least one of his melodies in its score'.[81] *Barbe-bleue*, burlesqued as *Bluebeard repaired*, appeared within four months of its Paris premiere (**1866**-1); the *Observer*'s balanced and informed review reckoned that 'there is scarcely a passage of music that is not lively and characteristic, whilst even in the greatest extravagances, a delicious tone of melody is preserved. Never has an *opéra bouffe* been so well given on the London stage'.[82] Francis Burnand's adaptation of *La belle Hélène* quickly followed (**1866**-2),[83] but to a lukewarm reception due to weak performers: '[O]ur artists want more training in the school of *opéra bouffe* before they can do complete justice to the sparkling [!] qualities of music so light and vivacious as that of M Offenbach'.[84]

While Offenbach's music normally survived largely intact, adaptation continued, original satire and innuendo typically being lost in the process (*pace* Senelick, the works were 'fumigated').[85] John Russell's production of *La Grande-Duchesse de Gérolstein* (**1867**-2), adapted by Charles Kenney, eschewed earlier burlesquing but fared little better with critics. Some music was already familiar, individual songs having crossed the Channel, while thousands of visitors to the Paris Exposition had seen the original. The *Observer* criticised the 'Bowdlerising process to which the text has been subjected',[86] but the *Orchestra* prophesied, nevertheless, that London audiences would not appreciate the work's ethos:

> The music is excellent of its kind – light, sparkling [!!], effervescent, French to the last degree ... We are about to introduce it to our matter-of-fact islanders, to audiences which require their comedy, like their liquor, full of body, ... people who derive their notions of the comic stage from slangy puns and breakdowns ... The idea of doing Offenbach in London is not new, but success in performing him, if it be achieved, will be unprecedented.[87]

The growing sense that adaptations were insufficient led to the invitation of Hortense Schneider, the *doyenne* of *Les Bouffes Parisiens*, and a complete French company to present Offenbach *au naturel* at the St James's (opened 22 June 1868). This proved controversial, as naïve audience members came face-to-face with previously expunged sexual innuendo; if the venture crowned Offenbach's reputation in fashionable London, it did so through titillation rather than critical approval. As Senelick argues, *opéra bouffe* introduced new character types: male leads were typically good-looking but comically unaware or stupid, while young female leads were 'clever, witty, alert; creature[s] of common sense bordering on wisdom ... [and] often from the proletariat ... [so] not constrained by codes of etiquette'.[88] Mature female roles, though, were most likely to shock as '[t]hey are granted the right to be capricious, moody, flawed, insufferable, authoritarian, jealous, angry, selfish, mendacious and desirable ... Most of all, however, they are endowed with libidos that find fulfilment'.[89] Schneider presented these mature roles with gusto and many London journalists were shocked (or affected to be), causing a flow of criticism and moral indignation directed not only at her but also the St James's' audience.

Opening with *La Grande-Duchesse* (played in opposition to Kenney's version, then at the Olympic), the *Orchestra* acknowledged Schneider's uniqueness:

> [N]o-one controverts her talent, even among those who often deplore the direction in which this is exerted. It is just to state in England that she has considerably modified that exuberance of demeanour that entrenched upon the unseemly. She does not dance the *cancan* [see below], [and] she is decorous in her love-making with Fritz ... Consequently, she was decent, to the obvious disgust of some of the audience.[90]

This was all too much for 'N D' in the *Musical World*:

> Not only was [the] theatre crowded on the first night sacred to Offenbach, but the list of visitors published in the papers looked like a compressed

edition of the Gotha Almanac, enriched with excerpts from the peerage ... The question is whether this is the sort of work that ought to command a general outburst of aristocratic enthusiasm ... In the fact that *La Grande Duchesse*, ably executed, is successful, there is nothing extraordinary. The sort of success that attends it is an evil sign of the times.[91]

Such criticisms became more pointed when Schneider appeared in *La belle Hélène*. The normally liberal *Observer* deemed her performance 'most remarkable for its astounding audacity ... [Schneider] makes use of every possible vulgarity of action that could be learnt in the worst haunts of Parisian coarse depravity'.[92] This may be less severe than it initially appears; the *Saturday Review* agreed that Schneider was vulgar, but acquitted her of immorality:

[A]lthough the piece itself compelled the actress to do a good deal more in the way of ogling, embracing, and hand-squeezing than an average husband would exactly like his wife to go through ... there was nothing in the mere doing of it so very atrocious ... The worst part, indeed the essential and crowning characteristic, of her acting seems to us, not its impropriety but its startling vulgarity ... The only class of characters which we can fancy Mdlle Schneider really suiting or excelling in is that ... in which some cook or housemaid suddenly becomes a countess and does not know how to carry off her novel position.[93]

Schneider's 'coarseness', meanwhile, was attributed to crude technique: on first seeing Paris, she allegedly gave a double-take similar to one 'a third-rate tragedy queen at a provincial theatre gives at discovering the strawberry-mark of her long-lost son'.

The 'can-can' caused particular excitement and censure. Omitted from Planché's version of *Orphée*, it was first performed in London by the well-known Finette at the Lyceum pantomime, causing only amusement.[94] The Olympic and St James's productions of *La Grande-Duchesse* also incorporated tame versions, by a ballerina and Schneider respectively, the latter provoking 'loud shouts from a not unimportant section of the stall occupants for [her] to kick her clothes higher'.[95] Despite her restraint, the mere act of her dancing, coupled with spectator encouragement, induced press criticism, though perhaps directed more at the audience than Schneider herself.[96]

In the midst of such distractions, Offenbach's music was often forgotten or regarded merely as a vehicle for Schneider, becoming tarnished as result; a sense of *ennui* is often also apparent, and a feeling that Offenbach was failing to 'advance'. A charitable assessment stated that the music of *La Grande-Duchesse*

is of the same taking order as Monsieur Offenbach's other works. In fact, there is much similarity in all; but we do not quarrel with this; the bright sparkling airs ring in our ears long after we quit the theatre; and as we go humming them on our way home we find that we have glided from *La belle Hélène* to *Orphée*, or to the *Grande Duchesse*, the last and newest favourite.[97]

Whilst acknowledging Offenbach's popularity, the writer argued that, '[t]here is always the danger that [his works] are vitiating and corrupting the taste which would appreciate better things. It would be better for art, society – everyone concerned in them – if they were at once expunged from the *repertoire*'.

Such indignation did not deter London's theatre managers; popular demand was formidable, and the easy memorability of Offenbach's music was a key factor. 1870 saw a rush of English adaptations of not only his works but also two by his contemporary and rival Hervé (see below), who had temporarily relocated to London.[98] Schneider introduced *La Périchole* (**1870**-5) to a generally positive reception,[99] and also visited in 1869 and 1872; there was no dimming of interest:

> [H]er voice was weaker and her action stronger. She now 'underlines' every *double entendre* and emphasises every equivocal gesture. What before was suggestive is now openly impudent. It is natural that the devil-may-care confidence of Mdlle Schneider should attract many men, but we cannot understand what fascination ladies can find in such a performance. Nay, we cannot but wonder why highly-bred women like to look upon a person who exhibits their sex in the most odious aspect … Such a performance would not be tolerated even at Christmas-time at an East End theatre … Nevertheless, ladies who would on no account go to the Alhambra think nothing of taking stalls at the Princess's. Of a truth, the inconsistencies of English morality are astounding.[100]

Yet, when Schneider toured in 1870 (visiting Dublin, Liverpool, Glasgow, Manchester, Birmingham and Bristol), reactions were less prudish.[101] In Ireland, Cardinal Cullen's thinly veiled condemnation did not deter theatregoers; nor did the performances cause press outrage.[102] *Saunders's Newsletter* commented, 'there was nothing … to offend the taste or delicate feelings of the most fastidious playgoer', and the *Freeman's Journal* concurred, finding 'nothing very wicked in *La Grande-Duchesse*. In many respects it is far more severely decent than the English version which we had here some months ago', although the writer claimed the production had been modified in unspecified ways to accommodate local sensibilities.[103] The 'can-can' again proved controversial, being a dance 'for which no respectable mind could offer a shred of defence', although 'most of the females in the dress circle used their glasses during the entire affair and its repetition – for it was redemanded – and seemed most anxious not to lose the least gesture in a performance which was a degradation to their sex'.[104]

Offenbach's popularity peaked around 1870 and then plateaued through the decade but, as his output slowed, his reputation was sustained by established rather than new works.[105] His only music composed specifically for London, the pantomime *Dick Whittington*, was a collaboration with Farnie (**1874**-6). This ran until May 1875, but not due to its music; Offenbach was ignorant of the genre's English conventions and the *Era* reckoned that Sullivan or Clay would have done better.[106] As such works typically turned over annually, there was little prospect of an after-life; Offenbach was paid handsomely but his direct association with the Alhambra encouraged a sense of decline in press reviews.[107]

Offenbach's last major success was Farnie's adaptation of *Madame Favart* (**1879**-3). Focused on disguise and amorous pursuit valiantly resisted rather than extra-marital flirting, it contained nothing to offend, and was described as 'so amusing in its plot and in its incidents' that a long run was prophesied, despite the composer appearing 'to have lost the art of inventing original and agreeable melodies ... [but h]e knows how to hash up old materials with piquant seasoning, and he trusts to strongly marked dance rhythms to keep the audience in good humour'.[108] *Madame Favart* ran for over 500 performances, was revived subsequently and toured the provinces.[109] Offenbach's last *opéra bouffe*, *La belle Lurette* (**1881**-7), was given posthumously by a Parisian company but generated only moderate interest; that the most striking musical moment was the interweaving of Strauss's 'Blue Danube' waltz seemed emblematic of the composer's decline.[110]

The British appetite for *opéra bouffe* drew other French composers to London (see Figure 3.2). The first was Offenbach's rival in Paris, Florimond Ronger, commonly known as Hervé, a jack-of-all-trades who composed, wrote libretti, sang, acted, directed and designed. *Chilpéric* (**1870**-1) was immensely successful and was followed shortly by *Le petit Faust* (**1870**-3); taking temporary refuge in London, Ronger also collaborated with Alfred Thomson on a burlesque pantomime, *Aladin II* (**1870**-9). Despite the first two's successes, Ronger never approached Offenbach in popularity and his career remained centred on Paris. Of greater importance was Charles Lecocq. Well-established in France, he came to notice in Britain with the runaway success of *La fille de Madame Angot* (**1873**-4), performed by the Brussels *Fantaisies-Parisiennes*. Although thought frivolous and somewhat *risqué*, there was no suggestion of immorality, and it gained consistently good reviews. The music, judged both tuneful and sophisticated, made up for a weak book and prolix dialogue: the *Musical Standard* argued that

> Lecoq's music is decidedly pretty ... Moreover, he shows considerable knowledge of dramatic effect and can write graceful melodies when required ... His harmonies are always effective, his style of writing being of the modern French school, as represented at the *Opéra Comique*.[111]

Madame Angot overshadowed other works in the Brussels season,[112] and, before the year's end, two English adaptations had appeared (by Byron (Philharmonic, Islington), and Farnie (Gaiety)). The work was a gift for

Fig 3.2 'Composers of *Opéra Bouffe*': Offenbach, Lecocq and Hervé (*Graphic*, 28 November 1874, p. 525)

touring companies: in 1874, the *Graphic* noted that there were four different versions in the provinces, while Gänzl claims six;[113] it remained in the repertory for many years. *Giroflé-Girofla* (**1874**-4), also introduced by the Brussels troupe, was equally successful; most critics viewed this as more elevated, and closer to *opéra comique* than *opéra bouffe*, with Auber as progenitor, not

Offenbach; again, translated into English, the work proved highly popular on the provincial circuit.[114] Although Lecocq remained active, only a few other works reached Britain, and none made the same impact as his first two successes.[115]

It took almost ten years after his establishment in Paris for Offenbach's music to become widely known in Britain, although solo piano arrangements appeared in London publishers' catalogues from the early 1860s.[116] From 1865, however, Offenbach's popularity grew rapidly and his full-length *opéras bouffes* became an essential part of West End and then provincial repertory: it is no understatement that between 1865 and 1880 he was the single most popular theatre composer in the country. As his production rate slowed, his dominance ended, and his decline was almost as rapid as his rise. Offenbach's most successful works were revived occasionally but had to compete against those of Lecocq, Hervé and Maillart, and then Planquette and Audran, plus an increasingly vibrant school of British operetta, dominated by Gilbert & Sullivan. Overall, Offenbach's music was rapidly superseded after his death until a modest revival in the late 1900s (see Chapter 5).

Offenbach's works were not originally regarded as morally suspect as English adapters toned down the characters' behaviour and replaced Parisian innuendo with British burlesque. Suggestive actions were made sufficiently anodyne to ensure that, even when *risqué*, they inclined to 'good taste'. Schneider's appearances led commentators – who could not ignore her, given the fashionable audience she attracted – to revise their views:

> There was a time … when society knew not Offenbach. Society may have been, even then, far from musically pure, but – it knew not Offenbach. That is to say, it was free from the influence of one whom, by uniting a certain form of art with positive absurdity and comparative indecency, not only degrades art in all its forms, but makes it attractive in its degradation … M Offenbach is with us … and Schneider is his prophetess … When one devil gains an entrance, seven others are pretty sure to follow.[117]

Schneider was both this reaction's catalyst and its initial victim, but Offenbach soon became the target, as the *fons et origo* of *opéras bouffes* bearing responsibility for their aesthetic. Nevertheless, it seems likely that some moral outrage was false indignation pandering to the assumed values of middle-class readers, given that as much – sometimes more – censure was directed at *beau monde* audiences as Schneider herself. Schneider's approach – flirtatious, pert and salacious – undoubtedly contrasted with her British contemporaries (even though music hall veterans such as Emily Soldene and Julia Mathews were well acquainted with lively audiences) but Schneider clearly also tailored her performances, perhaps even nightly, as she gauged reactions. Nevertheless, a narrative still emerged that the morally superior middle classes were either ignorant of Offenbach or deliberately avoided him. When Boosey published some solo songs in 1870, the *Graphic* commented that

M Offenbach's operettas attract the upper ten thousand, and his tunes are whistled by the lower million. But the serious part of the 'great middle class' regard him as a musical *enfant perdu*; one who has gone astray and allied himself with Schneider ... Hence an Offenbachian song has to them a flavour compounded of Cremorne and the Alhambra.[118]

The original words, 'the most innocent translation of which would be suspected of lurking naughtiness', were replaced with inoffensive versions by Kenney. As operetta, taken in its widest definition, would come to be regarded as archetypally middlebrow entertainment, its assignment here to the upper and working classes is striking. Moreover, the easy memorability of Offenbach's melodies meant they were widely re-used:

With all the best numbers [of *La Périchole*] we are perfectly familiar in this country ... [T]he catching air which La Périchole and Piquillo sing ... in the market place has been ground on every organ in the metropolis and may daily be heard as the Guards' band proceed from St James's Palace to the Wellington Barracks.[119]

The immense success of *opéra bouffe*, at least in English versions, suggests that either substantial parts of the middle class were not as censorious as journalists thought they were or ought to be, or that Schneider's individuality was greater than critics allowed; the former is the more appealing hypothesis.

Even adapted, however, *opéras bouffes* reinforced stereotypical images of Frenchness. The frequently used words 'sparkling' and 'naughtiness' played directly to British views of French levity, wit, *joie de vivre* and greater degrees of sexual openness and female autonomy than were sanctioned at home. Such tropes were scarcely new: the reach of *opéra bouffe*, though, surely reinforced British perceptions of the French at a broader level. While 50 or 100 years earlier, French fiction influenced British views, the decline of French literacy noted by Dames and Cohen increased the importance of other forms of engagement; tourism's role has been widely recognised but, especially outside musicological circles, that of *opéra bouffe* much less so, despite being familiar to an immeasurably greater number of people than visited Paris, or were acquainted with French literature or art. Offenbach's German origins were ignored, and his work became a quintessential representation of Frenchness and *la vie parisienne*.

Bizet and *Carmen*

While *Faust* appeared following advance publicity and the publication and performance of extracts and arrangements, *Carmen* arrived virtually unknown. Nor was its composer familiar, having previously merited only passing comments in the 'Musical Gossip' or 'Waifs' sections of the press. Indeed, between the London premieres of *Faust* and *Carmen*, French 'grand opera' and *opéra comique*, in contrast to *opéra bouffe*, passed through a quiet period, with only a few notable new works appearing, such as Meyerbeer's *L'Africaine* (**1865**-3), Thomas's *Hamlet* (**1869**-1), and Massé's *Galatée* (**1872**-3). Mapleson took the unusual step of reviving Gluck's *Iphigénie en Tauride* at Her Majesty's in 1866, while, at Covent Garden, Italian versions of *Le domino noir* and *Les diamants de la couronne* appeared in 1870 and 1873 respectively. Extended seasons of *opéra comique* were given at the Gaiety in 1870 and 1875, the Strand in 1872 and the Philharmonic, Islington, in 1875.

Carmen's Paris premiere received barely a glance in London other than from the *Athenaeum*, which noted a success but declared that 'Bizet's score has some strong points, but it is too laboured and ambitious', before unwittingly adding, 'Still, great things are expected from this young composer'.[120] Bizet's death three months later provoked no more coverage. Following successful European productions, British interest increased, though it was only in March 1878 that plans to perform *Carmen* in London became public when both Gye and Mapleson included it in their prospectuses, the former with Patti in the title role. Mapleson contracted Minnie Hauk, the American mezzo-soprano who had played Carmen in Brussels to significant acclaim. Gye, who, in retrospect, clearly misjudged the situation (as with *Faust*), dropped *Carmen*, giving Flotow's *Alma l'incantatrice* and Massé's *Paul et Virginie* (**1878**-7) instead, and left the field open for Mapleson, who presented *Carmen* after several postponements, in Italian and with recitatives replacing spoken dialogue (**1878**-9).

Despite being the work of a virtually unknown composer, critical reaction was overwhelmingly positive, although most interest alighted upon Carmen's character and Hauk's portrayal.[121] 'Her representation ... is one of the most remarkable things seen upon the stage in the present decade. It is perhaps the first operatic character with any marked or especial individuality,' stated the *Morning Post*.[122] This idea of Carmen being 'new' was widely replicated, sometimes with a sense of revulsion, so far was she from the meek and innocent heroines of English romantic opera, or the pious but misled Marguerite in *Faust*. Bizet's decision to cast Carmen as a mezzo-soprano rather than as a coloratura also made an impact. Although, as Susan Rutherford illustrates, the characters of *prime donne* had started to broaden beyond the *ingénue* stereotype, Carmen still came as a surprise.[123] In reviews of Hauk's portrayal there are partial parallels with Schneider, but Hauk was treated more leniently; few reviewers thought she lost propriety, while Carmen's fate raised her above the frivolous characters portrayed by Schneider in narratives of little depth.[124] The *Illustrated London News* asserted that '[t]he pert flippancy, the coquettish levity, and heartless frivolity of the part were admirably suggested, while still preserving a certain external grace and refinement of manner'.[125] The *Illustrated Sporting and Dramatic News* was unusual in its partial dissent, arguing that Hauk took little trouble

> to soften the unpleasing characteristics of the part, and seemed to think
> it indispensable that Carmen should appear coarse and vulgar, as well

as immoral. This view of the character may be defended, but we shall hope to see the part played in England with equal piquancy, coupled with greater refinement.[126]

Despite some audience crossover between Her Majesty's and St James's, the presentation of *Carmen* as grand opera smoothed Hauk's passage: in the Italian context, equivocal female characters were more familiar and subject to different scrutiny.

While Hauk's performance attracted greatest interest,[127] Bizet's music was also substantively appraised, with mainly positive results. Gounod, Meyerbeer and Wagner's influences were detected, the latter, though, only due to the recurring 'fate' motif and periodic use of more freely structured passages. The *Standard* praised the individualised musical characterisation, while the *Morning Post* deemed the work 'full of character and on the whole remarkable originality', asserting that Bizet 'has not written a single weak bar'.[128] The *Illustrated Sporting and Dramatic News* was one of several journals noting the prevalence of 'local colour' and 'Spanish rhythms', but continued, '[Bizet's] melodies are fresh and original, and are embellished by orchestral accompaniments of the utmost piquancy and grace'.[129] The *Examiner* detected two idioms, those of Spain and the Romani, and thought Bizet self-indulgent but continued,

> this fact ought not to blind us to the great beauties of an opera which, from a dramatic point of view, is the most important work the modern French school has produced since *La muette de Portici*, with the exception only of certain scenes in Gounod's *Faust*.[130]

Henry Frost reckoned that Bizet had compromised his Wagnerian principles by employing musical forms that 'might have been written by Auber', but had still exhibited an 'individuality truly remarkable' in adapting them to his own purposes; he singled out the rhythmic ostinato of the 'Habañera' and the descending sequence in 'Les tringles des sistres tintaient' for particular praise.[131] Critical consensus was that Bizet had produced a work of striking individuality and freshness worthy of joining the established repertory; for once, their advocacy was reflected by reality.

Carmen's popularity was evident immediately: despite its late appearance, Mapleson gave it twelve times that season, and it was repeated in the autumn with Zelia Trebelli as Carmen, as Hauk and Mapleson were touring the United States. Trebelli's portrayal aligned more with conventional expectations: the *Era* believed that 'she did not so completely realise the conception of the capricious gipsy girl as did Mdlle Hauk', but the *Academy* found her more musical and dramatically agreeable: 'the coarser features of the gypsy are gently toned down. The picture is less vivid, and therefore less repulsive'.[132] Trebelli, it seems, relied more on vocal quality and technique, less on physicality, and implicitly preserved a greater sense of conventional femininity than Hauk.

English-language productions followed. Carl Rosa, in mounting the first of these (Her Majesty's, 5 February 1879), decided to return *Carmen* to – or take it beyond – its *opéra comique* roots; Henry Hersee's liberal translation restored the spoken dialogue and Rosa recruited Selina Dolaro to play Carmen, an interesting choice given Dolaro's previous focus on light roles in *opéra bouffe*.[133] She received a variety of notices; most praised her characterisation and pluck but agreed that her voice was insufficiently strong.[134] Earlier reservations regarding the opera, however, had been swept away: the *Musical World* referred to the 'intrinsic charm of both story and music', and quoted an unnamed critic who stated that 'those who persist in thinking it naughty, are ready to grant that it is also nice', and 'the chief strength of Bizet's music does not lie in its national flavour so much as in the originality of description and expression'.[135]

Rosa retained exclusive rights to perform *Carmen* in English in the West End but sold a share in provincial rights to another *opéra bouffe* singer, Emily Soldene, who performed *Carmen*, along with *Geneviève de Brabant* and *La fille de Madame Angot*, in an extensive tour (starting at Leicester, 1 May 1879). Of a subsequent performance in Birmingham, a local critic stated: 'Madame Soldene herself, though not physically an ideal Carmen, is the life and soul of the opera – full of reckless Bohemian spirit, dash and vigour; but her acting is quite free from any suggestion of coarseness or vulgarity'.[136] To the music, however, 'though fairly effective, [she] did less obvious and invariable justice'. The critic reiterated earlier views of the opera:

> [I]t is the most dramatic, most characteristic, most successful opera, which has been produced since Gounod's *Faust*, not even excepting the works of Wagner ... Bizet possessed a dramatic faculty, a verve and command of local colouring rarely equalled, and never surpassed, by any of his contemporaries.

It was Soldene's version that was first seen by most provincial theatregoers; she performed *Carmen*, alongside two or three *opéras bouffes*, in tours in 1880, 1882 and 1883, covering 46 towns and cities, from Aberdeen to Plymouth and Dublin to Hull.[137] From 1880, Rosa also included *Carmen* in his touring repertory; between 1884 and 1899, doubtless determined to retain a box office certainty, his company exercised a virtual monopoly on English-language performances. The newly established Moody-Manners Company gave *Carmen* from 1900 and James Turner added it to his troupe's repertory in 1901. After Soldene's tours which, given their nature, almost certainly reached a broader audience than would otherwise have been the case, Rosa's troupes sustained interest; *Carmen* was included in every tour from 1880 to 1900. In Italian, *Carmen* also appeared regularly in the West End: after introduction at Covent Garden in 1882, it was produced every year but two until 1908, and in French from 1890. By 1914, there had been 130 performances in the main spring seasons; after a dip in the inter-war years, it became a regular fixture once again after 1945.

Beyond theatre: other French music in Britain 1863–78

The status and nature of French music performed in concerts remained essentially unchanged in this period, being overwhelmingly dominated by opera extracts, principally overtures and arias. The repertory of orchestral concerts, which played an expanding role in British musical culture, focused increasingly on 'great' works by 'classical' (and typically deceased) composers, but no French music was added to this corpus.[138] Although living French composers had started to produce significant amounts of instrumental music, little of it crossed the Channel; in writing vocal music specifically for British audiences during his exile, Gounod was a rare exception (see above). Berlioz was largely neglected, even by Manns and Hallé, who retained the works they had introduced up to 1860 but subsequently added little more; considering prevalent perceptions, this is unsurprising (see below). French music was just as sparsely represented in concerts of chamber music and solo recitals. Regarding French music in general, Hallé's Manchester programmes are in many ways indicative, despite certain oddities: opera overtures were a staple ending for selection programmes and include 80 performances of 20 Auber overtures between 1858 and 1870.[139] Hallé also presented less familiar music, including Gluck's *Orfeo* and *Iphigénie en Tauride*, and overtures by Méhul. From 1871 to 1878, however, French music appeared much less often, with only eleven performances of six Auber overtures and works by Gounod, Meyerbeer, Boïeldieu, Berlioz and Hérold also decreasing in frequency.[140] Curios apart, in concert halls French music remained largely confined to opera extracts.

Although largely isolated from other musical activities, organ recitals played a crucial role in disseminating music of many types, and programmes started to include purposely composed French music in the 1860s. The provision of recital venues, in the form of civic and private multi-function halls increased greatly from the 1830s: examples opened between 1830 and 1870 include Exeter Hall, St James's Hall and Crystal Palace in London; town halls in Birmingham, Leeds and Newcastle; Glasgow's Grand Hall; Colston Hall, Bristol; Free Trade Hall, Manchester, and the St George's Halls in Bradford and Liverpool. Technological innovations, competition between venues, and lobbying by British and visiting musicians resulted in the installation of new, large instruments (all the buildings mentioned were provided with organs either when they opened or shortly afterwards), and expansion of existing ones, widening repertory that could be played. In parallel, the role of music in liturgical services was also changing, with organ usage at the forefront: new or rebuilt organs were often ambitious in scope, especially in the new Anglican churches and non-conformist chapels of affluent suburbs, and the industrialised north and Midlands, while the Church of Scotland rescinded its ban on organs in 1864. All these changes facilitated an exponential increase in dedicated organ recitals from the 1850s, provided by a rapidly expanding band of players, many of whom sought to professionalise fully their musical careers, aided by a widespread feeling that such events were excellent examples of so-called 'rational amusement', which enabled 'the refining influence that good music, aptly interpreted, is calculated to exercise on the evil qualities of our nature'.[141]

The performance of French music initially was severely limited; other than a few compositions by Lefébure-Wély, original works were almost unknown, and recitals incorporated mainly arrangements and transcriptions.[142] This situation changed markedly from about 1870, enabled by the emergence of a new generation of organist-composers (Mailly, Salomé, Saint-Saëns, Guilmant, Dubois, Widor and Gigout, all born between 1833 and 1844) and a small but significant number of organ installations by the prized builder Aristide Cavaillé-Coll. The first of these, at the Carmelite Priory, Kensington, in 1866, was unimportant in itself, but demonstrates the significance of agency and cultural transfer: the founding priest, charismatic convert and former Liszt pupil and companion, Hermann Cohen, was invited to England by Cardinal Wiseman and, with his French co-founders, brought knowledge and esteem of Cavaillé-Coll's work; the inaugural recital on 15 July 1866 was shared by four organists, including Guilmant and Widor, in what were probably their first professional appearances in Britain.[143] Cavaillé-Coll's second organ, built for the barrister and former Liberal MP John Turner Hopwood at his country house in Bracewell, near Colne, in 1870,[144] was for private use but led directly to the installation of a Cavaillé-Coll instrument in Sheffield's new Albert Hall (1873), and indirectly to those installed at St Mary's, Blackburn (now Blackburn Cathedral, 1875) and Manchester Town Hall (1877).[145]

The organs at Sheffield and Blackburn were inaugurated by William Best; he and Albert Lister Peace were the most prominent British performers of purposely composed French organ music.[146] Both were indefatigable travellers who, in addition to regular home-town recital series (Best typically performed thrice each week), performed throughout the country; programmes published in the musical press show that they typically included one French piece in each recital, most commonly by Guilmant, Widor or Saint-Saëns; while the programmes comprised a small proportion of their overall repertory, they were consistent in their approach and added new works regularly.

French organists also appeared. Some of Saint-Saëns's earliest professional engagements were in 1871 when he played at Crystal Palace and, with Bruckner, was among those who inaugurated the organ in the Albert Hall; although subsequently focused on conducting and piano playing, he reappeared at the Albert Hall and also gave recitals in Manchester and Liverpool.[147] Following his visit in 1866, Guilmant became a particularly enthusiastic visitor, performing almost annually until well into the 1890s; he was particularly interested in the Cavaillé-Coll organ at Manchester but played at venues around the country;[148] Eugène Gigout also toured each spring between 1888 and 1890. Although all three performed a varied repertory, French works were particularly well represented.

Less high-profile British organists were influenced by both their prominent counterparts, and, by the 1900s, music by a reasonably broad range of French composers featured regularly in the majority of organ recitals reported in the musical press: programme summaries published in *Organist and Choirmaster* for January 1901, December 1902, and January and October 1903, show that between half and three-quarters of published programmes contained at least one French work; the best-represented composers were Guilmant, Widor and Dubois, but Boëllmann, Batiste, Lemaigre, Chauvet, Mailly and Lemmens also featured, with reports coming from towns as widely dispersed as Dublin, Perth, Winchester, Porthmadog and Norwich.

Analysing the reception of this music is problematic: organ recitals were such a central and ubiquitous part of Victorian culture that they rarely attracted detailed coverage, at least at a national level, and the musical press generally wrote little about repertory beyond supplying programme details, focusing instead upon the mechanics of performance. Music critics and other arbiters of taste appear often to have considered organ music a niche interest detached from the remainder of musical culture: when Widor conducted the Philharmonic Society in 1888, the *Musical World*'s preview article stated that, although his name was 'by no means unknown', it had been made 'familiar to cultivated amateurs by the charm of many of his songs which from time to time find their way to the concert platform'; following a detailed appraisal of the Piano Trio, Widor's organ music was referenced *en passant* in the final paragraph.[149] And yet, organ recitals made a significant impression upon audiences, for many of whom such events constituted their primary engagement with music, especially outside major urban centres; when Gigout visited in the late 1880s he played in Hanley, Dewsbury and Ashby-de-la-Zouch amongst other places, while both he and Guilmant gave several recitals at the Bow & Bromley Institute, in the heart of London's East End. In many places, organ recitals were intentionally aimed at less affluent citizens, with the overt intention of inducing moral 'improvement' and elevated musical taste. Undoubtedly this is an area in which further research, although challenging methodologically, would be of great value.[150]

The deaths of Meyerbeer, Berlioz and Auber

Obituaries of Meyerbeer, Berlioz and Auber, who died in 1864, 1869 and 1871 respectively, provide useful 'snapshots' of both the regard in which they were held as individuals and perceptions of French music and its characteristics in general. Appraisals of Meyerbeer were uniformly admiring though not without criticisms; notices in the *Athenaeum* (by Chorley) and *All the Year Round* regarded as paradoxical their assertion that 'not a tune of Meyerbeer's is on the organs or in the streets … [yet] he has ruled the musical stage of Europe for the past thirty years'.[151] The *Morning Post* declared that *Robert le diable* 'marked a new epoch in dramatic art',[152] and most writers asserted that the Parisian operas constituted Meyerbeer's noteworthy contribution to music. Another consistent thread was his cosmopolitanism; Chorley placed him in the 'brilliant phalanx of German musicians belonging to the days of Beethoven,

Weber and Mendelssohn', while his ethnoreligious status was mentioned by all, as was his time studying in Italy. Reflecting a common contemporaneous view of Jewishness, the *Orchestra* stated that Meyerbeer's 'genius was essentially eclectic', rather than national;[153] many writers noted his relative lack of success in Germany in later life, which *All the Year Round* attributed to Meyerbeer 'having made himself altogether French' after settling in Paris. Elsewhere, however, he was perceived as French in neither life nor musical style: for Chorley, he achieved success because he 'entirely satisfied the wants and wishes of the French public' through an 'instinct of the stage'. Other attributes were expertise in orchestration, 'a wondrous feeling for climax' and being 'most ingenious and subtle in his varieties of rhythm', but not facility as a melodist or national identity. Meyerbeer's success represented not France but the perceived Parisian demand for theatricality and eclecticism.

Obituaries of Berlioz were much more divided: the most positive presented him as a flawed genius, the least as an egotist with insufficient ability to support his ambitions. The *Athenaeum* declared his life a 'long mistake', although it recognised some works, such as *Harold en Italie* and *Roméo et Juliette*, as being 'filled with musical thoughts of rare beauty'.[154] Davison's notice in the *Musical World*, however, deemed Berlioz a 'great thinker', and opined that 'a more earnest man, a musician more thoroughly persuaded of the absolute truth and rectitude of his own adopted convictions, has never existed', while alleging that he had 'ideas which the world could not comprehend'.[155] Even Berlioz's supporters, though, did not conceive of him in national terms despite his incontestable Frenchness in the literal sense and his devotion to Paris equalling or exceeding Meyerbeer's. The perception of individuality placed Berlioz apart and too far from established notions of French style to represent it meaningfully.

The exact opposite was true for Auber. Critics found tropes of 'Frenchness' easily in his music, concurrently proving his nationality and the tropes' validity. No writer regarded Auber as a 'great' composer but all recognised his longevity, fecundity, and central role in giving a consistent ethos to *opéra comique*: he was, according to the *Athenaeum*, 'the acknowledged chief of the French opera school … [and] the real representative of the National Art at the Salle Favart'.[156] The writer continued,

> The qualities of grace, elegance, spontaneity, [and] originality have been cheerfully conceded to Auber by all critics, however adverse; but power and passion and grandeur are attributes which it is denied that he possessed. This, to a certain extent, is true: Auber's music was essentially gay and vivacious, coquettish and fascinating.

Qualities such as these were already associated with Frenchness: other positives included piquancy, sparkle, charm, brilliancy and freshness, countered by superficiality and lack of pathos; the only work widely thought to escape these weaknesses was *Masaniello*. Auber was easily presented as the quintessential French composer: to underline the point, comparisons were made with other Paris-based writers, including Rossini and Gounod (both too Italian) and Meyerbeer (too German).[157] Conversely, neither Berlioz nor Offenbach were referenced; the former defied categorisation, while the latter was widely regarded in 1871 as *infra dig*, rendering comparison with the veteran Auber who died, as it were, amidst the ruins of the city he loved, a tacit insult. In the words of the *Musical Standard*, Auber was not only 'the representative of French music, but he was a Parisian *par excellence*, and reflected with a marvellous fidelity the spirit of the scenes amid which he moved. His music, in its vivacity, finish and gracefulness, as well as in its superficiality, want of depth and solidity, exactly portrays Paris'.[158] Despite the trauma of the Commune, Paris was still for British observers the home of wit, frivolity and escapism.

Conclusion

French music's presence in Britain between 1863 and 1878 was in certain ways idiosyncratic. Relatively little new music appeared: compared to the previous 30 years, few new operas were produced, and very little new concert music; against a sympathetic background of improving relations, the 1860s and 1870s can be viewed as a period of consolidation rather than advance. While Meyerbeer's operas remained popular in the West End, they achieved relatively little traction elsewhere; knowledge of Auber was largely confined to three or four operas, though a wider selection of overtures and other extracts featured in concert programmes. Berlioz's music appeared infrequently, and, despite the increasing productiveness of French composers in this area, few other new concert works appeared. Nevertheless, in specific ways, this period was highly significant: the immediate and sustained popularity of *Faust*, and Gounod's four-year residence in London impacted substantially on British musical culture until the end of the century and beyond. *Carmen*'s popularity possibly exceeded *Faust*'s but was of a different nature: Bizet's premature death resulted in *Carmen*'s immediate monumentalisation but prevented any further development of his reputation, whereas Gounod remained active and often notorious, attracting attention from supporters and detractors alike. In terms of 'reach', the most important development was the craze for *opéra bouffe*; despite the intense reactions it provoked, heightened by Schneider's visits, the genre supplied the platform upon which Gilbert & Sullivan and others built a specifically British version of operetta, while the popularity of Offenbach's successors (see Chapter 4) shows that the appetite for *opéra bouffe* was sustained for some 30 years.

While both *Faust* and *Carmen* accorded neatly with a Victorian moralistic approval of retributive justice, aiding their popularity alongside the appeal of their scores, neither work made any significant impression on the British mindset in terms of their 'Frenchness', the cosmopolitan aspects of both operas militating against such assessments. The contrary applies to *opéra bouffe*, which in many respects fitted perfectly with stereotyped British conceptions, from both pro- and anti- standpoints. In 1874, the critic Clement Scott optimistically but precipitately predicted its demise on the grounds that the *risqué* aspects did not accord with superior British morality;[159] later criticisms by writers such as Hueffer (see Chapter 4) show how the genre's attributes continually offended part of the establishment. Scott believed *opéra bouffe* 'left behind it a train of unpleasant smoke', and attributed its success to its music:

> It was Parisian and anti-English to the backbone. We took it up ... because we were swayed and influenced by the siren voices of the light French melodists. We could hear nothing but the music, and for the sake of the music, we either refused to listen to the words or cheerfully forgave the uncongenial humour of the French libretti ... [W]e welcomed them all for the captivating melodies or feverish dances ... A stage that prided itself, somewhat puritanically and ostentatiously, on its purity has been handed over to 'can-can' dancers.

Scott identified the 1867 Exposition as the most important catalyst for *opéra bouffe*'s popularity: 'Where the world went, there, of course, the English folks were found; and those who were unable to be present in Paris besought their friends to bring home a score of [*La Grande-Duchesse*]', before observing (sardonically?) that, while British visitors to Paris might briefly be seduced by its lifestyle, 'the very instant the train arrives at Charing Cross, we call for a glass of stout and hurry off to Simpson's for a cut off the joint and a taste of English mutton'. Decrying Farnie's adaptations, which subjected the original works to a 'careful process of Bowdlerism', Scott clearly viewed *opéra bouffe* as representing seductive French Otherness and antithetical to English stoicism and nobility, a perspective traceable to the seventeenth century.

Scott was not the only writer to draw on long-established tropes: the émigré Viennese pianist Ernst Pauer, who settled in London in 1851 and remained for over 40 years, wrote a succession of works on art music for middlebrow audiences and also lectured extensively. Unsurprisingly, he believed German music superior to that of other 'national schools',[160] and drew on familiar images of Italy and France, reinforcing common perceptions: in a public lecture in 1878, Pauer stated that

> In military songs, and rhythmical and march movements the French are pre-eminent ... The glittering French characteristics, *savoir faire* and *savoir vivre* shine in their music no less than in their manner. Agreeable not deep, their music is best adapted for social intercourse, the melodies are not abstruse but aim at sweetness, and are replete with taste, piquancy, clearness and symmetry. With a correct and innate sense of roundness and smoothness, there is an absence of intensity, grandeur, and breadth, more technicality than fancy and inspiration.[161]

Musical transfers from France in the 1860s and '70s did little to revise generalised perceptions amongst a wide cross-section of writers, who were more likely to fit new arrivals into existing categories than to reconsider existing thoughts, especially when these accorded not only with tropes of French music, but French culture and nationality in general. An exception, at this point, was Gounod, whose music, partly as a direct result of his residency in London, was widely admired and respected; even critics who found his conduct egotistical (and contemporaneous reviews contain many barbed comments about his relentless self-promotion) praised much of his music, considering him France's foremost composer and a major figure in European art music. Temporarily at least, Gounod's religious music found widespread favour, especially those works composed for English consumers, whose appearance handily coincided with the popularity of Barnby and Stainer amongst church musicians, whose styles Gounod influenced significantly and who effectively acted as both heralds and acolytes. Gounod's music may at this point have broken free of the tropes of Frenchness imposed on others; his popularity in a field not previously associated in British minds with the French certainly brought stereotypes of Frenchness into question, even if, ultimately, they did not change them.

Notes

1 Napoléon spent several years between 1836 and 1848 in exile in London.
2 'A Flight', *HW*, 31 August 1851, p. 532.
3 'Mrs Lirriper's Legacy', *AYR*, 1 December 1864 (Extra Christmas Number), p. 8.
4 'Paris Improved', *HW*, 17 November 1855, p. 365.
5 *SR*, 9 November 1867, pp. 601–2.
6 See, for example, 'A Flight from Paris', *AYR*, 8 October 1870, pp. 443–6, and Denis Bingham, *Journal of the Siege of Paris* (London, 1871). The conductor Jules Rivière related his gratification that, at the Alhambra music hall's war-time Promenade Concerts, Mélanie Reboux's rendition of 'La Marseillaise' received the loudest cheer (*My Musical Life and Recollections* (London, 1893), pp. 134–6).
7 Napoléon died in 1873; Eugénie established Farnborough Abbey, Hampshire, as his mausoleum and was also interred there in 1920, as was their son Louis-Napoléon (d. 1879), a member of the British army.
8 John Ella noted that some forty professional refugee musicians contacted him, hoping for engagements; see Christina Bashford, *The Pursuit of High Culture: John Ella and Chamber Music in Victorian London* (Woodbridge, 2007), p. 308.
9 Frederic Harrison, 'The Effacement of England', *FR*, 1 February 1871, p. 148.
10 Harrison, p. 157.
11 *MW*, 24 September 1870, p. 639.
12 Edward Dicey, 'Paris After the Peace', *FR*, 1 April 1871, p. 494.
13 The foundation stone was laid in 1862; completion became urgent after the Salle Le Peletier, home of the Paris Opéra since 1821, was destroyed by fire in October 1873.
14 *Athenaeum*, 9 January 1875, p. 60; see also (curiously) *MW*, 1 January 1870, p. 4. *ISDN* noted that rival houses in St Petersburg, Munich, Berlin, Vienna, Venice

and Milan were all smaller, and published engravings (16 January 1875, p. 375, and 23 January, p. 398).

15 *Times*, 1 May 1878, p. 11.

16 Quoted in *Times*, 6 May 1878, p. 6; some parts of Edward's speech were delivered in French, which he spoke fluently. The phrase 'entente cordiale' was anticipated privately in 1843 by the Foreign Secretary, Lord Aberdeen ('a cordial, good understanding'), and used publicly shortly afterwards by Louis Philippe I; see Muriel Chamberlain, *'Pax Britannica'? British Foreign Policy 1789–1914* (London, 1988), p. 88.

17 *Times*, 6 May 1878, p. 9.

18 *Times*, 23 October 1878, p. 9.

19 *Athenaeum*, 22 June 1850, p. 668.

20 Probably an extract from or prototype for the opera *La nonne sanglante* (1854).

21 *Athenaeum*, 18 January 1851, p. 88.

22 *MW*, 18 January 1851, p. 41. Davison never liked Gounod's music but may at this point have been antagonised by Chorley's advocacy; a sceptical article, provoked by the *Athenaeum*'s support, appeared in *MW* the previous week (11 January, pp. 19–20).

23 *Times*, quoted in *MW*, 16 August 1851 p. 518.

24 Henry F Chorley, *Thirty Years' Musical Recollections* (2 vols, London, 1862), vol. 2, pp. 156 and 153.

25 *MW*, 3 December 1853, p. 763.

26 *MW*, 26 April 1856, p. 267

27 See *MGz*, 26 April 1856, p. 159; *Spectator*, same date, p. 443; *Athenaeum*, same date, p. 527.

28 *MW*, 14 November 1857, p. 735.

29 *MC*, 16 February 1860, p. 4; for more positive reviews see *MP*, same date, p. 5, and *DN*, same date, p. 2. Some negativity arose from antagonism towards the aesthetics of Roman Catholic liturgical music.

30 See James Mapleson, *The Mapleson Memoirs* (Chicago, New York and San Francisco, 1888), vol. 1, pp. 66–7. The arrangement's technical difficulty and high retail price (7s 6d) do not suggest a large circulation.

31 *Era*, 29 April 1860, p. 15; *MC*, 14 May, p. 6; see also *Athenaeum*, 19 May, p. 692. The Canterbury's proprietor, Charles Morton, was trying to raise its status: *Faust*, which had been preceded by *Dinorah* and *Macbeth*, was given in English but without the burlesquing typical of lower-ranking venues.

32 See Steven Huebner, *The Operas of Charles Gounod* (Oxford, 1990), pp. 53–5.

33 For his own convoluted and possibly partly fictional recollection of his production, see Mapleson, vol. 1, pp. 68–70. Gounod attended the first performance. See also Richard Northcott, *Gounod's Operas in London* (London, 1918), pp. 14–20.

34 Although Gye contracted Marie Miolan-Cavalho, the original Marguerite, most reviewers preferred Thérèse Tietjens's performance. Covent Garden's *mise en scène* was thought better. See *Era*, 5 July 1863, p. 10; *Observer*, same date, p. 7; *Times*, 6 July, p. 5; *ILN*, 11 July, p. 43; *SR*, same date, pp. 56–7.

35 *Athenaeum*, 20 June 1863, p. 817.

36 *Times*, 15 June 1863, p. 5.

37 *DN*, 15 June 1863, p. 2; see also *ILN*, 11 July 1863, p. 43.

38 *Observer*, 14 June 1863, p. 7; see also *SR*, 20 June 1863, p. 793.

39 *ILN*, 11 July 1863, p. 43.

40 See Huebner, p. 55, and Mapleson, p. 72.
41 In 1863 alone those issued in London included a waltz, galop and quadrilles by Charles Coote in versions for piano solo, orchestra, and cornet and piano; Fantasias for piano by Brinley Richards, Wilhelm Kuhe, George Osborne and Eugene Ketterer, and for piano and accordion by Richard Blagrove; selections for military band by A F Godfrey; 'All the Favourite Airs' for cornet, flute or violin and piano; and transcriptions for solo piano of individual items.
42 See Huebner, p. 71.
43 *Times*, 11 July 1864, p. 12.
44 See *Observer*, 5 March 1865, p. 3; *Times*, 6 March, p. 12 (reproduced in *MW*, 11 March, pp. 143–4).
45 *Examiner*, 11 March 1865, p. 151.
46 *Orchestra*, 19 August 1865, p. 326. Attempting to generate publicity, *Orchestra*, edited by Farnie (!), published an extended analysis of *Irene*: see 19 August, pp. 329–30; 26 August, pp. 345–6; 2 September, pp. 362–3; 9 September, p. 378.
47 See *Reader*, 19 August 1865, p. 214; *Athenaeum*, same date, p. 253.
48 *PMG*, 16 July 1867, p. 10.
49 *Standard*, 15 July 1867, p. 2.
50 *DN*, 15 July 1867, p. 2.
51 *Athenaeum*, 20 July 1867, p. 90.
52 For a summary of Gounod's relationship with Weldon and the consequences for Gounod's marriage, see Huebner, pp. 84–91.
53 *Sheffield and Rotherham Independent*, 2 May 1871, p. 8, and several other provincial newspapers that day, possibly originating in an untraced London journal.
54 *MW*, 6 May 1871, p. 272. See also *Standard*, 2 May, p. 5; *DN*, same date, p. 6; *MP*, same date, p. 5.
55 These are worthy of an independent study; Gounod's conduct provoked admiration, ridicule, astonishment and censure in almost equal measures.
56 See *MW*, 11 November 1871, pp. 724–5 and *MS*, 25 November, pp. 381–2. Gounod's lack of relevant experience and his being favoured over British candidates riled many observers.
57 See, for example, *MS*, 18 May 1872, p. 280. The inaugural concert was, nevertheless, attended by Queen Victoria in a rare public appearance and included a Te Deum by Gounod which celebrated Prince Edward's recovery from typhoid (**1872**-2).
58 *MS*, 3 August 1872, p. 70.
59 For sample reviews, see: *MS*, 15 February 1873, p. 103; 1 March, p. 134; 29 March, p. 200; 12 April, p. 232; 7 June, p. 359; 14 February 1874, p. 103; 28 February, p. 132; 14 March, p. 178; 28 March, p. 210; 18 April, p. 258.
60 See, for example, letters in *MW* commencing on 8 June 1872, p. 363, and appearing almost weekly until the end of July; these provoked a gleeful article in *MS* (13 July, pp. 18–19). Gounod later sued Henry Littleton of Novello, Ewer & Co over royalty payments (*MS*, 19 July 1873, pp. 19–21).
61 *MW*, 4 January 1873, p. 8.
62 While early concert performances had not been well received (see above), the 'St Cecilia' Mass was well-regarded by the 1870s (see *Times*, 10 February 1874, p. 10; *MS*, 14 February, p. 103).
63 See William Gatens, *Victorian Cathedral Music in Theory and Practice* (Cambridge, 1986), p. 14. This was followed by 'Daughters of Jerusalem' (originally 'O filiae Jerusalem' from *Seven Last Words* (1855)).

64   These are 'Come unto Him' (originally 'Prière du soir'); 'All ye who weep' ('Le crucifix'); 'O day of penitence' ('Le vendredi saint'); and 'As the hart' ('Sicut cervus').

65   *MW*, 18 February 1871, p. 101.

66   Gounod also published secular vocal works, including 'There is dew' (1871; solo song), 'Bells across the snow' (1872; part-song), and 'The message of the breeze' (1872; soprano duet).

67   See Jeremy Dibble, *John Stainer: A Life in Music* (Woodbridge, 2007), pp. 161–3.

68   John Stainer, 'On the Progressive Character of Church Music', in *Authorised Report of the Church Congress* (London, 1874), p. 537.

69   See *MP*, 18 May 1857, p. 5.

70   *Leader and Saturday Analyst*, 25 April 1857, p. 404.

71   See Andrew Lamb, 'Offenbach in London', in Rainer Franke (ed.), *Offenbach und die Schauplätze seines Musiktheaters* (Laaber, 1999), p. 186.

72   *Era*, 24 May 1857, p. 10; *MC*, 11 June, p. 5.

73   *MC*, 11 June 1857, p. 5.

74   See Lamb, pp. 195–202, who records over 60 productions between 1865 and 1874.

75   For further discussion see, Jim Davis and Victor Emeljanow, *Reflecting the Audience: London Theatregoing 1840–1880* (Hatfield, 2001), pp. 170–4.

76   See *Observer*, 14 May 1860, p. 7, and 19 January 1862, p. 5.

77   This was the sister venue of the Canterbury Hall, with a similar clientele, where a selection from *Faust* had been successful in 1860; a similar format was adopted with *Orphée* (see *Era*, 30 October 1864, p. 11).

78   Laurence Senelick, *Jacques Offenbach and the Making of Modern Culture* (Cambridge, 2017), p. 100.

79   *Athenaeum*, 30 December 1865, p. 933; see also *Era*, 31 December, p. 11.

80   *Times*, 27 December 1865, p. 10.

81   Kurt Gänzl, *The British Musical Theatre, Volume 1: 1865–1914* (Basingstoke, 1986), p. 6. For examples of 'filching' see *Era*'s review of *La Périchole* (3 July 1870, p. 11).

82   *Observer*, 3 June 1866, p. 6.

83   Following Sullivan's *Cox and Box*, for which Burnand wrote the libretto, at the same theatre. A selection from *La belle Hélène* had been playing at the Alhambra, Leicester Square, for several weeks.

84   *Observer*, 1 July 1866, p. 6. See also playwright John Oxenford's commentary in *The Times*, 13 July 1866, p. 10, reproduced in *MW* the following day (p. 448) under the by-line 'Joxoenhbonrd'.

85   Senelick, p. 102.

86   *Observer*, 24 November 1867, p. 3; see also *Examiner*, 23 November 1867, p. 44.

87   *Orchestra*, 2 November 1867, p. 91.

88   Senelick, p. 21.

89   Senelick, p. 23.

90   *Orchestra*, 27 June 1868, p. 213; see also *Examiner*, 27 June, p. 408. Aristocratic notables in attendance, headed by the Prince and Princess of Wales, are listed. Considering Isabelle Paul, Schneider's parallel at the Olympic, the writer observed that she was 'eminently gracious and graceful ... and invests [the role] with a spirit which does not in the slightest degree entrench on vulgarity'. Schneider saw Paul's performance (*Observer*, 21 June, p. 3) and possibly toned down her own, at least initially, in response.

91 *MW*, 18 July 1868, p. 503.

92 *Observer*, 19 July 1868, p. 7.

93 *SR*, 1 August 1868, p. 162.

94 Given with 'considerable modifications from the original, [so] there was nothing to arouse the indignation of a British audience' (*Observer*, 29 December 1867, p. 6, of the Boxing Day performance). Finette (stage-name of Joséphine Durwend) later performed a more *risqué* version at the Alhambra (*PMG*, 27 March 1868, p. 11) which, though still toned down, caused a scandal: according to Rivière (p. 134), the Alhambra consequently lost its dancing licence. All these versions differed greatly from that popularised by Louise Weber ('la Goulue') at the Moulin Rouge in the 1890s.

95 *London Review*, 4 July 1868, p. 16.

96 See, for example, 'One plea for censorship', *Orchestra*, 15 August 1868, p. 332.

97 *Examiner*, 18 July 1868, p. 457.

98 For Offenbach's works see **1866**-1, **1870**–2, **1870**–4, **1870**–7. Throughout 1870, John Hollingshead produced French opera at the Gaiety, including revivals of Adam's *La poupée de Nuremberg* (**1860**–4) and *Zampa*, led by Charles Santley.

99 See *MP*, 28 June 1870, p. 6; *Era*, 7 July, p. 11; *Graphic*, 2 July, p. 19. Several reviews noted that the music was mainly already familiar.

100 *Athenaeum*, 11 June 1870, p. 782. Opinions varied; *Era* (previous note) asserted that Schneider was 'not nearly so coarse in her acting as usual'.

101 See *Liverpool Mercury* (1 April 1870, p. 6; 4 April, p. 6); *Glasgow Herald* (9 April, p. 4; 12 April, p. 4; 15 April, p. 4; 20 April, p. 4); *BDP* (24 April, p. 8; 25 April, p. 8; 26 April, p. 8); *Bristol Mercury* (4 June, p. 8).

102 See *PMG*, 7 March 1870, p. 7; Cullen warned that 'the parent who allows his child to resort to such demoralizing scenes will have a fearful account to render to God'.

103 *SN*, 15 March 1870, p. 2; *FJ*, same date, p. 3; see also *Era*, 27 March, p. 12.

104 *FJ*, 24 March 1870, p. 3.

105 See Lamb, pp. 95–102, and Gänzl, pp. 34 and 40–1.

106 *Era*, 3 January 1875, p. 12.

107 See *DN*, 28 December 1874, p. 2; *MP*, same date, p. 2; *Lloyd's Weekly Newspaper*, 3 January 1875, p. 5. For further discussion see Gänzl, pp. 69–70.

108 *ISDN*, 19 April 1879, p. 106.

109 Gänzl, p. 144.

110 See *DN*, 7 July 1881, p. 3; *PMG*, 8 July, p. 10; *MP*, 8 July, p. 3; *Era*, 9 July, p. 8.

111 *MS*, 14 June 1873, p. 375. For other reviews see: *Observer*, 18 May, p. 3; *Athenaeum*, 24 May, pp. 670–1; *MW*, same date, p. 347; *Illustrated Review*, 1 June, pp. 611–2.

112 British premieres of Lecocq's *Les cent vierges* (**1873**–6) and Offenbach's *Les braconniers* (**1873**–8), and revivals of *La Grande-Duchesse* and *Les brigands*.

113 *Graphic*, 13 June 1874, p. 563; Gänzl, p. 66.

114 For sample reviews, see *Illustrated Review*, 1 June 1874, p. 395; *Observer*, 7 June, p. 6; *Orchestra*, 12 June, pp. 163–4; *Athenaeum*, 13 June, p. 804; *ISDN*, same date, p. 363; *Graphic*, same date, p. 563.

115 See **1874**–5, **1876**-4 and **1878**-3.

116 Stone's 'Fantaisie facile' on themes from *Orphée*, Isaac Strauss's 'Orpheus Quadrille' and an arrangement of the full *Orphée* score were issued in 1860.

117   *MW*, 29 January 1870, p. 74.

118   *Graphic*, 29 January 1870, p. 210.

119   *Era*, 3 July 1870, p. 11.

120   *Athenaeum*, 13 March 1875, p. 368.

121   For further discussion, see Paul Rodmell, '*Carmen* – As Seen and Heard in Victorian Britain' in Richard Langham-Smith and Clair Rowden (eds), *Carmen Abroad* (Cambridge, 2020), pp. 186–99.

122   *MP*, 24 June 1878, p. 6.

123   Susan Rutherford, *The Prima Donna and Opera 1815–1930* (Cambridge, 2006), pp. 213–30.

124   Nevertheless, the *Athenaeum* made a pointed comparison: 'If *opéra bouffe* is to be accepted here in place of refined vocalisation, and of polished and finished acting, then will the star of the American *prima donna* [Hauk] be in the ascendant' (29 June 1878, p. 836).

125   *ILN*, 29 June 1878, p. 611; see also *Academy*, same date, p. 591; *Graphic*, same date, p. 639.

126   *ISDN*, 29 June 1878, p. 377. The writer thought Carmen 'an ignoble copy of Violetta in *La traviata* [but] her immorality is suggested rather than revealed', making *Carmen* less offensive.

127   Hauk attributed the opera's success in part to more naturalistic acting than the established Italian style (see Minnie Hauk, *Memories of a Singer* (London, 1925, pp. 160–1)), although her claims are not especially credible: contemporaneous reviews do not mention a difference, although there may have been steps towards the presentational style practiced by French companies (see Chapter 2 and above), with which Hauk would have been familiar.

128   *Standard*, 24 June 1878, p. 2; *MP*, same date, p. 6.

129   *ISDN*, 29 June 1878, p. 377.

130   *Examiner*, 29 June 1878, p. 926. *Athenaeum* agreed, referring to the Romani as 'the Gipsies and their Hindoo blood' (as note 124).

131   *Academy*, 29 June 1878, p. 591

132   *Era*, 27 October 1878, p. 5; *Academy*, 26 October, p. 416.

133   These included West End productions of *Geneviève de Brabant*, *La Périchole* and *Chilpéric*. Durward Lely ('Signor Leli') made his West End debut as Don Jose; he later created the role of Nanki-Poo in *The Mikado*.

134   See *ISDN*, 8 February 1879, p. 502 (positive), and *Examiner*, 15 February, p. 212 (equivocal); Rosa seems to have agreed; this was Dolaro's only role with his company.

135   *MW*, 15 February 1879, p. 99.

136   *BDP*, 7 May 1879, p. 7.

137   For a full account, see Kurt Gänzl, *Emily Soldene: In Search of a Singer* (2 vols, Wellington (NZ), 2007), vol. 2, pp. 38–45, 126 and 138.

138   William Weber shows that the proportion of works by dead composers performed at Philharmonic Society concerts expanded from 48% in 1830 to 85% in 1870; see *The Great Transformation of Musical Taste: Concert Programming from Haydn to Brahms* (Cambridge, 2008), pp. 169–73.

139   See Thomas Batley (ed.), *Sir Charles Hallé's Concerts in Manchester* (Manchester, 1896).

140 In part this was due to changing tastes, as Hallé introduced works by Schumann, Schubert, Brahms, Wagner, Russian and eastern European composers, pushing other older works out. Nevertheless, given the sudden change after 1870, an anti-French reaction amongst Hallé's German subscribers may have occurred; this requires further investigation.

141 *MS*, 18 May 1872, p. 272. For further information, see Rachel Milestone, 'A Melodious Phenomenon: The Institutional Influence on Town Hall Music-Making', in Paul Rodmell (ed.), *Music and Institutions in Nineteenth-Century Britain* (Abingdon, 2012), pp. 55–77.

142 An analysis of William Best's first year of recitals at St George's Hall, Liverpool, states that, in 77 performances, the only original French works were 'Offertoires by Lefébure-Wély', while transcriptions comprised 'reminiscences' (i.e. selections) and/or overtures from operas by Meyerbeer, Auber, Méhul, Hérold and Thomas (*MW*, 6 September 1856, pp. 570–1).

143 *Orchestra*, 21 July 1866, p. 262.

144 *MS*, 16 April 1870, p. 192, and *MW*, 12 November, p. 793. The three-manual instrument comprised 38 stops, cost over £3,000, and was inaugurated over three days by the Leeds Town Hall organist, Frederick Spark; *MW* asserted that 'Assuredly, there is not a finer specimen of organ building to be found, at present, in England'.

145 Cavaillé-Coll also installed organs at Paisley Abbey and Bellahouston Parish Church in 1874 but this sudden interest was not sustained, and Manchester was Cavaillé-Coll's last major British project. For details of each instrument see the National Pipe Organ Register (www.npor.org.uk) and *Sheffield Daily Telegraph*, 11 January 1873, p. 2; *MS*, 7 March 1874, p. 153 (Paisley); *Blackburn Standard*, 18 December 1875, p. 8; *MS*, 21 July 1877, p. 42 (Manchester).

146 Best's principal role was organist at St George's Hall, Liverpool (1856–94); Peace was based in Glasgow from 1865 and succeeded Best at Liverpool, where died in post in 1912.

147 See *MS*, 11 October 1879, p. 226 (Manchester Town Hall); 22 May 1880, p. 326 (Albert Hall); 22 October 1881, p. 261 (St George's Hall, Liverpool). In Manchester and Liverpool, Saint-Saëns also appeared as pianist and conductor.

148 The Victoria University of Manchester awarded Guilmant an honorary doctorate in 1910 (*MG*, 4 July, p. 5), when he also gave his final recital at the Town Hall (*MG*, 2 July, p. 11); he died nine months later.

149 *MW*, 21 April 1888, pp. 306–7.

150 For a wide-ranging survey, see Makiko Hayasaka, 'Organ Recitals as Popular Culture: The Secularisation of the Instrument and its Repertoire in Britain, 1834–1950', unpublished PhD thesis, University of Bristol, 2016.

151 *Athenaeum*, 7 May 1864, p. 646; *AYR*, 28 May, pp. 374–7 (quoted, p. 374).

152 *MP*, 3 May 1864, p. 5.

153 *Orchestra*, 7 May 1864, p. 505.

154 *Athenaeum*, 13 March 1869, p. 376.

155 *MW*, 13 March 1869, p. 178.

156 *Athenaeum*, 20 May 1871, p. 632.

157 See *BDP*, 16 May 1871, p. 4; *Era*, 21 May, p. 10.

158 *MS*, 20 May 1871, p. 32; see also *MW*, same date, p. 299.

159 Clement Scott, 'The Rise and Fall of *Opéra Bouffe*', *London Society*, 1 January 1875, pp. 42–9.

160 Pauer's short book, *The Elements of the Beautiful in Music* (London, 1877), based on Ferdinand Gotthelf Hand's earlier *Aesthetik der Tonkunst*, used exclusively examples from German repertory, principally Beethoven.

161 Ernst Pauer, 'The Spirit of Italian, French and German Music', *MS*, 2 March 1878, p. 127; compare these remarks with those of Haweis (see Introduction).

4 *Fin-de-siècle*
French music in Britain 1879–1900

While the progress of French music in Britain in the 1860s and '70s was largely confined to specific genres, the *fin-de-siècle* decades were characterised by a steadily broadening spectrum of activity, the most significant of which was purposely composed concert music. Saint-Saëns was most successful, but Massenet was also well received, Gounod produced two popular large-scale choral works, and Berlioz's music received a greatly increased level of attention and support. For opera, however, circumstances were less stable: the mid-1880s were torrid years in the West End, where 'grand' opera briefly approached complete collapse. Nevertheless, Saint-Saëns and Massenet both enjoyed successes, and during Augustus Harris's management of Covent Garden, French works were enthusiastically promoted. Theatre and concert repertories were increasingly crowded: most of Wagner's operas arrived in Britain in the 1880s, while concert halls also added Brahms, Schumann, the rediscovered Schubert, Dvořák and Tchaikovsky amongst others to their programmes. A similar situation pertained in musical theatre; Offenbach's popularity declined rapidly, and his successors had to compete firstly with Gilbert & Sullivan and then musical comedy, largely surviving the former but falling victim to the latter. In parallel, after the balmy 1870s, Franco-British political relations declined, improving significantly only when both sides started working actively toward the *Entente Cordiale*.

Political and cultural relations 1879–1900

At inter-governmental level, conflicting imperial ambitions regularly put Franco-British relations under strain. Despite post-war rebuilding, France still felt vulnerable, aware of Bismarck's desire to maintain French isolation, exemplified by the Dreikaiserbund (1873). Britain, though less discomfited, was still drawn towards France, as many politicians and opinion-formers highlighted their commonalities as centres of liberal democracy, distinct from the autocrats further east. Simultaneously, though, both nations had complex domestic agendas,[1] and conflicting overseas interests.[2]

The main bone of contention was Egypt, the 'festering sore in Anglo-French relations'.[3] Britain bought the Egyptian government's share of the Suez Canal in 1875 and started to interfere in Egyptian administration, checking previously dominant French influence; four years later, Egypt was brought under dual French and British control. Following a local revolt in 1882, British troops unilaterally occupied Egypt, ostensibly to protect canal access (and becoming unintentionally entrenched until 1956), causing French resentment, which was only resolved by the *Entente Cordiale*. West Africa was also problematic, as France had imperial ambitions and Britain commercial interests in ports from Gambia to Nigeria, though few landholdings. During the 'scramble for Africa', France rapidly acquired territory, activity which some in Britain used to foment populist Francophobia. Tensions also existed in Burma and Siam; British fear of potential French aggression precipitated increased naval funding in 1889.

Tensions climaxed with the Fashoda Crisis of 1898. In retrospect, this seems primarily a conflict of abstract ideals as it turned on aspirations to create contiguous trans-continental colonies (Cairo to Cape Town for Britain and Dakar to Djibouti for France). In July, Fashoda (now Kodok, South Sudan) became the flashpoint when a small brigade of French and Senegalese troops arrived, hoping to create a French protectorate and advance France's east–west link. Within days a larger British force isolated the French, creating a stand-off. In October, the new French foreign minister, Théophile Delcassé, concluded that France's position was too weak; worried about German ambitions in Europe, he did not want to antagonise the British further. French troops withdrew but the episode reinforced perceptions of British unscrupulousness, a view further augmented during the Boer War: French public opinion strongly favoured the South Africans.

Despite these tensions, France and Britain remained deeply intertwined economically and culturally. The 1860 Cobden–Chevalier Treaty had stimulated trade, especially until the mid-1870s; in François Crouzet's view, even the more protectionist Méline Tariff introduced in 1892 had little effect, with France consistently enjoying a healthy trade surplus with Britain,[4] which, as France's best customer, bought around 30% of all French exports in the 1890s (declining to about 20% by 1911), while the French typically bought around 12% of British exports. Goods exchanged reflected national needs and values: about two-thirds of French purchases comprised raw and semi-finished materials, while sales were the inverse, about two-thirds being manufactured goods. Culturally, it is significant that 'French exports, though varied, were clearly specialised, and therefore occupied "niches"'.[5] The British liked 'high-end' products: wines and spirits, textiles (including silk, lace and embroidery) and other deluxe items such as clothing (principally for women and children), Limoges porcelain, Baccarat crystal and fine art; although the French exported fewer engineered goods, they led the field in cars, another luxury commodity.[6] Such patterns maintained historic trends and the result was circular: in Britain, French goods continued to be perceived as high-quality, bespoke, fashionable and predominantly feminine; their presence reinforced perceptions of their attributes, sustained their desirability, and encouraged more imports.

As shown in Chapter 3, responses to France's Expositions Universelles provide useful 'snapshots' of British views, and reactions to the events of 1889 and 1900 were significantly more cautious than hitherto. The 1889 Exhibition in part commemorated the French Revolution, which made sense domestically but deterred several European governments, including Britain's, from high-level involvement. Nevertheless, the Exposition was still a major event, and significant contributions came from European states, their colonies, and independent nations worldwide. Exhibits by non-European nations proved especially popular, though Gustave Eiffel's new tower was the greatest attraction;[7] new electric lighting reinforced Paris's status as world capital of leisure:

> All the principal streets, indeed, are ablaze with light, and all Paris is in the open air ... Numbers of people are supping or dancing in the streets, and processions of young men with flags are singing the 'Marseillaise' ... Never, indeed, has Paris presented a gayer, more brilliant spectacle.[8]

Generally, though, *The Times*'s coverage was factual and tonally neutral, lacking the emphasis on mutual affinities and interests evident in 1878.

In 1900, this shift was still more marked. Partly this was due to the Exposition being widely perceived as over-commercialised and even kitsch,[9] but it also took place against a tense backdrop; French support for the Boers led Britain to downplay its presence, with no high-level attendees in an official capacity. *The Times*'s Paris correspondent concluded his preview article by entreating Frenchmen not to 'allow themselves to be led astray by those who are the evil genius of France ... in preaching unremittingly discord at home and hatred abroad'.[10] His mood later improved slightly: 'It is a calumny ... to allege that [France] ... has been thus far on her good behaviour for fear of injuring the Exhibition', but he urged his readers to ignore 'the ambitious and discredited fanatics who are about to shout for Mr Kruger', claiming that France 'will now calmly turn to the serious [domestic] problems demanding her attention'.[11]

Despite these tensions, Britain remained a major exhibitor; the centrepiece, designed by Edward Lutyens, was a pastiche seventeenth-century mansion, intended to 'give an idea of how the most favoured class of English people live',[12] though displays from outside Europe proved of greater interest. Popular engagement arose not only through press reports: Paris was easier and cheaper to reach than ever and many British citizens went in person, including 2,000 inhabitants of Port Sunlight, paid for by their employers, Lever Brothers, at a cost of £7,000; travelling overnight from Manchester, they arrived at 9 am and thirteen hours later were on the train home. *The Times*'s correspondent was impressed by his working-class compatriots, whose first request on arrival was to get washed;[13] even during such a brief visit, the impression made upon the travellers must have been great.

Although significant, *fin-de-siècle* political tensions did not define the Franco-British relationship. While popular anti-French sentiment was roused periodically, this should be seen in the context of deeply entrenched cultural and economic links; Britons might be inclined to dismiss, ridicule or despise French culture, while being simultaneously entranced by it. The desire for French goods, widely available by 1900 though only as an occasional treat below the middle classes, was strong and consistent. Knowledge, both factual and fictional, of Paris was more widespread than of any other European city and its reputation as a cosmopolitan pleasure centre was undimmed.

Grove's *Dictionary of Music and Musicians*

More than any other reference work, Grove's *Dictionary* has shaped anglophone perceptions of music, French works not excepted.[14] Although presented as an authoritative factual source, the content of the first edition also provides a valuable insight into how music was viewed and valued in the 1870s; such was its status and ubiquity in places such as public libraries, that *Grove* rapidly acquired the mantle of an 'official history'.

Early editions of *Grove* did not contain articles on nations or cities, and so there was no overview of France or Paris. Composer entries came from a large pool of contributors, but for French composers in the first edition the great majority came from the prominent critic Gustave Chouquet (1819–86).[15] Those on Adam and Auber were written by Francis Hueffer, and on Berlioz by Eduard Dannreuther, both German émigrés resident in London; only Florence Ashton Marshall's article on Meyerbeer might be said to originate in a primarily insular way.

The centrality of German and British composers in *Grove* has been noted elsewhere.[16] Meyerbeer's is the longest 'French' entry (six pages); most French composers merit two or three sides. Given the extent of Chouquet's contribution, the perspective presented is predominantly Parisian; he wrote most positively of Ambroise Thomas, stating that he had

> a remarkable gift of interpreting dramatic situations of the most varied and opposite kinds ... With a little more boldness and individuality of melody this accomplished writer, artist and poet ... would rank with the leaders of the modern school of composers.[17]

Saint-Saëns also merited significant praise: 'He is an excellent contrapuntist, shines in the construction of his orchestral pieces, has a quick ear for picturesqueness of detail, and has written enough fine music to procure him an honourable position among French composers'.[18] By contrast, the surprisingly short article on Gounod was quite critical; Chouquet dismissed almost everything prior to *Faust* although *Faust* itself placed Gounod 'at once in the first rank of living composers'.[19] Chouquet's conclusion was fairly even-handed but came with a final barb:

> Gounod is a great musician and a thorough master of the orchestra ... [H]is dramatic compositions seem the work of one hovering between mysticism and voluptuousness ... In the chords of his orchestra, majestic as those of a cathedral organ, we recognise the mystic – in his soft and original melodies, the man of pleasure. In a word, the lyric element predominates in his work, too often at the expense of variety and dramatic truth.

Chouquet viewed Halévy as talented and under-appreciated ('His countrymen have never done him justice') but erratic and indiscriminate; he 'took any libretto offered him, no matter how melancholy and tedious, [and] wrote in a hurry and carelessly', never surpassing *La juive*.[20] Entries on Bizet and Massenet were inevitably brief; Bizet, though, was 'a musician of superior abilities' and *Carmen* 'a fine score',[21] while 'if M Massenet will refrain from all mere cleverness ... he will prove an honour to the French school'.[22] Chouquet's most damning criticism was directed at Offenbach:

> [His] melodies are often vulgar and often wanting in piquancy. He never hesitates to repeat a good phrase, or to break a rule, if any purpose is to be served by it; but this, and other faults, are much concealed by the bustle, gaiety and extravagance of his effects, the frequent happy hits, and the strong natural vein of irony ... [His works] too often display merely a vulgar scepticism, and a determination to be funny even at the cost of propriety and taste.[23]

Lecocq, principally because he was not Offenbach, suffered less: 'His style is not a very elevated one and makes no demand on the poetry or the intellect of the composer; but it requires tact, ease, freedom, and above all, animation'.[24]

The articles by other authors contain various judgements; Hueffer was somewhat critical of Adam, but rated Auber highly:

> [He was] the last great representative of *opéra comique*, a phase of dramatic music in which more than in any other the peculiarities of the French character have found their full expression. In such works as *Le maçon* or *Les diamants de la couronne* Auber has rendered the chevaleresque grace, the verve, and amorous sweetness of French feeling in a manner both charming and essentially national.[25]

Marshall's article on Meyerbeer deemed him unique rather than original and emphasised his German origins as much as his association with Paris. There is an underlying thread of antisemitism; Ashton argued that Meyerbeer lacked creativity but could adapt, chameleon-like, to produce what was needed, supported by superb technical facility. However, she still acknowledged his achievements: of *Les Huguenots*, she wrote, 'The splendours and the terrors of the sixteenth century ... are all here depicted and endued with life and reality, while the whole is conceived and carried out on a scale of magnificence hitherto unknown in opera'.[26]

The most striking article, however, is Dannreuther's on Berlioz, a piece of advocacy made more significant by its extensive reach. The image of composer as tortured genius was fully on show:

> He stands alone – a colossus with few friends and no direct followers; a marked individuality, original, puissant, bizarre, violently one-sided; whose influence has been and will again be felt far and wide, for good and for bad, but cannot rear disciples nor form a school. His views of music are practically if not theoretically adhered to by all eminent composers and executants since Beethoven.[27]

Although earlier critics, especially Davison, had supported Berlioz, Dannreuther surpassed them, emphasising qualities valued by Victorian arbiters of taste:

> [C]ertain of Berlioz's attainments are phenomenal. The gigantic proportions, the grandiose style, the imposing weight of those long and broad harmonic and rhythmical progressions towards some end afar off ... The originality and inexhaustible variety of rhythms, and the surpassing perfection of his instrumentation are points willingly conceded even by Berlioz's staunchest opponents.

Berlioz's true weakness was a moral one, which led even admirers to 'recoil with instinctive revulsion'; citing the 'Devils' chorus' in *Faust* and finales of *Symphonie fantastique* and *Harold en Italie*, Dannreuther argued that grotesque subject matter inspired 'bloodthirsty delirious passion such as ... may have been excited by gladiators and wild beast shows in Roman arenas'.[28] Nevertheless, he conceded that 'these same reprehensible pieces contain some of their author's most astonishing technical achievements'.

Dannreuther excepted, the *Grove* articles largely reiterated extant thinking. Chouquet did not allow personal acquaintance to prevent him from expressing critical views. From a British perspective, his enthusiasm for Thomas was uncontroversial; criticism of Gounod was more surprising given British enthusiasm for the composer but, from Chouquet's Parisian perspective, Gounod had never surpassed *Faust*. Many readers would have endorsed Chouquet's view of Offenbach; the idea of talent frivolously wasted was familiar and regularly applied to Sullivan also. Offenbach's popularity, though, was undeniable and doubtless some readers saw Chouquet's view as moralising snobbery.

As in his obituaries, Auber was seen as the quintessential French composer, thanks to his achievements in *opéra comique*, the genre most strongly associated with France in British minds. Hueffer's presentation was there-fore familiar: a diligent, accomplished composer whose works encapsulated stereotypical French characteristics of wit, verve and elegance, albeit tinged with superficiality. Dannreuther's positive view of Berlioz, although unusual, echoed earlier suggestions of an untameable eccentric genius defying categor-isation, and coincided with renewed British interest in Berlioz's music (see below).

The first edition articles on French composers largely echoed and summarised British thought and, more importantly, reinforced them for decades: Fuller Maitland's second edition (1906) replicated almost all of the original articles[29] and some of Chouquet's entries appeared in Eric Blom's fifth edition (1954), which remained in use until replaced by the first *New Grove* in 1980; Chouquet's own position almost certainly imbued his articles with an additional sense of 'authenticity'. In an age when national attributes were widely believed to be biologically determined, *Grove* tied British perceptions of French music to ethnicity in a more enduring way than ever before.

Saint-Saëns in Britain

Of all nineteenth-century French composers, Saint-Saëns engaged most extensively with Britain. Due to the Franco-Prussian War, he spent sev-eral months in London in 1871, during which he made his first professional appearances, including at Ella's Musical Union;[30] his last appearances were in 1913.[31] As he came from Paris with solid credentials, London critics paid him some attention but, up to 1876, notices are typically brief. The C minor Cello Sonata (**1873**-9) was deemed 'choice and charming' by the *Musical Standard*,[32] but the earlier Suite for Cello and Piano (**1874**-2) was dismissed by the *Academy*: 'For nearly half an hour the audience sat and listened to a succession of passages, often brilliant, always ingenious, but without a trace of anything which really appealed to the feelings'.[33] Other early performances included the Variations on a Theme of Beethoven (**1875**-2) ('a clever, brilliant and remarkably taking composition'), *Introduction et rondo capriccioso* (**1875**-3) ('will sustain his reputation for melodiousness and facility of inven-tion') and the A minor Cello Concerto (**1876**-2) ('his tendency is towards the modern erratic school of Germany, rather than towards the more agreeable mannerisms of the land of his birth').[34]

An appearance at the Philharmonic Society in 1874 further raised Saint-Saëns's performer profile,[35] but as a composer his visit in July 1876 was more important: the B flat Piano Quartet, Op. 41, was introduced at the Musical Union (**1876**-5) and an independent concert dominated by his own music at St James's Hall two days later included the British premiere of *Marche héroïque*, Op. 34 (**1876**-6). Charges of 'academicism', stylistic eclecticism (or inconsistency) and lack of feeling, familiar later, were already appearing; the *Musical World* thought his compositions 'decidedly clever … but that they are calculated to arrest any attention by any freshness or marked originality of idea we are by no means disposed to admit'.[36] After hearing the Second Piano Concerto (**1878**-8), the *Athenaeum* was relieved: 'His Wagnerian tendencies are well known but there were no signs of them ... in this concerto'; its departures from conventional forms were deemed successful.[37] The A minor Symphony (**1879**-4) was also well reviewed:

> It contains sufficient adherence to rule to satisfy musicians of the old school, while there is an amount of freedom which indicates the inclination to progress and development. The adagio movement is very sweet and delicate and the prestissimo finale is irresistible.[38]

Appraising the Third Piano Concerto (**1879**-9), however, the *Examiner* found the first movement 'dry and diffuse, though a marvel of orchestration for the band and brilliancy for the solo instrument', and the finale 'striking for its enormous executive difficulty, but for no other reason'.[39] At the same concert, *Le rouet d'Omphale* (**1878**-10) was deemed 'thoroughly clever and genuinely artistic ... [though] a mere trifle,' by the *Musical Standard* and 'pleasing and fantastic,' by the *Examiner*.[40] *Danse macabre* (**1879**-6), however, was condemned by the *Daily News*, which thought that Saint-Saëns had produced

> effects the most horrible, hideous and disgusting ... [including] the use of the xylophone, the effect of which inevitably suggests (as doubtless intended) the clattering of the bones of skeletons. Another disagreeable (scarcely less hideous) device is the [retuned solo violin] ... The piece is one of the many signs of intense and coarse realism that is entering into much of the musical composition (so-called) of the day.[41]

The successful demand for an encore was noted ruefully. As with Offenbach, a disjunction between excitable audiences and censorious journalists is apparent; for the latter, certain subjects were inappropriate for musical representation and composers were expected to set a moral example (see also Dannreuther on Berlioz, above).

The Birmingham Festival's commission, resulting in the cantata *La lyre et la harpe* (**1879**-8), indicates British regard for Saint-Saëns by the late 1870s. This guaranteed widespread press coverage but achieved only a *succès d'estime*, the work being too removed from festival conventions.[42] The *Monthly Musical Record* outlined its challenges, but argued that musicians would

> appreciate its construction and the evident effort of the author to give a poetical character to his work ... Of the two new cantatas done at the festival, *The Lyre and the Harp* has the greater chance of popularity, but it not likely to be a sudden one.[43]

The *Musical Standard* praised the music but criticised the abstract subject, 'which is quite outside the ordinary walks of life',[44] while Henry Lunn argued that Saint-Saëns had fallen victim to the malign influences of Wagner and Gounod.[45] *La lyre* garnered puzzled respect rather than enthusiasm; accusations of 'Wagnerism', though inaccurate, were harmful, and no further performances are known.[46]

When he visited in 1880, Saint-Saëns's reputation had reached a plateau. While well-regarded and widely accepted as France's most versatile living composer, his status did not advance;[47] London concert programmes in the 1880s comprised mainly repetitions, and reviews tended to be more respectful than enthusiastic. At Hallé's concerts some resistance is apparent; Saint-Saëns's music featured regularly only from 1884 (typically two or three works per season plus short vocal items) and, of the sixteen major works performed, all but three were written before 1880.[48]

Only two major works arrived in London in the 1880s: the twenty-year-old setting of Psalm 18 (**1885**-4), received indifferently, and the new 'Organ' Symphony (**1886**-1). The latter arose from a Philharmonic Society invitation, a proposal Andrew Deruchie suggests Saint-Saëns accepted in the hope of finally producing an acclaimed 'monument'.[49] Any such aspirations were initially disappointed as critical reception was predominantly hostile.[50] Critics rejected the work's expanded orchestra and formal innovations, the latter offending their sense of propriety in the genre regarded as the supreme instrumental form; some argued that it was not a 'symphony' at all. Despite clear precedents, Saint-Saëns was thought self-indulgent, while unorthodox structures and instrumentation papered over a lack of substance. The *Graphic* was unusually blunt:

> [It] is, in point of fact, an even more than usually weak species of orchestral fantasia, in the course of which, by way of compensating for lack of ideas, the ordinary orchestra is reinforced by parts for an organ, a piano *à quatre mains*, and a cymbal that is thwacked with the butt-end of a kettle-drum stick ... [Its] most satisfactory feature seemed to be that it never once interrupted the flow of conversation on the part of the Philharmonic subscribers.[51]

The *Pall Mall Gazette* agreed, declaring that there were 'not more than half a dozen bars here and there that we should ever care to hear again'.[52] The *Musical Times* was more positive, deeming the slow movement 'the gem of the composition' and finding in the finale 'infinite variety of colour ... in the orchestration ... [while] a brilliant Coda, unduly prolonged, forms an exciting conclusion' but decided that while '[t]here is a great deal to admire in this Orchestral Rhapsody ... we distinctly decline to term it a "Symphony"'.[53] Thomas Southgate also found the work too idiosyncratic, arguing that in the finale 'the impetuous steeds have, as it were, escaped from the control of the charioteer and literally run riot'.[54] Hueffer, however, placed Saint-Saëns alongside Beethoven, Mendelssohn and Schumann (antecedents no doubt carefully chosen), asserting that the symphony came to a 'triumphant close' and made 'a favourable impression'; he concluded that 'Saint-Saëns is a master of his craft, and what is more, he makes that mastery subservient to the expression of a poetic idea'.[55] In terms of immediate after-life, Saint-Saëns was unlucky; the symphony was hardly more radical than works by Wagner and Berlioz but, following the largely hostile initial reception, there was little short-term incentive for more performances. The Philharmonic's revival (14 June 1894) fared as badly, but Lamoureux's (16 April 1896) was somewhat more successful.[56]

Recognition by the academic establishment came with the award on 12 June 1893, at Stanford's initiative, of an honorary doctorate by Cambridge, alongside Bruch, Tchaikovsky and Boïto.[57] Although of little immediate consequence, it indicates the regard for Saint-Saëns maintained by Britain's leading educators and connoisseurs; after Gounod's death four months later, he was widely regarded as France's leading living composer.

Of greater practical import was the establishment, in concert form, of *Samson et Dalila* (**1893**-5). Certain extracts were familiar, but the effective prohibition on portraying biblical characters ruled out a staged performance, so *Samson* was presented as an oratorio by the singer-cum-concert-promoter Farley Sinkins. Despite under-preparation, Sinkins's hope that the opera's renown would generate interest was well-founded,[58] though press coverage focused on the performance, the acceptability of 'biblical opera' and trans-formation from opera to oratorio. The *Musical Standard*, while acknowledging Saint-Saëns as 'a man of talent and at the very top of his profession', thought *Samson* 'essentially dull and lacking in the vital spark of inspiration'; concert performance was no disadvantage to a work that was 'essentially undram-atic'.[59] The *Musical Times* disagreed, arguing that 'the impressiveness and charm of the opening and closing acts, in which religious feeling predominates, are remarkable, while the second, dealing with Samson's fall and betrayal, shows dramatic strength and works up to an exciting climax'.[60] The *Athenaeum* agreed, referring to the work's 'melodic grace, sensuous beauty, and effective contrasts', and concluded that it showed 'Dr Saint-Saëns at his best'.[61]

After a short hiatus, *Samson* was taken up elsewhere, encouraged by the publication of an English vocal score; the Hallé gave the work in 1895, 1896 and 1897; it appeared in Glasgow and Liverpool in 1896, Leeds in 1897, at the Sheffield and Norwich Festivals in 1899 and at Nottingham in 1900. In London, Robert Newman included *Samson* at the Queen's Hall Promenade concerts in 1896 and 1897. Critical perspectives remained diverse; the *Musical News* appreciated the 'clearness and directness of expression and appropri-ateness of colouring', but John Runciman reckoned that Saint-Saëns had 'written the cleverest and dullest opera in the world'.[62]

Samson's popularity may have induced the Grand Opera Syndicate to produce *Henri VIII* (**1898**-5), the first of Saint-Saëns's operas to be staged in Britain, but critical reception was again mixed, varying from positive in the *Lute* ('the entire opera is engrossing in the most agreeable sense' even if Saint-Saëns did not 'shine so brightly as an inventor as he does in *Samson*') to boredom in the *Musical Standard*.[63] This time, there was no popular success: lavishly produced late in the season but without star singers, the work was given twice and then discarded.

Overall, Victorian reception of Saint-Saëns has a high degree of consistency: early evaluations were reinforced rather than modified. Regarded as supremely versatile and erudite (both as a performer and composer), Saint-Saëns was as easily able to shock, entrance or bore;[64] as early as 1876, the *Monthly Musical Record* had been struck by the contrast between the B flat Piano Quartet and *Danse macabre*.[65] His facility bemused critics and became a doubled-edged sword: reviewing *Henri VIII*, 'R Peggio' wrote:

> It is very difficult to find the real Saint-Saëns ... [H]e most assuredly possesses a kind of musical tarn-helm which enables him to conceal himself fairly successfully. Apparently he can write music in any style you choose. Do you want a little Wagner? Very well, Mons. Saint-Saëns gives you a passable imitation of the second act of *Lohengrin* in 'vous tous qui m'écoutez'. Do you admire Meyerbeer? If so, you will find much to your taste in *Henry VIII* ... [But] the real Saint-Saëns? Has he anything to say for himself?[66]

'R Peggio's' answer was no; accusing him of being merely 'a lover of sensuous beauty', he concluded that 'Do what he will, Saint-Saëns cannot be great; he does not even escape the common'. Despite its technical accomplishment, Saint-Saëns's music was widely felt to lack profundity and individuality; the pejoratives 'dry', 'academic', and 'dull' recur regularly. Yet, despite such reservations, Saint-Saëns's abilities, regular visits to London, urbanity and the popularity of works such as the Second Piano Concerto resulted in agreement that he was the most important French composer of his generation. Compared to Auber and Offenbach, Saint-Saëns was rarely viewed explicitly through a prism of Frenchness yet, implicitly, qualities attributed to him draw on established tropes: suavity, clarity and lightness were balanced by superficiality and frivolity, making him an archetypal Parisian. His long career and sustained engagement with Britain reinforced these perceptions in the twentieth century.

Massenet

Although Massenet also became known in Britain in the 1870s, his dedication to opera limited dissemination of his music; unlike Saint-Saëns, he visited Britain only occasionally and did not so actively court its cultural agents. Nevertheless, Massenet was soon recognised as a major composer whose activities, especially before 1900, were reported regularly in the musical press, with new operas gaining generous coverage.

Orchestral music arrived first: *Scènes pittoresques* (**1875**-4) made a favourable impression due to agreeable melodies, colourful orchestration and evocative moods; the *Musical Standard* referred to its 'Fête Bohème' as 'exceedingly characteristic, sparkling and full of vivacity, and suggestive of scenes most picturesque to the dullest imagination'.[67] Massenet visited Britain to introduce *Scènes dramatiques* (**1878**-4) and selections from *Le roi de Lahore* (**1878**-5) and *Les Errinyes* (**1878**-6).[68] His music's accessibility was highly rated; the *Musical Standard* was happy to be entertained:

> The appearance of M Massenet amongst us is an event of real import-ance, for he is undoubtedly a great man of the day, if not in the fullest sense, as some assert, *l'homme de l'avenir* ... His conducting is like his music, graceful, energetic and unaffected; his orchestration is masterly in the extreme, yet there is no apparent search after effect: his melodies are telling and never commonplace, sometimes even broad and imposing.[69]

As with Saint-Saëns, early impressions formed the basis for subsequent judgements; in line with general expectations of French music, Massenet's strengths were perceived to be in illustrative rather than 'absolute' genres, and attractiveness rather than profundity.

A major step came when *Le roi de Lahore* was staged at Covent Garden (**1879**-7), receiving extensive publicity and favourable reviews. The exotic mythical setting was variously linked to Wagner, *Aïda* and *L'Africaine*, while the opulent production compensated for excessive length, essentially conven-tional characters and the lack of a fascinating Carmenesque lead.[70] The opera was viewed as significantly better than most other recently introduced works, and Massenet as having potential; the *Academy* argued that, despite clear antecedents, there were 'traces of the working of an individual mind ... [and] much that is very charming in the quieter portions'.[71] Indicative of shifting attitudes, the *Saturday Review* declared that

> Whilst the influence of Wagner is clearly felt, and felt for good rather than harm, M Massenet never is driven to imitation. Thus, whilst he takes romantic legend for his subject, subordinates musical to dramatic effect, abjures strictly formal melodies, and often gives the most important and melodious part to the orchestra, rather than to the voices, we find that he does not disdain to use unaccompanied recitative ... and that he is not always using violin harmonics, restless changes of key, abrupt modulations and startling discords.[72]

It was Hueffer, however, who best predicted the opera's future:

> If we look in an opera for the emanation of highest dramatic pathos ... we most certainly shall be disappointed in Massenet's work. If, on the other hand, we are satisfied with flowing, though not very deep or very new melodies expressive of sentiments common to heroes and heroines of

the lyrical stage, with admirable musical workmanship aided by gorgeous scenery ... [It] contains all the elements of at least temporary success.[73]

After five performances in 1879 and three in 1880, *Le roi de Lahore* was dropped, and eleven years passed before Massenet got his next opportunity.

In the interim, extracts from operas such as *Hérodiade* became familiar, as did certain orchestral pieces: the popular *Scènes pittoresques* was joined by the 'Danse galiléenne' and the still-familiar 'Dernier sommeil' from *La Vierge* (**1880**-10). A short *scena*, *L'invocation d'Apollon*, performed by Joseph Maas at the Norwich Festival (**1884**-3), was also well received and repeated elsewhere but Maas's premature death in January 1886 seems to have led to its being forgotten.[74] In one respect Massenet fell foul of divergent national sensibilities: his *légendes sacrées* would initially appear to be ideal for British choral societies but no performances have been traced. Reviewing the vocal score of *Ève*, the *Musical Times* declared:

> It is easy to understand the reluctance of choral societies to present to the public with works in which the sacred characters are travestied in a manner likely to be regarded as blasphemous ... It would, of course, be absurd to look for the essential features of oratorio... breadth, power, and fugal writing. [*Ève*] is highly esteemed in the land of its birth, but public taste must undergo considerable change if it is to become popular in this country.[75]

The Carl Rosa Company achieved a coup by introducing Massenet's newest work, *Manon*, at Liverpool (**1885**-1) (see Figure 4.1).[76] The *Liverpool Evening Express* declared the work 'essentially French' and influenced by Thomas,[77] while the *Musical Times* singled out the orchestration and ensembles for particular approval, with recurring motifs and eschewal of extractable items proof of Massenet's modernity.[78] The *Magazine of Music* concurred; although 'essentially representative of the modern French school', Massenet was 'an unprejudiced student of the whole range of music, and incorporates into his work, without the slightest suggestion of plagiarism, the spirit and essence of what he deems good in contemporaneous music'.[79] Rosa subsequently gave *Manon* at Drury Lane, where it was more fully reviewed. The *Athenaeum* was tempered but thought it would succeed: '*Manon* cannot in any sense be regarded as an elevated work of art ... [but it] is certainly the most acceptable comic opera since *Carmen*'.[80] Comparing the two lead characters, the *Musical World* found Manon more sympathetic; while Carmen was 'profoundly sensual and revoltingly heartless', Manon lacked 'coarsely vicious propensities' and her downfall came only from 'vanity or mere love of pleasure'.[81] George Bernard Shaw, in one of his early pieces of music criticism, was impressed, referring to Massenet's music as 'pretty, spirited, easy to follow, varied with considerable fancy and ingenuity, never dull, and only occasionally trivial or

Fig 4.1 Massenet's *Manon*, Royal Court Theatre, Liverpool (*Graphic*, 16 May 1885, p. 492)

vulgar', although sometimes, due to Massenet's fondness for 'stage tumult', Shaw found *Manon*, literally, too loud: 'The quartet with chorus in the fourth act must be almost as audible on Waterloo Bridge as in the first row of stalls in Drury Lane Theatre'.[82]

Considering its success, it is surprising that *Manon* survived in Rosa's repertory for only two seasons. No single aspect explains this, suggesting that it simply failed to displace established favourites or to escape displacement itself by other novelties, but easy parallels with *Carmen* may have proved problematic, especially as Marie Roze played both eponymous roles, as may the lack of easily extractable solo items. Harris's revival at Covent Garden succeeded only modestly (see below) and Massenet's best opportunity to establish himself as an opera composer passed: although other works followed, including the specially commissioned *La Navarraise*, Massenet never achieved the (very differently constructed) renown of Saint-Saëns.

'Grand opera' in the West End, 1879–1900

The mid-1880s were difficult years for West End opera companies; challenges had long been accumulating but now finally combined to bring the network to virtual collapse.[83] Although recovery was relatively quick, French composers lost opportunities that were not later recouped. While many commentators believed Italian opera had run its course, seeing no successor to Verdi, French composers, though widely thought to produce interesting and accessible work, had yet to surpass either *Faust* or *Carmen*.[84] Meanwhile, Wagner's mature operas arrived in London, performed in German rather than Italian, as had been the case hitherto; *Der Ring*, *Tristan und Isolde* and *Die Meistersinger* were premiered in 1882 but, while they highlighted the Italian troupes' stale repertories, neither audiences nor critics were ready for Wagner wholly to displace them. *Die Meistersinger* and *Tristan* were repeated in 1884 but then left until 1889 and 1892 respectively, when *Der Ring* also reappeared. At Covent Garden, Ernest Gye relied on a small number of stars, while Mapleson found touring the United States with Patti more profitable; lucrative opportunities in South America also drove up singers' fees in London. In 1885 and 1886, several impresarios, including Mapleson, suffered embarrassing failures in the West End. Victoria's Golden Jubilee in 1887 proved fortuitous: Augustus Harris, a long-established West End manager, was induced by a select number of the 'upper ten' to mount a short season of popular works at Drury Lane. Assured of continuing support, Harris moved to Covent Garden in 1888 and remained there until his death in 1896, managing seasons as musically successful and socially desirable as ever before. In terms of repertory, Harris proceeded cautiously up to 1890,[85] and, consequently, few French operas were introduced in the 1880s: besides *Manon*, only Delibes's *Lakmé* (**1885**-2) and Bizet's *Les pêcheurs de perles* (**1887**-1) were given, neither of which became established.[86]

The make-up of West End opera repertory throughout the period examined in this study was somewhat paradoxical. Unlike concert repertory, there was little sense of a developing corpus of masterpieces deemed worthy of preservation, while audiences expected that new works would be regularly introduced; these factors, combined with relatively short seasons and high production costs, meant that new operas, if successful, could only gain a place in the regular repertory by displacing other, usually older, works; from the 1880s, operas by Meyerbeer, Auber, Rossini, Bellini and Donizetti were all produced less frequently than previously; after 1890, Auber, Bellini and Rossini disappeared almost entirely. Conversely, however, audience preferences were quixotic; there was no reliable way to predict a new work's acceptance, either temporarily or permanently.

Despite the risks involved, Harris realised that re-establishing Covent Garden's 'gatekeeper' status was an essential criterion for success. His rationale for selecting new operas is unknown: although a Francophile and fluent French-speaker, Harris was not a trained musician and he was probably influenced as much by leading subscribers, performers and connoisseurs as by his own preferences. While British repertory and German composers except Wagner were *infra dig*, French works were supported; the popularity of singers Jean and Edouard de Reszke and Victor Maurel, all with strong Parisian connections, almost certainly helped. During Harris's tenure, five of the ten most frequently performed operas originated in Paris (in descending order: *Faust*, *Carmen*, *Roméo et Juliette*, Gounod's *Philémon et Baucis* and *Les Huguenots*), to which might be added Gluck's *Orfeo* given its particular history.[87] Harris also introduced new French operas: in addition to *Philémon* were *Le rêve* and *L'attaque du moulin* (Bruneau; **1891**-3 and **1894**-4), and *Werther* and *La Navarraise* (Massenet). Notable revivals included *L'Africaine* (1888), *Les pêcheurs de perles* and *Roméo* (1889), *Le prophète* (1890), *Manon* (1891), and *Fra Diavolo* (1895).

A further innovation was the production of French and German operas in their original languages; in 1892, the 'Royal Italian Opera' became the 'Royal Opera' and, by 1896, the Italian versions of most French operas had been abandoned. The first work to benefit was *Roméo et Juliette*. Gounod's revised version, made for the Paris Opéra in 1888, was used; the decision to perform in French was widely praised though it was casting Nellie Melba and the de Reszke brothers as Juliet, Romeo and Friar Lawrence that ensured success. John Shedlock summed up critical consensus: the music was 'very charming', though 'with only moderately good singers, [it] might prove somewhat tedious'; the incongruity of 'Je veux vivre' was felt as strongly as previously (see Chapter 3).[88] With audiences, however, *Roméo* was popular: it was the third most frequently performed opera in Covent Garden's main seasons between 1889 and 1905 (100 performances), after *Faust* (130) and *Lohengrin* (104) (see Figure 4.2). Following Harris's revival, the Rosa company gave the first English-language and provincial performances in the 1890s.

Fig 4.2 Emma Eames as Juliette in Gounod's *Roméo et Juliette*, Covent Garden (*Illustrated London News*, 18 May 1901 (cover))

Harris produced *Philémon et Baucis* (**1891**-2) in what was effectively a dedicated autumn French season staffed almost entirely by Parisians; of the seven operas performed, only *Lohengrin* was not French. *Philémon* proved unexpectedly popular: the *Athenaeum* noted Auber's influence and commended Gounod's 'extremely fine music' and its 'dreamy tenderness', while the *Monthly Musical Record* believed it Mozartian, 'bright and attractive' and 'essentially French' with 'dainty and original music'.[89] Shaw, whose praise for Gounod was usually highly qualified, was also impressed, calling *Philémon* 'a charming work, all pure play from beginning to end, but play of the most exquisite kind'.[90] Its success was temporary; performed with spoken dialogue, *Philémon* required *opéra comique* specialists, viable only in a dedicated French season, a venture Harris's successors were unwilling to undertake; after his death the opera was quietly dropped.

Harris also showed great interest in Massenet but with indifferent results. His production of *Manon* (19 May 1891) was roundly criticised (a weak soprano lead and poor stage management), as were aspects of the work, echoing reviews of the original production; for the *Musical News*, 'in its literary, dramatic and moral aspects *Manon* is as sordid and unsympathetic as any of the now discarded works of the conventional Italian school', although the writer added that while 'by no means a great work, *Manon* is a fresh and winning opera, and on the whole far more equal than any of the composer's more ambitious efforts'.[91] Despite such reservations, *Manon* achieved a middling eighteen performances until its final appearance in 1903, but was not performed elsewhere.

With *Werther* and *La Navarraise* Massenet was unlucky, as they were overshadowed by acclaimed productions of Puccini's *Manon Lescaut* and Verdi's *Falstaff*.[92] Harris's decision to introduce two operas by the same composer in one season seems strange but the choice of *Werther* (**1894**-2) was probably due to lobbying by Jean de Reszke, who had successfully performed the title role in New York. Equivocal reviews focused on the scenario; the *Observer* found it dull: 'Here are two worthy middle-class people, whose fate differs in no way from that of their fellows … [but] we are asked to believe that their troubles are worthy of furnishing materials for a music-drama of quite heroic proportions'.[93] The *Athenaeum* searched for the positive, suggesting that 'Although the dramatic interest is feeble and the subject itself rather morbid … [t]he score glows with colour and freshness in melody and instrumentation and, as usual with the French composer, the love music is remarkable for sentiment and tenderness'.[94] De Reszke was uniformly praised and the first performance well attended, but it was not enough.[95]

La Navarraise (**1894**-3), a one-act *verismo* opera, was a rare Harris commission, and conceived for the highly popular Emma Calvé.[96] Reviews all noted first-night audience enthusiasm, and most were positive; Massenet attended but did not appear on stage. Obvious affinities with *Cavalleria rusticana* led the *Musical Standard* to declare that it was 'Mascagni out-Mascagnied',[97] while the *Manchester Guardian* argued that

It is not so much the music – though a great deal of that is beautiful and all of it appropriate – as the intensity of the drama and the acting that worked up the emotions of the spectators. Never on the operatic stage have the horrors of war been depicted with such absolute realism.[98]

The fifty-minute duration helped: according to the *Musical Times*:

[T]he musician is chained to the wheel of the rapid drama, and hurries along with it, doing his best with transient themes and instrumental colour ... It certainly held the Covent Garden audience as in a grip of iron. We never saw a house so absorbed in the fortunes of the stage, and seldom have witnessed a success so thorough and instantaneous.[99]

Several reviewers perceived a change in Massenet's music: the *Athenaeum* noted 'a measure of virility and individuality' from a composer known for 'sensuous, and what may be termed feminine, melodies and orchestration'.[100] The *Observer* also referred to 'virility', while the *Musical News* simply stated that 'the music is the most masculine that Massenet has written';[101] the presumption that French music was 'feminine' and sensuous remained sufficient for Massenet's score to be a surprise.

As with *Manon Lescaut* and *Falstaff*, however, *La Navarraise*'s success at Covent Garden was brief: after four performances in 1894 and one in 1895, it disappeared, excepting an unsuccessful revival in 1904. This was partly due to there being no obvious partner work,[102] but also a *volte face* in critical and possibly audience views. In 1895 critics were dismissive: the *Musical News*, having previously called *La Navarraise* 'an excellent example of the modern short tragic opera', now condemned it: '[T]ime does not increase respect for the music, whilst the ghastly realism with which the story is treated becomes more objectionable with further acquaintance ... [T]he opera presents the supreme effort of the morbidly sensational school'.[103] Runciman referred to 'an eminently silly opera, eminently French, ... [that] is even destitute of virile vulgarity',[104] refuting another earlier judgement. Such stark reversal is puzzling, especially given the contemporaneous popularity of *Cavalleria rusticana* and *Pagliacci* (although *La Navarraise* lacks a 'big tune' to equal *Cavalleria*'s Intermezzo). Harris may have 'manufactured' his commission's initial success, although his ability to sway so many observers is debatable. The principal victim, though, was Massenet; while *La Navarraise* remained popular in Paris until the 1940s, its London failure, alongside previous lack of outright success, inhibited his prospects in Britain: none of his operas introduced after 1900 lasted more than one season (see Chapter 5), and he showed less interest in promoting his music in Britain than Saint-Saëns.

Harris had secured a completely dominant position for Covent Garden when he died unexpectedly in 1896. Production standards had improved, and repertory broadened; French composers were notable beneficiaries. These changes were restricted to the West End: Harris had limited interest in touring and no other companies performed his new French operas.[105] Needing to keep influential subscribers on-side, Harris had limited room for manoeuvre and was forced to maintain the 'star system' of singers; the Grand Opera Syndicate, quickly established after his death, was driven by the same subscriber clique and fundamentally conservative. Nevertheless, during Harris's tenure French opera was better represented at Covent Garden than ever before, a position maintained until around 1905 when a resurgence in Italian opera, led by Puccini, started to displace it; even then, French opera remained a principal pillar of Covent Garden's repertory.

After Offenbach: French operetta in the 1880s and '90s

While Offenbach's popularity declined and British light opera flourished, several other French operetta composers also prospered in London until the popularity of the 'variety musical' diminished the fortunes of light opera from both nations. The most successful French works of the 1880s remained popular with touring troupes and also with the flourishing movement of amateur companies. Although no single French composer outpaced Offenbach, Robert Planquette, Edmond Audran and André Messager each experienced significant popular success in the 1880s and '90s. Central to their acceptance was respectability; most works were only seen in translation and there was no successor to the scandalous Hortense Schneider. Careful adaptation was essential to ensure that English versions remained (if only just) on the right side of good taste; reviewers continued to censure French 'naughtiness' and either to commend British authors (the indefatigable H B Farnie above all) for toning down saucy plot elements or to criticise them for going insufficiently far.[106] Reviewers regularly mentioned 'silly' or formulaic plots, excision of *risqué* elements, undistinguished music, the prominence of decoratively dressed female choruses, and expressed perplexity that such works were so popular.

Planquette developed the closest association with Britain. His first operetta, *Les cloches de Corneville*, achieved a major success in Paris before opening in London (**1878**-1), where he was praised for 'an inexhaustible flow of tune' and even the elitist Hueffer, in one of his first reviews for *The Times*, deemed the work 'light and agreeable'.[107] The routine plot was relieved of impropriety by Farnie: in Hueffer's words, 'it is free, as, indeed, is the whole piece, from any suspicion of indecorum', although he partly attributed the success to 'pretty scenery, pretty dresses, pretty faces, and a liberal display of the beauties of the female form'. Running for over 700 performances, *Les cloches* outpaced *HMS Pinafore* and became a standard work on the touring circuit; these, together with occasional West End revivals in the 1880s, ensured its popularity with amateurs for several decades.[108]

Les voltigeurs (**1881**-8) was less successful but Planquette's direct collaboration with Farnie on an adaptation of Irving's well-known *Rip van Winkle* (**1882**-3) did well. The more sober plot did not enthuse everyone: the *Academy* opined that 'it is feeble in comedy … and yet its serious interest … is never worked up quite strongly enough', though the *Saturday Review* argued that it was 'bright [and] untainted with the less agreeable peculiarities of Offenbach'.[109] The *Observer*, however, felt that *Rip* surpassed *Les cloches* and singled out the Act II finale as evidence of Planquette's ability to construct extended scenes, as well as catchy melodies.[110] Recalling Auberian *opéra comique* through less whimsical drama and more complex music did no harm: *Rip* ran for almost a year, with Violet Cameron's portrayal of Rip's wife, Alice, drawing particular praise. Despite this achievement, Planquette never surpassed *Les cloches*; *Nell Gwynne* (**1884**-1) managed only 86 performances before touring, and *Captain Thérèse* (**1890**-2) fared no better.[111]

Between Planquette's two successes came two equally popular works by fellow-tyro, Audran. *Olivette* (**1880**-8), yet another Farnie adaptation, provoked a somewhat weary reaction from the *Daily News* that typifies many critics' attitudes: Audran's music was characterised by a 'complete absence of originality' but 'the popularity of *opéra bouffe* ... is now so well assured that any composer having a natural feeling for tune, and furnished with a suitable libretto, may depend upon obtaining a public verdict in his favour'; leading singers Violet Cameron and Florence St John were praised.[112] Hueffer predicted a short after-life, arguing that *Olivette*'s songs would be 'played on the domestic piano and on the noisy street organ ... and sung for a season, till they go to the limbo of things forgotten'.[113] Unashamedly highbrow, Hueffer found *Olivette* formulaic, deftly aligning characters and plot elements with various precursors:

> That entertainments of this class at present command a vast amount of popularity in London is a fact which one may regret but cannot deny. They, of course, do not call for serious criticism, neither would it be of any use to preach the canons of high art to audiences intent only upon admiring pretty faces, pretty dresses and pretty, though commonplace, tunes ... [O]ne cannot suppress a feeling of pardonable pride at the thought of the marked superiority of English burlesque opera as created by Messrs Gilbert and Sullivan ... How infinitely more refined its humour; how pure its sentiment and diction; how much more artistic also its music!

Olivette ran for 466 performances, illustrating Hueffer's distance from popular taste.

Audran's follow-up, *La mascotte* (**1881**-9), opened just six days after *Patience*.[114] The coincidence allowed Hueffer to reiterate earlier points, comparing Audran unfavourably with Gilbert & Sullivan, and noting the 'lavish display of female charms', and the 'large audience, including the Prince and Princess of Wales',[115] expected, it seems, to set a better example. Hueffer conceded another popular success, however, stating that 'For all we know, it may extend its run over any number of weeks or months or years'. Others reviewers were more charitable but still critical; some had seen the Paris production and William Beatty Kingston marvelled at Farnie and Reece's ability to reduce its saucy plot to 'a harmless idyll'.[116] The *Manchester Guardian* was representative in finding the music 'decidedly better, the stream of melody being richer, and the orchestration more elaborate and piquant' than that of *Olivette*, but censured the hugely popular comic duet in which Bettina (Cameron again) and her suitor Pippo imitated gobbling turkeys and bleating sheep.[117]

André Messager is more distinctive. Though he was almost unknown in London when *La Béarnaise* was produced (**1886**-2), critics noted his pedigree: taught privately by Saint-Saëns and Fauré, Messager had been deputy organist at St Sulpice and composed in several serious genres, though this drew the implicit criticism that, like Sullivan, he had lowered himself by turning to light opera. Echoing Hueffer, the *Saturday Review* argued that *La Béarnaise* contained 'none of the literary finish' found in Gilbert, while noting how Florence St John's popularity, alongside 'bright dresses and gay music' secured audience approval.[118] Messager's score, however, was praised for its dexterity and elevated approach:

> We were so greatly pleased with ... [his] contrapuntal treatment of a chorus 'Ambassador? That tale don't tell', that we were very favourably disposed towards what followed. This chorus was unmistakably the work of a musician ... The melodies will not ring through the town as the airs of *La Grande Duchesse* and *La Fille de Madame Angot* so speedily began to do; but there is much in M Messager's score to gratify hearers.

A run of over 200 performances suggests that critics and audiences were better aligned than usual.

Reviews of *La Basoche* (**1891**-4) (see Figure 4.3) were also supportive. It was used by D'Oyly Carte at the Royal English Opera House as a replacement for Sullivan's *Ivanhoe*, putting Messager in a potentially difficult situation: *Ivanhoe* had achieved a record-breaking run for a serious British opera but interest was flagging, and the irony of a French light opera being used as a rescue attempt was obvious. Fortunately, no criticism was directed at Messager personally; according to the *Athenaeum*, 'the only feeling of regret ... is that no lyric drama by an English composer was secured to follow ... *Ivanhoe*'.[119] Commending Carte, the *Saturday Review* argued:

> Music should be of no nationality ... In going to the Opéra Comique ... Mr Carte has shown a wise discretion; for nowhere else in Europe does anything like a living school of opera exist ... Some disappointment at seeing what proposed to be the home of English opera occupied by so thoroughly French a work as *La Basoche* may be natural; but the lesson is one to be taken to heart and profited by.[120]

Many reviewers appreciated the work's humour despite the implausible plot; the *Monthly Musical Record* thought *La Basoche* a great success

SCENE FROM THE NEW OPERA "LA BASOCHE" AT THE ROYAL ENGLISH OPERA
Act I.—A Public Place in Paris in 1514.   Clement Marot (Mr. Ben Davies) disowns his wife Colette (Miss Lucille Hill)

Fig 4.3 Messager's *La Basoche*, Royal English Opera House (*Graphic*, 7 November 1891, p. 9)

and Messager's music 'of a high character. The melodies have a plaintive charm that reminds the hearer of the beautiful old madrigals',[121] while the family-orientated *Bow Bells* wrote of 'freshness and spontaneity that at once attract the ear'.[122] *The Times*'s new music critic was also positive: John Fuller Maitland, although no populist, had more catholic tastes than Hueffer, and thought *La Basoche* a 'work of very great beauty and charm ... [While it] contains passages which are light enough for *opéra bouffe*, it is clear from its general design that the composer is an earnest and highly cultivated musician'.[123] Despite this support, *La Basoche* ran only until January 1892 and, unusually, there was no provincial tour,[124] and none of *Fauvette* (**1891**-6), *Fanchette* (**1894**-1) and *Mirette* (**1894**-5) performed well.[125] Messager's next success, *Véronique*, did not come until 1903 (see Chapter 5).

Kurt Gänzl argues that London audiences' preferences changed sharply around 1893 in favour of 'variety musicals', a new subgenre lacking *opéra bouffe*'s intricate plots, and characterised by modern settings, topical jokes and glamorous costumes (copies of which could be bought).[126] Established works remained popular, especially outside London, but new pieces often struggled. An exception was Audran's final British success, *La poupée* (**1897-1**), whose popularity was driven primarily by the fantastical story, in which a real woman takes the place of a life-size automaton intended for use in a fabricated marriage to a novice monk. Reviews praised the sheer comedy value of this plot device; the *Musical Times*, which generally eschewed light opera, noted 'many diverting situations and humorous incidents' and music of 'melodic interest and graceful vivacity'.[127] According to the *Speaker*, ' "suggestiveness" has been kept (almost) within the limits of becoming mirth', which complemented the 'ear-tickling music'.[128] The *Lute* happily found *La poupée* 'widely removed from things of the *Gaiety Girl* or *Geisha* class. There is an atmosphere of refinement and neatness about *La poupée* which is infinitely pleasing'.[129] Reversing Hueffer's view, Maitland declared that, 'It is high time that comic opera, of the type made familiar in hundreds of examples from the French, came back to amuse English audiences' and praised Audran's 'charmingly vivacious and tuneful' music;[130] a genre previously derided as too lowbrow had been undercut and consequently rose in estimation.

Although no-one outperformed Offenbach, Parisian *opéra bouffe* remained a prominent part of London and provincial theatre repertory until the mid-1890s; despite critics' sniffiness, public appetite remained strong, weakened significantly only by the 'variety musical' and 'Girl' subgenres. Careful adaptation by Farnie and others was vital; faced with a robust British tradition from the late 1870s onwards, French operettas would almost certainly have failed had they retained overt Parisian 'naughtiness'. But adaptation also excised distinctiveness: critics typically saw little difference between French and British works as the former were anglicised, becoming cautious hybrids in the hope of securing favour; Hueffer's reviews were unusual in explicitly placing Sullivan firmly above Audran *et al*. Equally, light opera continued to be the most widely known French music in Britain, retaining its leading role in creating perceptions of what French music was for a large part of the public.

Concert music old and new: Berlioz, Gounod, Fauré and Chaminade

The range of French concert music performed in Britain broadened substantially in the *fin-de-siècle* decades. In addition to Saint-Saëns and Massenet, interest in Berlioz grew rapidly from the late 1870s, and Gounod remained prominent, primarily due to his oratorio, *The Redemption*. In the 1890s, several other French composers were briefly boosted by the Lamoureux and Colonne concerts, while, amongst others, Fauré and Chaminade also made an impression. This expansion should be placed within the context of the continuing prominence of German music; the canon, while still undergoing a process of consolidation, dominated programmes, and new music from across

Europe had to compete for attention. Further expansion in concert provision, especially in London, created additional performance opportunities in absolute terms, but it is worth recalling that the most prominent conductors active in Britain in the 1880s and 1890s (Manns, Hallé, Richter, Cowen, Sullivan, Mackenzie and Stanford) all had strong German connections of some form or other.[131] Exemplary evidence of the popularity of canonic repertory is given in Colin Eatock's examination of public votes held at Crystal Palace in the 1880s: French music barely features in the lists of works nominated for performance.[132] Such caveats notwithstanding, however, it is clear that opportunities to hear French concert music increased significantly and were widely appreciated.

Berlioz's music had mainly been neglected since his final appearance in London in 1855.[133] Although Hallé and Manns gave some shorter works in the late 1850s, their interest then plateaued (see Chapter 3). From 1875, though, and principally between 1878 and 1885, most of Berlioz's large-scale choral and orchestral works received their British premieres. Dannreuther's article in *Grove's Dictionary* (see above) re-energised the argument that Berlioz was an iconoclastic genius. By 1885, although his popularity did not approach Beethoven, Mendelssohn or Wagner's, Berlioz was widely accepted as one of Europe's most original composers, and his music, despite its technical challenges, was heard regularly in major venues.

The first 'rediscovery', *Harold en Italie* (by Hallé, Manchester, 28 January 1875), attracted little national attention and did not immediately inspire other activity, but was the first performance of a major work for over twenty years.[134] Three years later, Hallé repeated *Harold* and Manns also introduced it at Crystal Palace (30 November 1878). Critical views recalled those of the 1850s: the *Musical World* thought *Harold* 'full of beautiful passages and original thought [but] it lacks the continuity and coherence of the great works of the mighty masters ... and we are often startled by effects without being impressed or charmed'.[135] Ebenezer Prout believed Berlioz, like Mozart and Schubert, had been undeservedly neglected, and argued that Berlioz and Wagner were 'composers of great originality, writing in a style in advance of their age', who made 'not the slightest concession to popular taste', but whose trenchant prose writings had 'tended to embitter the contest raised over their music'.[136] Like others, Prout thought *Harold*'s first three movements inspired but the finale 'might just as easily have been taken for an orgy in a lunatic asylum'.[137] The *Symphonie fantastique* followed (**1879**-1); like *Harold*, it succeeded modestly with the last two movements provoking bewilderment and hostility: orchestral illustrations of diabolical depravity particularly offended Victorian sensibilities.[138] The *Manchester Guardian* was unusual in allowing that the 'Marche au supplice', 'though a morbid fancy, has a lurid brightness which exercises a singular fascination on the mind'.[139]

For Victorian audiences, Hallé's most significant contribution was the first complete performance of *La damnation de Faust* (**1880**-1).[140] The *Manchester Guardian* eulogised the entire work and noted the enthusiastic public reception;[141] the story was familiar, and, unlike *Harold* or *Symphonie fantastique*, *Faust*'s sung text provided an unambiguously moral ending. By 1890, Hallé had conducted twelve performances in Manchester; in 1880, he also conducted four performances at St James's Hall (21 and 22 May, 20 November and 11 December), where it also received overwhelmingly positive coverage. Shedlock's view is representative; finding the music 'strikingly original, and full of dramatic power', he added that Berlioz

> exhibits a wonderful versatility of style: the pathetic, the solemn and the terrible, the gay and the humorous, are blended together with skill and discrimination; and clear form without formality, and tuneful music without triteness combine to render the work pleasing and acceptable.[142]

Guarded agreement came from the *Musical Times*: *Faust* 'was bound to succeed sooner or later', as, even if 'the music belongs to the ultra-romantic school, it is recommended by so much melody, descriptive power and brilliant colouring that even those who most dislike the ultra-romantic are constrained to admire and applaud'.[143] Quickly established as Berlioz's most popular large-scale work, *Faust* was performed regularly by choral societies up to 1914; the Carl Rosa Company produced a staged version in 1894.[144]

More works followed, though with mixed results. *Nuits d'été* (**1881**-10) was found too lugubrious at a time when vocal items were expected to provide relief from weightier orchestral works,[145] and *L'enfance du Christ* (**1880**-12), though thought to contain beautiful music, was judged uneven.[146] The *Grande messe des morts* (**1883**-1) was more widely appreciated, despite a sense that it lacked religiosity, but its sheer scale inhibited regular performances.[147] More practical and better received was the *Te Deum* (**1885**-3), although this too was performed only occasionally; the *Saturday Review* called it 'a colossus among choral works', while the *Musical Standard* praised its overall design, counterpoint and orchestration.[148]

The revival's rapidity attracted attention.[149] While Berlioz's music puzzled many, a contemporaneous sense of curiosity is evident, from which not only Berlioz benefitted, but also Brahms, Wagner, Dvořák, Saint-Saëns, Massenet and many others, principally in London but also other large cities. In part, Berlioz was a 'flavour of the month'; after initial excitement dissipated, several works were neglected and hampered by technical and logistical challenges. Nevertheless, it was a striking reversal for a composer dismissed only a few years previously as an eccentric egotist whose music, however fascinating, was rarely found attractive.

Though based on only two works, Gounod's popularity also increased. Following his departure from London in 1874, interest had plateaued and his reputation continued to rely primarily on *Faust*; nevertheless, he was still popular and viewed as a good commercial prospect when approached by the Birmingham Festival committee in 1881, which sought a centrepiece work for its meeting the following year. By coincidence, Gounod had long been working on an oratorio, *The Redemption*, and was eager to see it performed; the committee bought it for the unprecedented sum of £4,000.[150] Exemplary marketing in the musical press, in which Gounod's opinion that *The Redemption* was the 'opera vitae meae' was regularly repeated, heightened interest;[151] its premiere was widely regarded as Birmingham's most important since *Elijah* in 1846 (**1882**-2).[152]

Critics tended to be dissatisfied. Dislike of Gounod personally, excessive hype, and resentment or incredulity regarding his fee surely played a part, but the publicly stated view was that *The Redemption* was weak. The *Musical Standard*'s writer confessed himself, 'somewhat disappointed ... The work is certainly one of a very and high refined order [but] I am doubtful ... as to its ultimate acceptance as a great work ... The composer, although he attains the grandiose in his choral movements at times, does not seem to touch the region of the sublime'.[153] The *Daily News* was more positive, despite finding the work 'occasionally somewhat secular in tone'; the *Standard*, however, stated that, although 'some beautiful thoughts are embodied in the score [and] occasion-ally we find an ennobled idea ... generally the feeling produced is one of mon-otony and depression', while the *Athenaeum* pithily declared that 'for posterity the great work of Gounod's life will be *Faust* rather than *The Redemption*', and also criticised the recitative sections, for being 'set either on a monotone or on ascending or descending chromatic scales ... [He] has used chromatic chords to such an extent as to become absolutely wearisome'.[154] Despite previous scepticism, the *Musical World* gave a positive review, arguing that 'the obvious beauties of the work are many ... the choral numbers produce an effect not to be denied';[155] wider critical reservations, its writer felt, arose from Gounod's partial eschewal of the understood conventions of the oratorio genre.

With choral societies and audiences, however, *The Redemption* proved popular: before the end of 1882 there were performances at the Bristol and Brighton Festivals, Albert Hall, Crystal Palace, Wolverhampton and Reading, with many more others following.[156] Selections appeared in organ recitals and single items as anthems in church services, as Gounod had doubtless hoped.

While many reviewers loftily criticised a musical style they felt lay below *Elijah* and *Messiah*, *The Redemption*'s popularity was sufficient to induce Birmingham to commission a successor.[157] *Mors et vita*'s premiere (**1885**-5) was complicated by Gounod's being mired in a libel action taken against him by erstwhile companion Georgina Weldon.[158] Considering the case trivial, Gounod was stunned when Weldon won and was awarded £11,640 in damages but, as these could only be enforced if Gounod visited Britain, he withdrew his commitment to conduct in Birmingham.[159] Disregarding this embarrassment, *Mors et vita* gained better reviews than *The Redemption*. Partly this was because Gounod made no pretence that it was a conventional oratorio: *Mors et vita* comprises three parts (a Requiem Mass, the Sleep of the Just and Last Judgement, and the vision of new Jerusalem from Revelation);

there are no 'characters' and only a broad narrative trajectory. The Latin text (novel for an English choral festival, though entirely appropriate for a piece dedicated to Pope Leo XIII by a devout Catholic) attracted some criticism. Extensively analysed before the premiere, the work was generally thought successful, though not without qualification.[160] Shedlock found it too long and criticised certain mannerisms, including Gounod's 'habit of repeating short vocal phrases in sequence – three, four times and even oftener ... [and] the continual, and at times very harsh chromatics' but praised 'the extreme beauty and pathos of some of the pages, the power and brilliancy of others, and throughout the splendid clearness and vivid colouring of the orchestration'.[161] For Joseph Bennett, the work was a success: 'It cannot be heard without emotion; or without a sense, at the end, that the spirit of the hearer has been raised to higher than earthly things'.[162] Shaw, agreed in part but overall found it too naïve and, ultimately, boring:

> [Gounod] is the romantically pious Frenchman whose adoration of the Virgin Mother is chivalrous, whose obedience to the Pope is filial, and whose homage to his God is that of a devoted royalist to his King. It follows that he is not a deep thinker. But his exquisite taste, his fastidious workmanship, and an earnestness that never fails him even in his most childish enterprises, make him the most enchanting of modern musicians within the limits of his domain of emotion and picturesque superstition ... At bottom, [however,] M Gounod's piety is inane, and so, at bottom, his music is tedious.[163]

Despite this warmer critical reception, *Mors et vita* was never as popular as *The Redemption*. At three and a quarter hours it was exceptionally long, even by Victorian standards; perceptions of repetitiveness militated against it, as did the Latin text, although an English adaptation was soon published. After initial interest, the work never threatened to displace established predecessors. Ultimately, perceived unevenness proved the biggest handicap: the *Standard* argued that

> much that is full of exquisite charm and unaffected grace suffers from juxtaposition with a great deal that is harsh and unnecessarily discordant ... Another detracting quality is the constant employment of the sequential method of composing ... too lavish indulgence in such an easy means towards an end discounts the value of the workmanship.[164]

Mors et vita was Gounod's last British success. His death in 1893 provoked press coverage that in many respects anticipated future British perceptions. *Faust* was considered his best work: in Shedlock's words,

> It may be found that the sentimental side of Goethe's dramatic poem has been unduly emphasised, that Gounod was not altogether oblivious of

the gallery; and yet the music is irresistible. There is true feeling in it: it goes from the heart of the composer straight to the heart of the hearer.[165]

The *Saturday Review* was more direct: 'The impresario knows he cannot stand without *Faust*. Every new operatic tenor, every young operatic soprano, is of the same mind. The public all the world over demand it with one voice. It is *toujours Faust* and *Faust partout*'.[166] Excepting *Roméo et Juliette*, Gounod's other operas were regarded as failures. His relationship with Britain was mentioned by all, but his liaison with Weldon variably treated. Considering works premiered in Britain, Shedlock's view that *The Redemption* 'enjoys a reputation here which its music does not altogether justify',[167] was widely shared, although the *Athenaeum* attributed this to Gounod's 'absolute sincerity and earnestness', continuing, '[H]is methods were not those employed by the great masters of the past, [but] they were his own, and they impress with all the force of intense and unswerving faith'.[168] Maitland raised the inevitable question of Gounod's legacy and his conclusion exemplifies the view of establishment commentators:

> The large admixture of a weak sentimentality in his professedly sacred compositions ... makes it difficult for thoughtful musicians, at least in England, to accept them as wholly sincere ... His highest flights in the way of sacred, if not devotional, music are undoubtedly to be found in places where they would not at first be expected; the second, fourth and fifth acts of *Faust* ... have a vigour of expression which is sadly to seek in *The Redemption*. The winsome grace which is to be found in his greatest opera, as well as in *Roméo et Juliette* ... has far more of the element of permanence in it, and while opera lasts it is probable that the best of these will not be forgotten.[169]

Of all French composers known in Victorian Britain, Gounod aroused both greatest enthusiasm and ambivalence. Although never, unlike Offenbach, publicly accused of immorality, there was a recurrent underlying sense that he was an outsider whose music appealed to a weak, sentimental aspect of British taste and did little to improve it. Above all, Gounod was thought to write down to audiences; whatever reservations critics had about Berlioz, causes of admiration were his aspiration, perceived independence and disinterest in popularity. With Gounod, most British commentators never rid themselves of the suspicion that he sold out.

Among other composers whose reputations developed at the *fin-de-siècle* were Fauré, Franck and Chaminade, the first and last of whom gained from personal appearances. Excepting an isolated rendition of his Violin Sonata (**1880**-5),[170] Fauré's music was virtually unknown in Britain until its repetition, with the G minor Piano Quartet (**1891**-5), by Belgian virtuoso Eugène Ysaÿe. Neither work enthralled critics: the *Musical News* thought the sonata 'full of *esprit*, clever writing and effective passages, but built on themes lacking in individuality and developed in a rhapsodical manner that ... often seemed to approach incoherence'.[171] The *Athenaeum*'s review of the Piano Quartet also focused on form, arguing that

> [Fauré] does not seem to be able to handle the larger forms of the art with much success ... [He] seeks to gain effects by singular changes of tonality and this device is pursued in the slow movement to such an extent as to be positively ear-torturing.[172]

Progress was slow: Fauré came to London to perform the Violin Sonata, the C minor Piano Quartet (**1894**-6) and selected songs with Francis Thomé; he also met Frederick and Adela Maddison, who became keen supporters.[173] Maitland wrote positively of the quartet, referring to it as a 'thoroughly interesting, original and in some passages beautiful work, revealing a mastery of construction that few of his countryman have surpassed'; doubtless its Brahmsian turns of phrase made the individualistic harmonies more palatable.[174] More intense exposure came in 1896 and '97, when Fauré appeared in London on several occasions, though performances were dominated by previously heard chamber music. A salon hosted by Alberto Visetti featured the C minor Piano Quartet and *Caligula* (**1896**-4);[175] the former was repeated at St James's Hall, while Ysaÿe also repeated the Violin Sonata.[176] The G minor Piano Quartet still mystified reviewers when heard in a dedicated Fauré concert at St James's Hall on 10 December,[177] and a similar concert on 5 June 1897 also does not appear to have advanced Fauré's reputation;[178] nor did composing incidental music for the British premiere of Maeterlinck's *Pelléas et Mélisande* (**1898**-4).[179]

The first large-scale work to be heard was *La naissance de Vénus* at the Leeds Festival (**1898**-6) but this inhibited rather than enhanced Fauré's reputation: 'dreary' and of 'very little character' was the *Manchester Guardian*'s view,[180] while Edward Baughan was contemptuous:

> The French composer has a certain vogue among the tireless searchers after new sensations, and, to be frank, there is a certain elusive charm to many of his smaller pieces, although the charm often borders on the eccentric ... [*La naissance*] is pretty in its way, but the prettiness is of a very sugary order, and the composer wanders about from key to key with that ineffective restlessness that is particularly characteristic of the modern French school at its worst.[181]

By 1900, Fauré's reputation had advanced only slightly; despite his own conspicuous effort and valuable support from others, little of his music had been professionally performed and it had met with limited success. Perhaps unsurprisingly, it was almost ten years after appearing at Leeds before Fauré returned (see Chapter 5).

While Fauré could promote his music in person, Franck had already died by the time any significant British interest arose. When the Violin Sonata was introduced (**1893**-2) it was tolerably received: the *Athenaeum* thought that, despite tonality that 'is almost painfully restless', the work was characterised by 'great earnestness of purpose [that] has little in common with ordinary French music', while the *Magazine of Music* offered a rounded appreciation, deeming Franck

> one of those unassuming characters, whose real merit is only known to the world after their death ... A strong sense of artistic form combined with a science which it would be hard to surpass ... distinguish [his] music ... [and] all these qualities were noticeable in the beautiful sonata.[182]

Other performances gained some positive comments; Franck was more highly regarded than Fauré at this point, though no more frequently performed. Colonne conducted one movement from *Psyche* (**1896**-6), and Lamoureux both the Prelude to Part II of *Rédemption* (**1896**-10) and the D minor Symphony (**1896**-12); the latter gained several positive comments ('a nobly conceived and finely carried out work' in the *Observer*'s view, which was 'remarkable for its loftiness of purpose and dignified expression' and 'one of the best examples of modern French music' according to the *Musical Times*).[183] The Glasgow Choral Union's innovative performance of *Les béatitudes* (**1900**-1) was praised but the work itself viewed as uneven and uninspired.[184] Despite some positive reviews, especially of the Violin Sonata and Symphony,[185] the lack of an advocate in a posthumous context proved a persistent handicap, with only limited progress before 1914.

Like Fauré, Chaminade built her British reputation almost entirely on chamber music but with considerably greater success. Her works originally appeared in the late 1880s, but the first significant marker was her personal debut at St James's Hall on 23 June 1892. For the remainder of the decade, Chaminade performed annually in London, typically at the height of the social season, promoting her music assiduously and building a significant following, especially in affluent circles. Initially, London critics were impressed: of the Piano Trio in A minor, Shedlock wrote, 'We do not remember any work by a female composer showing such breadth of conception and treatment, sustained power and fertility of ideas', while the *Athenaeum* thought it one of 'great merit, not only in the symmetry of its construction, but in the remarkably fresh treatment of the subject matter'.[186] In part, Chaminade gained attention due to her gender – London critics were then showing considerable interest in the phenomenon of the 'lady composer' – but compliments in early reviews are typically direct and lack condescension.

Within two years, Chaminade was well known; she was interviewed by the *Magazine of Music*, appeared at Bristol in late 1894 and undertook a provincial tour in spring 1895.[187] Sympathetically reviewing her annual St James's

Hall recital in 1895, Arthur Hervey stated that 'Her music is typified by a peculiar grace and piquancy. It is melodious and flowing, while her harmonies are both refined and uncommon'.[188] In addition to her own appearances, her short pieces, especially songs, featured regularly in other recitals; her reputation peaked with performances of the *Concertstück for Piano and Orchestra* at the Philharmonic Society (**1895**-2), and *Callirrhoë* (**1896**-5) at Queen's Hall and Crystal Palace. The *Concertstück* was not so well received,[189] but *Callirrhoë* was judged 'a work of much charm, fresh in tone [and] most cleverly scored'.[190]

A rapidly emerging reservation, however, was that Chaminade's music, while well-crafted, cultivated and amiable, tended to be stylistically and sonically uniform, a perception inadvertently encouraged perhaps in her recitals, which were dominated by her own music. While treated even-handedly by some critics, others were dismissive, and a current of sexism verging on misogyny characterises several reviews from 1896 onwards. The *Musical Standard* was consistently unimpressed, snidely commenting of *Callirrhoë* that

> the work bears out the truth of Dr von Bülow's *dictum* that no woman ever originated a new musical idea. What *seems* novel in it is due to the interpolation of borrowed Grecian or Oriental tunes, dressed up with noisy and sensational orchestration ... [T]he suite is thoroughly French in its frivolity and would have suited the Promenade Concerts of a few years back much better than the Crystal Palace.[191]

Runciman was still more dismissive: 'We all know how the Chaminade ceases not by day nor yet by night to spin a web of pretty music without an original or striking or ugly bar in it'.[192]

Nevertheless, like Offenbach and Gounod in other contexts, Chaminade's chamber music, especially her songs, proved popular with performers and audiences; snobbish misogyny from certain critics did not prevent wider popularity, though she made few significant advances after the late 1890s. Less hostile writers thought her style had failed to develop; following her annual recital in 1899, the *Athenaeum* commented that

> Everything she write displays skill, taste and fluency ... it is sure to be graceful or brilliant, and in its way effective. All these qualities, however excellent in themselves, yet do not fully satisfy. As piece follows piece, we feel that we are listening to music with which we can find no technical fault, yet to music which seems as if the first impression it creates would be the strongest. It may well be ... that she knows exactly the measure of her strength [and] the limitation of her powers.[193]

Chaminade herself seems to have concluded around 1900 that performing in London had become less rewarding, and reduced her visits; of her last recital, in 1907, Maitland wrote, with typical condescension, 'All Mme Chaminade's favourite idioms and all her most popular devices were displayed in a way that was both telling and successful … [S]he understands her own limitations, and only writes what she knows she is capable of writing well'.[194]

While French singers and instrumentalists performed regularly in London,[195] and opera troupes visited occasionally from the 1840s, conductors were rarely seen unless, like Saint-Saëns, they were also composers. Two exceptions were Charles Lamoureux and Edouard Colonne, who created a brief frisson in London concert halls in the late 1890s. Lamoureux often visited London in a private capacity and had made his professional début with a specially formed orchestra at St James's Hall in March 1881 in two concerts of French music. Widely appreciated by critics, the concerts introduced major compositions by Gouvy (**1881**-1) and Widor (**1881**-5) amongst others.[196] Attendance was, perhaps, not as good as hoped, as Lamoureux did not reappear until April 1896, when, at Robert Newman's invitation, he brought his own orchestra to Queen's Hall. On this and subsequent occasions, Lamoureux conducted French, German and Russian repertory; many reviewers discussed at length whether a Frenchman could truly 'understand' Beethoven and Wagner.[197] Although initially praised, doubts crept in and Lamoureux was widely regarded as being best when conducting French music, though he regularly drew broader appreciation.[198] His initial season, which also included whistle-stop appearances in Manchester, Birmingham and Brighton, was judged successful and Lamoureux returned in November 1896, April 1897, and then, conducting the Queen's Hall's resident orchestra, in November 1897 and February 1898. Various premieres, including works by D'Indy and Franck, were incorporated, although the repertory became more conservative and less French as time progressed.[199] Indicative, perhaps, of over-kill, Colonne's visit, in October 1896, was less successful, initially possibly due to tiredness and under-preparation: his orchestra gave its first concert in Queen's Hall on the day it left Paris.[200] Colonne presented mixed programmes and was most highly rated when conducting French music, though Lamoureux was preferred; three short works were introduced (**1896**-6 to **1896**-8).[201] Colonne and his orchestra revisited in 1908 and 1913, conducted by Pierné on the latter occasion following Colonne's death; on both occasions, though, the programmes were unadventurous.[202]

Conclusion

Following consolidation in the 1860s and '70s, the *fin-de-siècle* decades comprised a period of incremental expansion of French music in Britain. Gounod's reputation became founded as much on religious music as on opera, Saint-Saëns and Massenet achieved significant progress, Berlioz's music underwent a major revival, and there was a big increase in non-theatrical music in concert programmes, based initially on the composers mentioned and followed, mainly in London in the 1890s, by works by several lesser-known composers, including Fauré, D'Indy, Chaminade and Franck, who acted, in effect, as an advance guard for a younger generation of musicians after 1900. Only in operetta and *opéra bouffe* did French music undergo a reverse, undermined in the 1890s by the runaway success of 'variety musicals', whose popularity pulled attention away not only from *opéra bouffe* but also from the 'Savoy' operas and their imitations.

Grove's Dictionary provides a useful reference point from which to consider the evolving reputations of French composers at the *fin-de-siècle*. A notable feature is differing levels of consistency in perceptions; views on Saint-Saëns and, to a lesser extent, Massenet, crystallised within a few years of their music becoming known and, in the case of Saint-Saëns particularly, have hardly changed since. Berlioz, however, underwent a major reappraisal, with many commentators tempted to put him in the 'genius' category alongside Beethoven, assuming that, as with Beethoven and Wagner, further acclimatisation to his music would vindicate their judgements in the longer term. Among critics, Gounod's reputation, conversely, started to decline even before his death, though his music remained widely popular until 1914 and beyond; as with Offenbach, part of the critical establishment looked down on Gounod's music and was frustrated by its ubiquity. The conservative critic Joseph Bennett, writing in 1897, articulated a common future view when surveying the church music of Gounod's supporters, Stainer and Barnby;[203] the tendencies towards 'sentimentalism' and 'a full measure of languorous tenderness carried on the wings of a pretty tune' that Bennett perceived in Stainer, and of 'an expression of feeling which sometimes inclines to the effeminate' in Barnby were attributed to Gounod's influence which, in Barnby's case, was 'too obvious to escape note'. Bennett nevertheless remained positive: 'For my own part, I welcome this strain of French sacred music in our English amalgam. It would be easy – very easy – to have too much of its mannerisms but, kept in their proper place, these make possible some excellent effects and furnish materials which no sensible composer can wholly ignore'. Others viewed this 'sentimentalism' less charitably, though, and criticism on these grounds became a running thread in British attitudes to Gounod in the twentieth century, *Faust* to some extent excepted.[204]

Overall, however, the period 1879–1900 can be viewed as the second big step forward for French music in Britain, following the preceding plateau. Moreover, this expansion took place against a backdrop of declining political relations, further demonstrating, as with trade, that diplomatic tensions had little effect on British interest in French culture and produce. Developments in the 1890s set the stage for a further expansion, both in volume and stylistic diversity, from 1900 to 1914.

Notes

1 In France, there was extensive debate on restoring the monarchy, while Britain addressed a sustained agricultural depression and Irish Home Rule.

2 See T G Otte, 'From "War-in-Sight" to Nearly War: Anglo–French Relations in the Age of High Imperialism, 1875–1898', *Diplomacy and Statecraft*, **17** (2006), pp. 693–714, and John Lowe, *The Great Powers, Imperialism, and the German Problem 1865–1925* (London & New York, 1994).

3 Otte, p. 700.

4 See François Crouzet, *Britain Ascendant: Comparative Studies in Franco-British Economic History* (Cambridge, 1990), especially pp. 442–63.

5 Crouzet, p. 451.

6 Cars worth 2.6 million francs were exported to Britain in 1899, rising to 65 million in 1910.

7 See *Times*, 25 April 1889, p. 8. For an examination of music at the Exposition, see Annegret Fauser, *Musical Encounters at the 1889 Paris World's Fair* (Woodbridge, 2005).

8 *Times*, 7 May 1889, p. 5.

9 See Alexander Geppert, *Fleeting Cities: Imperial Expositions in* Fin-de-Siècle *Europe* (Basingstoke, 2010).

10 *Times*, 13 April 1900, p. 4.

11 *Times*, 13 November 1900, p. 5. Paul Kruger had been deposed from the Presidency of the Boer Republic in September and forced into exile. He was received enthusiastically in Marseilles on 22 November, followed by Paris, Cologne and The Hague.

12 *Times*, 24 May 1900, p. 10.

13 *Times*, 28 May 1900, p. 8.

14 George Grove (ed.), *A Dictionary of Music and Musicians* (1st ed, 4 vols, London, 1878–89). Although the first edition was published over ten years, the content was written in the 1870s; post-1879 updates comprise an Appendix to Volume 4.

15 Appendix updates were supplied by the Paris-based critic Adolphe Jullien, who also wrote new entries on Fauré and Franck.

16 See, for example, Robert Stradling and Meirion Hughes, *The English Musical Renaissance 1840–1940: Constructing a National Music* (2nd ed, Manchester, 2001), pp. 24–6.

17 Grove, vol. 4, p. 104.

18 Grove, vol. 3, p. 215.

19 Grove, vol. 1, p. 614.

20 Grove, vol. 1, p. 645.

21 Grove, vol. 1, p. 246.

22 Grove, vol. 2, p. 236.

23 Grove, vol. 2, p. 493.

24 Grove, vol. 2, p. 110.

25 Grove, vol. 1, p. 102.

26 Grove, vol. 2, p. 323.

27 Grove, vol. 1, p. 232.

28 Grove, vol. 1, p. 233.

29 Only Dannreuther's article on Berlioz was entirely replaced (see Chapter 5, note 142); others were updated to account for post-1889 developments and Maitland expanded Chouqet's article on Bizet.

30 Stephen Studd, *Saint-Saëns: A Critical Biography* (London: 1999), pp. 82–5.

31 Stéphane Leuturé states that Saint-Saëns visited Britain 22 times ('Saint-Saëns: The Travelling Musician', in Jann Pasler (ed.), *Camille Saint-Saëns and his*

World (Princeton and Oxford, 2012), p. 136)). For his appearances as an organist, see Chapter 3.

32 *MS*, 13 December 1873, p. 370.

33 *Academy*, 7 March 1874, p. 272.

34 *MMR*, 1 August 1875, p. 118; *MS*, 20 November 1875, p. 335; *MW*, 4 March 1876, p. 174 (for a more positive review see *MS*, same date, p. 142).

35 Playing Beethoven's Fourth Piano Concerto (Studd, p. 99, and *MS*, 18 July 1874, p. 38).

36 *MW*, 22 July 1876, p. 499; see also *Athenaeum*, 8 July, p. 59.

37 *Athenaeum*, 22 June 1878, p. 807; see also *MW*, same date, p. 405.

38 *MS*, 31 May 1879, p. 335.

39 *MS*, 13 December 1879, p. 367; *Examiner*, 20 December, p. 1636.

40 As previous note; Sullivan's earlier performance received little attention (see Appendix). *La jeunesse d'Hercule* (**1877**-2) fared less well; see *Athenaeum*, 27 October 1877, p. 541.

41 *DN*, 3 June 1879, p. 6. *MW* later described the piece as 'a perversion of talent', 'a degradation of pure and beautiful art to low and repulsive purposes' and 'musical prostitution' (26 March 1881, p. 196, of Lamoureux's performance at St James's Hall on 22 March).

42 Victor Hugo's text juxtaposes 'voices' of paganism and Christianity; Saint-Saëns illustrated these via orchestral texture, tempo, major and minor modality etc., but the work lacked a conventional narrative and personifications by soloists.

43 *MMR*, 1 October 1879, p. 153; the other cantata was Bruch's *The Lay of the Bell*.

44 *MS*, 6 September 1879, p. 144; see also *Athenaeum*, same date, pp. 314–5; *Orchestra*, 1 October, p. 44.

45 *MT*, 1 October 1879, p. 526;

46 *MW* stated that *La lyre* 'is not the result of a desire to win popular applause at any cost, otherwise it would have been much more full than it is of cheap claptrap' (13 September, p. 576).

47 See *MW*, 8 May 1880, p. 289; *MS*, 22 May, p. 326; *MT*, 1 July, pp. 344–5.

48 Works performed before 1884 were the Second Piano Concerto and *Le rouet d'Omphale* (1878), Third Piano Concerto (1879), and 'Danse des prêtresses' from *Samson et Dalila* (1880). The post-1879 works were the ballet music from *Henri VIII* (1886), *Suite algérienne* and the Third Violin Concerto (both 1894).

49 See Andrew Deruchie, *The French Symphony at the Fin-de-Siècle* (Woodbridge, 2013), pp. 16–19. The Philharmonic's initial invitation to perform a piano concerto soon changed to introducing a symphonic work; see Sabine Teller Ratner, 'Saint-Saëns in England: His *Organ* Symphony', in Pasler, p. 163.

50 Curiously, many daily newspapers mainly ignored the concert, despite the Philharmonic's status and the presence of Saint-Saëns and the Prince and Princess of Wales.

51 *Graphic*, 22 May 1886, p. 558.

52 *PMG*, 20 May 1886, p. 5. See also *Athenaeum*, 22 May, pp. 688–9; *Academy*, same date, p. 372.

53 *MT*, 1 June 1886, p. 335.

54 *MS*, 29 May 1886, pp. 334–5.

55 *The Times*, 22 May 1886, p. 5, largely reproduced in *MW*, 29 May, p. 349.

56 Of the Philharmonic performance, George Bernard Shaw stated that 'It is a pity that this particular work of Saint-Saëns degenerates so frightfully at the end. All

that barren coda stuff, with its mechanical piling of instruments, its whipping of rhythms, and its ridiculous scraps of fugato, should be ruthlessly excised: it has no real theme, and only spoils the rest' (*The World*, 13 June 1894, quoted in Dan H Laurence (ed.), *Shaw's Music: The Complete Musical Criticism of Bernard Shaw* (3 vols, London, 1981), vol. 3, pp. 240–1). See also *Academy*, 16 June 1894, p. 502; *Athenaeum*, same date, p. 783; *MS*, same date, p. 505; *Academy*, 25 April 1896, p. 351; *Athenaeum*, same date, p. 553.

57 Boïto and Bruch were second choices, Verdi and Brahms having refused Cambridge's invitations; Grieg was absent due to illness; see Gerald Norris, *Stanford, the Cambridge Jubilee and Tchaikovsky* (Newton Abbot, 1980); *MT*, 1 July 1893, p. 408, and *MN*, 17 June, p. 568. At the post-congregation concert Saint-Saëns was the soloist in his *Afrique*, Op. 89 (**1893**–4); he and Tchaikovsky also appeared at the Philharmonic, the latter introducing his Fourth Symphony.

58 Frederic Cowen conducted; see his *My Art and my Friends* (London, 1913), pp. 231–2.

59 *MS*, 30 September 1893, p. 266.

60 *MT*, 1 October 1893, p. 600.

61 *Athenaeum*, 30 September 1893, p. 461; see also *Academy*, same date, p. 279; *SR*, same date, pp. 381–2.

62 *MN*, 12 December 1896, p. 509; *SR*, same date, pp. 622–3, of the Queen's Hall performance on 10 December; see also *MS*, same date, pp. 363–4.

63 *Lute*, 1 August 1898, pp. 723–4; *MS*, 23 July, pp. 52–3; see also *MN*, same date, p. 87; *MG*, 15 July, p. 6; *MT*, 1 August, pp. 531–2.

64 Adolphe Jullien's supplementary comments in *Grove* exemplify this: '[He]is a consummate master of composition ... but the creative faculty does not keep pace with the technical skill of the workman' (Vol. 4, p. 778).

65 *MMR*, 1 December 1876, p. 191.

66 *MS*, 23 July 1898, p. 53.

67 *MS*, 23 November 1875, p. 353; see also *Observer*, 21 November, p. 7; *MMR*, 1 December, p. 178.

68 See *Athenaeum*, 4 May 1878, p. 581, and 11 May, p. 613; *MS*, 4 May, pp. 271–2; *Academy*, 11 May, p. 427; *MT*, 1 June, p. 327; *MMR*, same date, p. 94.

69 *MS*, 11 May 1878, p. 286.

70 See *MT*, 1 August 1879, p. 426; *Athenaeum*, 5 July, pp. 24–5.

71 *Academy*, 12 July 1879, p. 40.

72 *SR*, 19 July 1879, p. 82.

73 *Times*, 30 June 1879, p. 13.

74 See *MW*, 25 October 1884, p. 668; performances have been traced at Crystal Palace, Edinburgh and Birmingham over the following six months.

75 *MT*, 1 February 1888, p. 109; the score included an English translation by Hueffer.

76 A provincial premiere was unusual and caused local satisfaction (*MT*, 1 February 1885, p. 79). Rosa persistently tried to undermine the West End Italian companies' 'gatekeeper' status and introduced several new foreign operas in addition to his British commissions; see note 85 and Paul Rodmell, *Opera in the British Isles 1875–1918* (Aldershot, 2013), pp. 48–53 and 132.

77 Quoted in *MS*, 24 January 1885, p. 53.

78 As note 75.

79 *MoM*, 1 February 1885, p. 11.

80 *Athenaeum*, 16 May 1885, p. 640.

81 *MW*, 16 May 1885; see also *MG*, 8 May 1885, p. 8. For more critical views see *Academy*, 16 May, p. 356, and *MoM* (note 79).

82 *Dramatic Review*, 16 May 1885, quoted in Laurence, *Shaw's Music*, vol. 1, p. 244.

83 See Rodmell, pp. 35–48 and 53–61.

84 Opinions of Verdi were revised following *Otello*'s triumph in 1887 but it was widely regarded as a one-off.

85 Rosa's death in 1889 deprived his troupe of its driving force, which scaled back its innovative activities; Harris, by then a director, deliberately marginalised the company in London, although, outside the capital, it introduced Bizet's *Djamileh* (**1892**-2), Godard's *La vivandière* (**1896**-1) and Gounod's *Cinq Mars* (**1900**-2).

86 L Mayer integrated *Lakmé* (with Marie van Zandt, for whom the role was written), Gounod's *Mireille* and Thomas's *Mignon* into his established French drama season; *Lakmé* was moderately successful (*MW*, 13 June 1885, p. 364). His subsequent season of French opera and operetta at Her Majesty's in November 1886 was heavily criticised (see *Era*, 13 November, p. 9), but the two seasons between them included the first London performances in French of *Carmen*, *Faust, Les cloches de Corneville* and *Mignon*.

87 *Cavalleria rusticana* was the most popular work; the only German opera was *Lohengrin*.

88 *Academy*, 22 June 1889, p. 438; see also *SR*, same date, p. 760; *Athenaeum*, same date, p. 801.

89 *Athenaeum*, 31 October 1891, p. 592; *MMR*, 1 November, p. 256. See also *MN*, 30 October, p. 699; *MS*, 31 October, pp. 346–7; *MT*, 1 November, p. 662.

90 *The World*, 25 November 1891, quoted in Laurence, *Shaw's Music*, vol. 2, p. 465.

91 *MN* 22 May 1891, p. 235; see also *MS*, 23 May, pp. 418–9; *SR*, same date, p. 623.

92 Initial excitement dissipated rapidly: *Manon Lescaut* was dropped until autumn 1904 while *Falstaff* was repeated in 1895 but then dropped until 1914.

93 *Observer*, 17 June 1894, p. 6; see also *MS*, 16 June, p. 499, and *MN*, same date, p. 562.

94 *Athenaeum*, 16 June 1894, p. 782.

95 Allegedly, advance bookings for the second performance were so poor that de Reszke feigned illness, forcing its cancellation; see Harold Rosenthal, *Two Centuries of Opera at Covent Garden* (London, 1958), pp. 260–1.

96 Harris possibly steered Massenet in this direction: *Cavalleria rusticana* was hugely popular at Covent Garden but Harris was piqued that he had not introduced it to London himself.

97 *MS*, 23 June 1894, p. 523.

98 *MG*, 21 June 1894, p. 5; see also *SR*, 23 June, p. 662, and Shaw's review in *The World*, 20 June, quoted in Laurence, *Shaw's Music*, vol. 3, p. 243.

99 *MT*, 1 July 1894, p. 460.

100 *Athenaeum*, 23 June 1894, p. 815;

101 *Observer*, 24 June 1894, p. 6; *MN*, 23 June, p. 516.

102 *Cavalleria rusticana* was too similar and its leading role also strongly associated with Calvé; in 1895, *La Navarraise* was played with *Philémon et Baucis* and in 1904 with Saint-Saëns's *Hélène*.

103 *MN*, 23 June 1894, p. 586, and 27 July 1895, p. 76; see also *Speaker*, same date, p. 99.

104 *SR*, 3 August 1895, p. 140.

105 Harris mounted short tours in 1888, 1893 and 1894; works performed include *Philémon et Baucis* (Dublin and Birmingham, 1893) and *La Navarraise* (Dublin, Belfast, Edinburgh, Liverpool, Manchester and Newcastle, 1894).

106 John Lowerson argues that Farnie's adaptations 'were a guarantee of respectability, covering any *frisson* of foreign naughtiness with the assurance that no offence could be caused' (*Amateur Operatics: A Social and Cultural History* (Manchester & New York, 2005), p. 82).

107 *Era*, 3 March 1878, p. 5; *The Times*, 1 March, p. 10; see also *Observer*, 24 February, p. 6.

108 Lowerson (p. 84) cites evidence of over 80 productions up to 1910, not far behind Gilbert & Sullivan.

109 *Academy*, 11 November 1882, p. 354; *SR*, 22 October, p. 537.

110 *Observer*, 15 October 1882, p. 6.

111 *Captain Thérèse* was commissioned by the Carl Rosa Light Opera Company following the success of *Paul Jones*, an English version of *Surcouf*, from which, however, most of Planquette's music was discarded.

112 *DN*, 21 September 1880, p. 3; see also *MW*, 25 September, p. 610, which was marginally more positive.

113 *Times*, 21 September 1880, p. 8.

114 Inaugurating the Comedy and Savoy theatres respectively; *Olivette* later transferred to the Strand.

115 *Times*, 17 October 1881, p. 11.

116 *Theatre*, 1 November 1881, p. 292. The original scenario is based on the premise that farm-worker Bettina ('la mascotte') will bring luck to whomever possesses her, as long as she remains unmarried, i.e. a virgin.

117 *MG*, 17 October 1881, p. 5. Audran remained productive; *Gillette* (**1883**-3) was moderately successful and *La cigale* (**1890**–3) a hit, though much of its score was replaced. Other attempts (**1884**-4, **1886**-3 and **1891**-1) fared less well.

118 *SR*, 9 October 1886, p. 484.

119 *Athenaeum*, 7 November 1891, p. 625.

120 *SR*, 7 November 1891, p. 524. Simultaneously, Messager's *Fauvette* was playing at the Coronet, Notting Hill, also coinciding with Harris's French opera season at Covent Garden, which introduced *Philémon et Baucis* (see above) and Bruneau's *Le rêve* to London: this sudden rush of new French works did not go unnoticed.

121 *MMR*, 1 December 1891, p. 278.

122 *BB*, 13 November 1891, p. 479.

123 *Times*, 4 November 1891, p. 6; see also Shaw's review in *The World*, 11 November, quoted in Laurence, *Shaw's Music*, vol. 2, p. 450.

124 Carte was in difficulty, and sold the Royal English Opera House shortly afterwards to Harris, who turned it into a music hall; this was also the time of Gilbert and Sullivan's infamous 'carpet quarrel'.

125 Produced by Carte at the Savoy, *Mirette* was withdrawn after 41 performances, the theatre's shortest ever run; revised, it reappeared in October 1894, lasting for 61 nights.

126 Kurt Gänzl, *The British Musical Theatre, Volume 1: 1865–1914* (Basingstoke, 1986), p. 454. The earliest instances were *In Town* and *Morocco Bound* (both 1892), followed by a series of 'Girl' shows, starting with *A Gaiety Girl* (1893).

127 *MT*, 1 April 1897, p. 246; see also *MN*, 6 March, p. 222.

128   *Speaker*, 6 March 1897, pp. 270–1.
129   *Lute*, 1 March 1897, p. 587. Sidney Jones's *The Geisha* was the musical hit of 1896 and barely half-way through its 760-performance run when *La poupée* opened.
130   *Times*, 25 February 1897, p. 6.
131   Hallé's equally strong links with France are reflected in his somewhat more eclectic programming but possibly countered by the preferences of German subscribers to his concerts in Manchester; see Chapter 3.
132   See Colin Eatock, 'The Crystal Palace: Canon Formation and the English Musical Renaissance', *Nineteenth-Century Music*, **34** (2010), pp. 87–105.
133   For an account of Berlioz's music in London, see Leanne Langley, 'Agency and Change: Berlioz in Britain 1870–1920', *Journal of the Royal Musical Association*, **132** (2007), pp. 306–48.
134   *MW* stated that the audience enjoyed the first three movements of this 'remarkable work' but found the finale an anti-climax (6 February 1875, p. 99).
135   *MW*, 2 February 1878, p. 87; see also *MG*, 19 January, p. 9.
136   *Academy*, 7 December 1878, p. 551.
137   See also *Athenaeum*, 7 December 1878, p. 732; *MS* was unusual in finding the finale 'consistent, symmetrical, perfect' (same date, p. 351).
138   Reviewing the first London performance, *MW* called Berlioz 'a showman who explains in words the pictures he puts before the eye', in contrast to Beethoven, 'a god who draws us upward' (7 May 1881, p. 291); see also *MS*, 21 May 1881, p. 324, and reactions to Saint-Saëns's *Danse macabre*, discussed above.
139   *MG*, 11 January 1879, p. 5; Shaw, reviewing a London performance six years later, agreed: 'There is an infernal fascination about Berlioz's music that never fails to impress imaginative hearers when the performers get adequate steam up' (*Dramatic Review*, 5 December 1885, quoted in Laurence, *Shaw's Music*, vol. 1, p. 418).
140   A substantial selection, conducted by Jules Pasdeloup at Her Majesty's on 1 June 1878, made little impression.
141   *MG*, 7 February 1880, p. 9, which noted the reactions of Hallé's German subscribers.
142   *Athenaeum*, 29 May 1880, p. 411.
143   *MT*, 1 December 1880, p. 604.
144   Possibly inspired by Jean de Reszke's performance at Monte Carlo; the visual effects were outweighed by musical compromises and the production discarded (see *Athenaeum*, 10 February 1894, p. 187; *MT*, 1 March, pp. 173–3; *Lute*, same date, pp. 302–3).
145   See *MW*, 29 October 1881, p. 691; *Academy*, same date, p. 338; *MT*, 1 November, p. 570.
146   See *MS*, 8 January 1881, pp. 19–20; *Athenaeum*, same date, pp. 63–4; *MT*, 1 February, pp. 75–6.
147   See *SR*, 2 June 1883, pp. 693–4; *Academy*, same date, pp. 390–1; *Athenaeum*, same date, pp. 707–8.
148   *SR*, 25 April 1885, p. 544; *MS*, same date, p. 255.
149   *Athenaeum*, 25 April 1885, p. 544.
150   *MT*, 1 December 1881, pp. 617–8. Of this, £3,250 came from *MT*'s publishers, Novello. *MW* later mocked that, despite his 'grievance against England', Gounod now 'perhaps, thinks better of the perfidious island, and rejoices in the £4,000 with which the committee and publishers have bought his oratorio, neither having previously seen or heard a note of it' (22 July 1882, p. 451).

151 See, for example, *Tonic Sol-Fa Reporter*, 1 May 1882, pp. 105–6.

152 *MS*, 2 September 1882, p. 142. Unusually, the work was performed twice.

153 As previous note, pp. 144–5.

154 All quoted in *MS*, 9 September 1882, pp. 161–2; see also *Academy*, 2 September 1882, p. 177.

155 *MW*, 9 September 1882, p. 555.

156 In the first half of 1883 these include: Edinburgh, Glasgow and Dundee (January); St James's Hall (February and April); Westminster Abbey, Manchester and Liverpool (March); Dublin (April) and Oxford (May). The Royal Choral Society gave annual Ash Wednesday performances at the Albert Hall throughout the 1890s.

157 *Athenaeum*, 16 June 1883, p. 773.

158 One of Weldon's allegations was that Gounod had guaranteed her choir exclusive performing rights of *The Redemption*; upon attempting to prevent its Birmingham premiere, she was escorted from the Town Hall. For an account of the court proceedings, see *Standard*, 8 May 1885, p. 3.

159 Weldon was in Holloway Prison during the trial, having herself been found guilty of libel. An appeal by the Birmingham committee to withdraw her action so that Gounod could conduct a command performance at the Albert Hall on 26 February 1886 was rebuffed (*Edinburgh Evening News*, 14 January, p. 4).

160 The virtual hagiography in *MT* (1 September 1885, pp. 532 and 541–2) is exceptional but, as Novello published both journal and work, unsurprising.

161 *Academy*, 29 August 1885, p. 142; see also *MS*, 29 August, p. 129, and *Sunday Times*, quoted in *MW*, 5 September, p. 558. The 'Justice' motif comprises four pitches of a descending whole tone scale.

162 *Daily Telegraph*, quoted in *MW*, 29 August, pp. 541–2.

163 *Our Corner*, 1 December 1885, quoted in Laurence, *Shaw's Music*, vol. 1, pp. 298–9 and 300.

164 *Standard*, 2 December 1885, p. 3, of the previous evening's performance at St James's Hall.

165 *Academy*, 21 October 1893, p. 349.

166 *SR*, 21 October 1893, p. 458.

167 As note 165, p. 350; see also *National Observer*, same date, p. 577; *MH*, 1 November 1893, p. 340.

168 *Athenaeum*, 21 October 1893, p. 562; see also *MN*, same date, p 352.

169 *Times*, 19 October 1893, p. 10.

170 See *MT*, 1 July 1880, p. 351: '[It] appears somewhat hazy and indistinct. The subjects, although pleasant in themselves, apparently lead nowhere, and the feeling of listening to them for the first time is one of dreamy uncertainty. The last movement, however, appears far in advance of its predecessors in point of merit'.

171 *MN*, 5 June 1891, p. 275; see also *Athenaeum*, 6 June, p. 741

172 *Athenaeum*, 14 November 1891, p. 656; see also *MT*, 1 December, p. 725, and (more positive) *SR*, 14 November, p. 558.

173 J Barrie Jones, *Gabriel Fauré: A Life in Letters* (London, 1989), p. 71.

174 *Times*, 26 November 1894, p. 4; see also *MN*, 1 December, p. 456.

175 *MN*, 9 May 1896, pp. 436–7.

176 *MT*, 1 June, p. 387 (performance on 1 May); *MN*, 20 June, p. 581 (performance on 13 June). Jones (pp. 84–8) states that during these visits Fauré's music

was mainly performed in private houses, going unreported; in addition to Visetti and the Maddisons, Fauré was supported by Frank Schuster, and Earl and Lady de Grey.

177 *Academy*, 19 December 1896, p. 570; *MS*, same date, p. 387.

178 *Times*, 7 June 1897, p. 8.

179 Play reviews were inevitably written by drama critics, for whom incidental music was rarely of interest: *Academy*'s only comment was that 'the strange, bizarre significance of the text is preserved and not infrequently heightened by the … charmingly expressive music' (25 June 1898, p. 691).

180 *MG*, 10 October 1898, p. 6.

181 *MS*, 15 October 1898, p. 243.

182 *Athenaeum*, 22 April 1893, p. 515; *MoM*, 1 May, p. 99; see also *MMR*, same date, p. 112.

183 *Observer*, 22 November 1896, p. 6; *MT*, 1 December, p. 807; see also *Academy*, 21 November, p. 434.

184 See *MS*, 17 February 1900, pp. 105–6; *MT*, 1 March, p. 189.

185 See, for example, *MP*'s review of the Violin Sonata, played by Ysaÿe at St James's Hall (13 June 1899, p. 5, and probably written by the Francophile critic and composer, Arthur Hervey).

186 *Academy*, 2 July 1892, p. 19; *Athenaeum*, same date, p. 41.

187 See *MoM*, 1 October 1894, pp. 222–4; *MN*, 24 October 1894, p. 442 (Bristol); *MP*, 5 February 1895, p. 2 (tour incorporating Manchester, Oxford, Brighton, Cheltenham, Doncaster, Glasgow, Edinburgh and Liverpool).

188 *MP*, 8 June 1895, p. 5; see also *Standard*, same date, p. 5.

189 See *Times*, 15 June 1895, p. 6. When repeated at Crystal Palace with *Callirrhoë*, *MN* found 'no pretence to depth of tender emotion … [and] some of the music is commonplace and noisy' (14 November 1896, p. 415).

190 *MN*, as previous note.

191 *MS*, 14 November 1896, p. 306.

192 *SR*, 21 November 1896, p. 541.

193 *Athenaeum*, 17 June 1899, p. 763.

194 *Times*, 22 October 1907, p. 6.

195 The vast majority were short-term visitors; Prosper Sainton and Jules Rivière, who settled in London in 1845 and 1857 respectively, were relatively rare examples of Frenchmen who focused their careers on Britain, Sainton as a teacher, violinist and orchestra leader, and Rivière as a conductor of light music.

196 See *MW*, 19 March 1881, p. 174, and 26 March, p. 196; *MS*, 19 March, p. 181, and 26 March, p. 195; *MP*, quoted in *Orchestra*, 1 April, pp. 276–7; *SR*, 26 March, pp. 398–9.

197 See, for example, *MS*, 18 April 1896, pp. 243–4; *MMR*, 1 May, pp. 111–2.

198 See *Lute*, 1 March 1898, pp. 681–2; *MS*, 19 March, p. 184; *MT*, 1 April, p. 246.

199 For new works, see Appendix for years 1896–8.

200 After the final concert, on Saturday afternoon, the orchestra returned immediately to Paris in order to play their regular Sunday engagement.

201 See *Academy*, 17 October 1896, pp. 290–1; *MS*, same date, pp. 238–9; *MoM*, 1 November, pp. 702–3.

202 See *Times*, 9 October 1908, p. 11; 16 April 1913, p. 11; 17 April 1913, p. 11.

203 Joseph Bennett, 'Victorian Music (V)', *MT*, 1 May 1897, pp. 299–302.

204 See, for example, Kenneth Long's appraisal of Barnby in his *The Music of the English Church* (London, 1972), p. 363.

5   *Entente Cordiale*
French music in Britain 1901–14

While the *fin-de-siècle* was characterised by the significant but incremental progress of French music in Britain, more intense change occurred after 1900. From around 1905, performances of new music from across Europe proliferated in London. Although Covent Garden, operating mainly without serious competition, focused on new Italian sensation, Puccini, 1909 saw the premieres of Debussy's *Pelléas et Mélisande* and Charpentier's *Louise* while, from 1910, Joseph and Thomas Beecham had big successes with Russian opera and ballet. French light opera was largely sidelined, as home-grown musical comedy and Viennese operetta topped the bills. It was often in concert halls, though, that the most challenging new music was heard: French composers, fronted by Debussy and Ravel, were best represented in chamber recitals, but orchestral concerts followed a similar trajectory with London's most exciting programmes provided by Henry Wood at Queen's Hall. The capital's 'gatekeeper' status was maintained, although many new works also reached major provincial cities. All these activities took place against the backdrop of improving Franco-British political relations, characterised by a mutual desire to emphasise synergies and accommodate differences.

Franco-British political and cultural relations 1901–14

Improvements in the Edwardian years, though genuine, were driven ultimately by self-interest and epitomised by the *Entente Cordiale* (1904).[1] Though often presented as a singular transformative event resetting relations and ending old animosities, the *Entente* was, in reality, a staging post in a process.[2] Momentum built steadily from 1900. France feared losing its pre-eminence among world powers as its population and economy were surpassed by Germany and the United States; an alliance with Russia was inaugurated in 1894 but, while Franco-German relations improved, German possession of Alsace-Lorraine prevented close co-operation. Britain was an alternative ally, but strong economic and cultural ties were countered by imperial rivalries. Meanwhile, widespread condemnation of Britain's conduct of the Boer War, its near defeat, and other colonial antagonisms, shook British faith in 'splendid isolation'; similarly unsettled by American and German prosperity, Britain felt its naval supremacy under threat. Although wary of formalised alliances, Balfour's government wanted to build closer relations with other European powers. The Foreign Secretary, Lansdowne, looked first to Germany but, despite strong connections, Germany's vociferous support for the Boers led him to conclude that insufficient trust existed. A fluent French-speaker whose army-general grandfather was reputedly Talleyrand's illegitimate son, Lansdowne next looked to France. In 1902, with Théophile Delcassé and Paul Cambon (French foreign minister and ambassador to London respectively), Lansdowne started working to resolve outstanding differences. Circumstances were opportune; tensions over Egypt were indirectly solved by the Moroccan regime's collapse, as France conceded her Egyptian interests in return for Britain's approving a French protectorate in Morocco. Disputes in Newfoundland, the South Pacific and Siam were also resolved. The *Entente Cordiale* was neither an alliance nor even a single document, but the ending of outstanding rivalries, enabling Franco-British relations to move on.

Differences remained. France desired an alliance, while Britain wanted no new obligations. Nevertheless, mutual diplomatic support was forthcoming: at the 1906 Algeciras Conference, Britain backed France against Germany; such incidents strengthened Franco-British ties while simultaneously cooling British relations with Germany.[3] In 1907, the Anglo-Russian Convention resolved more colonial tensions and evolved into the Triple Entente. Despite the two power blocs that fought the Great War consolidating, European relations remained nuanced and complex, and few in the British establishment expected major hostilities. In clandestine talks following the 1911 Agadir Crisis, Britain aimed to avoid firm commitments to support France in the event of German aggression, creating 'a position of extraordinary uncertainty and ambiguity'.[4] Bell notes that only on 2 August 1914 did the British position change and due to the invasion of Belgium, whose integrity Britain had guaranteed since 1830, not Germany's declaration of war on France.

Widely reported demonstrations of Franco-British friendship aimed to garner popular support for the improved relationship. From a British perspective, Edward VII's visit to Paris in 1903 is most familiar, but the prewar French Presidents (Loubet, Fallières and Poincaré) all made state visits to London. *The Times*, a long-standing advocate of strong Franco-British relations, stated that Fallières's visit in 1908 (see Figure 5.1) was 'the best possible proof that the *entente*, which we all prize so highly, is working and wearing well'.[5] When the *Entente*'s tenth anniversary was celebrated in 1914, *The Times* was equally positive:

> King George goes to Paris to confirm and to carry on the work of King Edward. He goes to bear public witness that after ten years of trial the policy of the Entente is the policy of England as it is the policy of France. He goes to testify that it is more firmly rooted in the minds of both nations than at any former point of its history.[6]

Fig 5.1 'What the President saw at the Opera': President Fallières at Covent Garden (*Illustrated London News*, 30 May 1908, p. 782)

Many newspapers published translations of Poincaré's welcome speech as evidence of mutual regard: '[Your visit] responds to the desire of two powerful nations equally attached to peace, equally enthusiastic for progress and equally accustomed to the habit of liberty'.[7] Nevertheless, the liberal-minded *Manchester Guardian*, though supporting strong Franco-British relations, rejected 'any attempt under the guise of improvement of our relations with France to give diplomatic form and reality to the Triple Entente', reflecting its distrust of Tsarist Russia,[8] and advocated instead an alliance between Britain, France and Germany. Such opinions reflect the complex politics of 1914, in which the *Entente* was only one thread.

The improved relationship was successfully encapsulated by the Franco-British Exhibition of 1908, which took place at the purposely constructed 'White City' complex, with the Olympic Games held on adjacent ground.[9] Though far smaller than the 1900 Paris Exposition, the 'Franco' was London's biggest such event to date: the king and Fallières were among 8.4 million visitors. Excursion trains came from around Britain and many visited from France;[10] the site even became the setting for Act II of Caryll and Monckton's musical comedy, *Our Miss Gibbs*. Media coverage highlighted the nations' affinities: the popular *Penny Illustrated Paper* endorsed the view of the Exhibition president, the Duke of Argyll:

> When the working men of different communities really get to know each other and the appreciate each other's good qualities, they bind their people together with bonds which are stronger than steel, more lasting than bronze, for, if nothing is weaker than hate, nothing is stronger than love, and love, at all events between two nations, is the child of sympathy and understanding.[11]

Despite stressing affinities, however, the nations appeared as co-existent, not intertwined, entities; the official guide played upon familiar 'chalk and cheese' tropes: 'When Anglo-Saxon energy blends with French *savoir vivre*, when British Empiricism is ordered by French method, when British solidity is adorned by French grace, a combination is reached which embraces the highest achievements of the human race'.[12] Showground space was allocated equally but lacked any shared areas; British exhibits exploited national stereotypes in the 'Tudor House', 'Old London' and 'Irish Village' (Ballymaclinton, sponsored by McLinton's Soap).[13] Scant attention was paid to music: none of the subject subcommittees was tasked with its presentation and the 300-seat Palace of Music also regularly housed horticultural exhibits.

While not transformative, the *Entente* initiated and symbolised change. It was used regularly as justification for promoting cultural and commercial ventures, as a marketing tool for French products and services, and by professionals, including artists, writers, actors and musicians. Cultural exchanges, wider in the nineteenth century than often realised, only benefitted from closer political and diplomatic ties.

Theatre music: opera and operetta

In the 1900s, Covent Garden dominated opera, though the Grand Opera Syndicate, which presided over the principal spring seasons after Harris's death, took an inconsistent approach to new repertory. Its leading figures (Harry Higgins, Neil Forsyth and Lady Constance de Grey) were amateurs whose management strategy was dominated by financial and social considerations. Covent Garden's audience finally embraced Wagner in the late 1890s, with complete *Ring* cycles appearing every second or third year and *Tristan* and *Die Meistersinger* several times per season. Puccini's operas were introduced, the most popular being *La bohème* (regularly from 1901), and *Tosca* and *Madama Butterfly* (both 1905). These interests, amplified by the Syndicate's relative inattention to artistic matters, resulted in a decline in French opera. Although Messager joined the Syndicate in 1901 and conducted regularly from 1902, he does not appear to have influenced repertory; despite conducting the Paris premieres of *Louise* (1900) and *Pelléas et Mélisande* (1902), neither work appeared at Covent Garden during his tenure. Such were the changes in fashion that in spring 1913 and 1914 both *Faust* and *Carmen* were discarded.

New French operas were often received indifferently, including Saint-Saëns's *Hélène* (**1904**-2), and Massenet's *Hérodiade* (**1904**-3), *Le jongleur de Notre-Dame* (**1906**-1) and *Thaïs* (**1911**-4) (see Figures 5.2 and 5.3). Only 1909 was exceptional, with *Samson et Dalila*, *Louise* and *Pelléas* all generating significant interest. *Samson* was hardly new, but its production ended the ban on the stage portrayal of biblical characters.[14] It opened the season on 26 April and Saint-Saëns attended but press reaction was lukewarm; although approving the policy change, *The Times* summed up sentiment in finding *Samson* 'curiously old-fashioned'.[15] Audience reaction was more positive; the work received 31 performances up to 1914.

Louise (**1909**-8) was a genuine success, with press and public sentiment coinciding, and 29 pre-war performances. Presenting Paris as a city of both dreams and ordinary citizens appealed to critics; Edwin Evans found *Louise* 'almost aggressively French', while *The Times* rhapsodised:

> In the exquisite scene … [in which] the great town lying in darkness at the feet of the lovers gradually begins to glimmer with glow-worm lights, the sky takes on the glow, rockets whistle softly up into the blue, and Paris, the city of pleasures, calling [Julien and Louise] to the life of freedom, lights up for them on their bridal night.[16]

Fig 5.2 Massenet's *Le jongleur de Notre-Dame*, Covent Garden (*Illustrated London News*, 23 June 1906, p. 927)

MASSENET'S RECHRISTENED OPERA: THE FIRST PERFORMANCE OF "SALOMÉ" IN ENGLAND.

DRAWN BY W. RUSSELL FLINT.

Madame Calvé.

SCENE FROM ACT III.: MADAME CALVÉ IN THE RÔLE OF SALOMÉ.

This work by Massenet was on its first production known as "Hérodiade." On another page we give an appreciation of the composer's work.

Fig 5.3 Emma Calvé as 'Salomé' in Massenet's *Hérodiade*, Covent Garden (*Illustrated London News*, 9 July 1904, p. 46)

The characters were thought realistic and sympathetic; Alfred Kalisch saw a precedent in *La bohème* but lauded Charpentier's achievement:

> He has the skill to make us sympathise in turn with the girl who longs for life and freedom and the parents who would keep her by their side ... He writes in a very modern way, and the orchestra is fully symphonic, but he gives melodies to his characters and they have dramatic meaning independently of the orchestra.[17]

A widespread consensus was that Charpentier had struck a judicious balance between dramatic 'realism' and 'operatic' music, being modern but not modernist; the *Musical Times* stated that 'it can fail to please only those who care for a cheerful story and ear-catching melodies of a conventional type'.[18]

The reception of *Pelléas et Mélisande* (**1909**-7) a few weeks earlier was more varied. Although some of Debussy's music was familiar (see below), a full-length opera challenged Covent Garden's more socially focused audience. The Paris premiere had attracted some press attention with 'ultra-modern' a popular summary; S Marchesi thought *Pelléas* 'another step downwards'.[19] By 1909, Debussy was the most high-profile 'new' French composer and, of the season's French 'novelties', *Pelléas* received most scrutiny.[20] Even if bemused, most critics engaged positively: the *Musical Times* recalled that 'it took many years before [*Der Ring*] was understood and appreciated'.[21] While the *Illustrated London News*'s headline was 'The opera that is without a tune', its below-picture text stated that *Pelléas* was 'likely to provide the musical sensation of the year' (see Figure 5.4). Kalisch was more sceptical:

> All the characters speak precisely the same idiom, and the constant recurrence of the same pattern of sound does cease to interest after a time ... The peculiar harmonic idiom of Debussy, which is so piquant and fresh in smaller works, also loses its power when it is spoken for the whole evening ... [E]verything from rapturous ecstasy to bewildered boredom was expressed by members of the audience, musicians no less than mere amateurs.[22]

Having evoked Wagner, the *Musical Times* made clear its puzzlement, suggesting that 'Debussy's music by itself is disjointed, meaningless – though it perfectly fulfils its purpose', but continued, 'The French composer has written in a forcible yet wonderfully restrained style ... *Pelléas et Mélisande* is a remarkable and impressive work'.[23] The composer George Clutsam, though, was enthusiastic, opining that

> If you are sensitive, appreciative and sympathetic you will find many [thoughts and emotions] in the score of Debussy's wonderful work. If you cannot immediately perceive them go again and again. It is all so new. It is the opera of another planet.[24]

THE OPERA THAT IS WITHOUT A TUNE: DEBUSSY'S "PELLÉAS ET MÉLISANDE."

DRAWN BY A. FORESTIER.

Golaud (M. Bourbon).   Mélisande (Mlle. Féart).   Pelléas (M. Warnery).

A WORK THAT IS A REVOLUTION AND A REVELATION: PELLÉAS AND MÉLISANDE ARE DISCOVERED TOGETHER BY GOLAUD.
IN "PÉLLEAS ET MÉLISANDE." AT COVENT GARDEN.

Debussy's great work, produced at Covent Garden last week, brings London face to face with one of the most startling developments in the world of music. The music is without any consecutive melody, and is written in a scale of six whole tones with frequent use of the augmented triad. It seeks throughout to emphasise the action on the stage without interfering with it in any way. There are no arias and no concerted numbers, and there is absolutely nothing in the score that the audience can carry away, nothing that can be said to come under the definition of a tune. The house accepted this startling innovation with the greatest enthusiasm. "Pelléas et Mélisande" is likely to provide the musical sensation of the year.

Fig 5.4 'The opera without a tune': Debussy's *Pelléas et Mélisande*, Covent Garden
(*Illustrated London News*, 29 May 1909, p. 779)

The Times's critic took Clutsam's advice. Initially he had complained of 'monotonous singing, which often becomes a sort of a wail', despite the music having 'a special and peculiar fitness' in creating 'the archaic atmosphere that is aimed at'.[25] Nevertheless, he praised the orchestration and recognised that

> It is wonderful that with this strangely restricted art Debussy … should succeed in making the impression … not merely of pleasure, but of keen delight to a good many people, in spite of the manner in which all the older and newer canons of musical beauty have been set at naught.

Closer acquaintance increased appreciation; in a follow-up review, the same writer stated 'that there is not a single passage which is not actually beautiful sound' and admired 'the extraordinary aptness with which it fits the play'.[26] Unsurprisingly, given its distinctiveness, *Pelléas* was less popular than either *Samson* or *Louise*, but still achieved fourteen pre-war performances at Covent Garden. Elsewhere, the reach of *Pelléas* and *Louise* was limited; Beecham gave *Pelléas* once in 1910, and Oscar Hammerstein produced *Louise* in 1912, while performances outside London were restricted to large companies and cities; *Louise* appeared only in Thomas Quinlan's tour in 1912 and *Pelléas* in Ernst Denhof's aborted venture in 1913.[27]

Excepting five major works (*Carmen*, *Faust*, *Louise*, *Samson* and *Pelléas*), performances of French opera in London's elite theatres were sporadic. Hammerstein's London Opera House opened with Nouguès's *Quo vadis?* (**1910**-2) but it failed; Hammerstein also promised seven operas by Massenet, but produced only three (*Hérodiade*, *Le jongleur* and *Don Quichotte* (**1912**-2)).[28] Beecham, more adventurous and successful, focused on German and Russian opera; his most interesting French venture was a staged version of Debussy's *L'enfant prodigue*, but Missa's *La muguette* (**1910**-3) and Leroux's *Le chemineau* (**1910**-6) excited neither critics nor audiences.[29]

The Edwardian decade was a meagre one for French operetta. Having been largely displaced by 'variety musicals' and 'Girl' shows in the 1890s (see Chapter 4), the arrival of Léhar's *Merry Widow* in 1907 marginalised French works further; Messager's *Véronique* and *Les p'tites Michus*, were two rare successes. The former's production at the Coronet (**1903**-2), in French, was well received, aided by support from the Grand Opera Syndicate and many notables, including the Prince and Princess of Wales.[30] Arguments that French comic opera was superior to British reappeared; for *Country Life*, *Véronique* proved that 'there is no reason why the monopoly of the apparently all-conquering musical comedy – a distinctly retrograde form of the lighter lyric art – should continue',[31] while the *Morning Post* thought French works had more substantive plots and praised Messager's music for being 'light and catchy … [but] invariably refined, never vulgar and scored with great delicacy'.[32]

Inspired by this success, an English version, produced by George Edwardes, appeared at the Apollo in 1904.[33] Although it ran for 496 performances,[34] some critics found the adaptation heavy-handed; in Edward Baughan's words, 'it was funny, but it was not French'.[35] Messager's music was presented intact; *Country Life* reverted to a favourite epithet: '*Véronique* is champagne. The music is as light and sparkling and merry and sentimental as that wine can be'.[36] The success led Edwardes to produce *Les p'tites Michus* (**1905**-2) twelve months later, which ran for 400 performances.[37]

These successes aside, French light opera was largely sidelined. Wearing shows no West End appearances by Planquette, Lecocq or Chassaigne and one each by Audran (*La poupée*) and Serpette (*Amorelle*; **1903**-3). A Parisian company gave a brief season at the Coronet in April 1907, including revivals of *La mascotte*, *Les cloches de Corneville*, and *La fille de Madame Angot*; the *Musical Standard* welcomed a 'pleasant change from the usual detestable musical comedy', but its view was clearly not shared by audiences.[38] Provincial Britain followed, albeit with a delay: *The Era*'s 'On the Road' reports for the first six months of 1900, 1905 and 1910 show that in 1900 there were two (and sometimes three) troupes performing *La poupée* plus an intermittent tour of *Les cloches*, and in 1905 full-season tours of *Amorelle*, *La poupée* and *Véronique*, but in 1910 no French works at all.

April 1907 also witnessed the Berlin Komische Oper's introduction of Offenbach's *The Tales of Hoffman* (**1907**-1). Consistently praised, critics found the largely unknown work more 'elevated' than anticipated; the *Observer* noted that 'the impish character of Offenbach is entirely absent; he is suave, mystic, emotional and sensuous', before jibing at musical comedy, that 'there are no show girls, picture hat business, panterloonery [*sic*] or the song and dance turn'.[39] *Hoffman*'s more serious mood distanced it from entrenched perceptions of Offenbach and tropes of French 'naughtiness'; conversely, adjectives such as 'sensuous' and 'voluptuous' maintained an association with Frenchness familiar to British readers. *Hoffman* proved popular: Beecham produced it in English (1910, London and provincial tour), Hammerstein in French (London, **1911**-12), and Quinlan on provincial tours (**1911**-13); it was also performed regularly during the Great War.[40]

Hoffman's success induced a modest revival of Offenbach's *opéras bouffes*: *La fille du tambour-major* and *La Grande-Duchesse* appeared in short runs in French at the Shaftesbury in June 1908,[41] while Herbert Tree presented *Orpheus in the Underground* as his post-Christmas offering in 1911. This version illustrates changing mores: Offenbach's satirised censor, Public Opinion, was recast as Mrs Grundy, the archetype of prudish Victorian morality who, in poke bonnet and crinoline, attempts to keep the gods in order in their louche Louis-Quinze surroundings. She fails, though, to 'make quite English what proceeds from France',[42] with Jupiter's intrigues presented as indulgently as in Second Empire Paris. The *Academy*'s critic reminisced:

> Some of us remember the extraordinary enthusiasm which *The Grand Duchess* aroused in the playgoers of the 'sixties … The sparkling music, the careless frivolity, the complete abandon were as a goblet of nectar to the

staccato mid-Victorian palate. Steeped in goody-goodiness and arrayed in crinolines, the French revelation was an astonishing pick-me-up.[43]

The 'can-can' now merited only passing comment and *The Times* praised Offenbach's 'delicious, pulse-quickening, nerve-titillating, brain-maddening music ... [He] is a kind of virus that gets into the blood'.[44]

A discursive article in *The Times*, probably by its new chief critic, Henry Colles, re-examined Offenbach's work; taking an unashamedly high-minded view, he treated *Hoffman* separately; after praising its melodies and character-isation, he declared that Offenbach had 'succeeded in reproducing the strange blended atmosphere of beauty and *diablerie* which makes the phantasies of ... Hoffman unlike anything else in German literature, and by doing so he has succeeded in writing something unlike anything else in music.'[45] Colles found the *opéras bouffes* too homogeneous, though, arguing that 'younger music lovers' need only see *Hoffman* and *Orphée* to understand 'what it was that made the name of their composer a household word'.

Although French theatre music declined in prominence in the 1900s, this was due to changes in fashion and taste rather than outright rejection. *Carmen* and *Faust* remained popular but were far from novelties and the same was true for operetta; the unknown variable was not if change would come, but when. *Pelléas*, like Wagner's operas previously, did not instant-aneously appeal and in London acculturation was hampered by a deluge of Russian opera and ballet, followed by the war; *Louise* fared better but faced the same circumstances. Operetta, more stylistically consistent, arguably lost its sense of freshness. A lack of committed advocates for both genres further undermined their positions.

Concert music

While French theatre music became less popular, concert music prospered. In London, following the abandonment of Crystal Palace's regular orches-tral concerts in 1900 and Manns's consequent retirement, Queen's Hall became the principal venue for orchestral music; its resident band, directed by Henry Wood, gave many premieres and repeat performances, especially during 'Proms' seasons, while Thomas Beecham's eclectic taste resulted in performances of rarely heard works by Grétry, Méhul, Berlioz, Franck and D'Indy between 1906 and 1909.[46] Manchester fared less well: after a four-year interregnum following Hallé's death in 1895, Richter took over until 1911 but his limited interest in French music meant its presence in Hallé programmes decreased;[47] his successor, Michael Balling, was more catholic, but also favoured German repertory. Elsewhere, the lack of professional orchestras continued to limit dissemination of new music, especially works requiring large ensembles or non-standard instruments.

The importance of the 'Proms' has been widely acknowledged; after starting with a 'populist' approach, more 'highbrow' works, as Leanne Langley notes, were included from 1902, thanks to Edgar Speyer's involvement.[48] Langley shows that, between 1895 and 1914, of the 32 composers most frequently performed, Wagner was the most popular (2,383 appearances), with Beethoven a distant second (681); six French composers feature in her list: Gounod (5th, 487); Saint-Saëns (9th, 269); Ambroise Thomas (12th, 229); Berlioz (14th, 209); Bizet (17th, 188); and Debussy (28th, 39).[49] Inviting composers to conduct their own music added cachet; Debussy, Ravel and D'Indy all appeared at Queen's Hall.

Chamber recitals, dominated by pianists and singers, were organised by many promoters and performers, mainly as one-off events or short series. The most active promoter of dedicated French music concerts was the *Société des Concerts Français*, but the bulk of performances took place within mixed programmes. The relative cheapness of providing small-scale recitals meant that outside London chamber works by composers such as Debussy and Ravel were often heard before their orchestral pieces.

As with organ recitals (Chapter 3), the sheer volume of activity and lack of detailed press coverage renders comprehensive analysis impractical: the July 1913 issue of the *Musical Times*, for example, covering 21 May to 20 June, the peak of London's social season, briefly reviewed eleven orchestral concerts (under 100 words each) and listed 106 chamber recitals (46 vocal, 40 piano and 20 others), commenting on just 17; weekly publications also managed only selective coverage. Extant collections of programmes are equally partial, as are the music press's provincial reports: the *Musical Times*'s 'Music in Yorkshire' articles from December 1908 to March 1909 mention several French works but are far from comprehensive.[50] Unimpeachable analyses of works' dissemination and comprehensive records of first performances (other than major works in London), are unachievable; errors by omission are supplemented by sometimes inaccurate claims by press or performers.[51] Any account of the reception of French instrumental music in this period must acknowledge these methodological challenges.

The 'modern French school': Debussy, Ravel and beyond

The 'modern French school' was used regularly to refer to composers whose music arrived after 1900 and covered various styles and aesthetics. Despite his relative seniority, D'Indy was usually placed in this category, as was Chausson, although the term was later more usually applied to composers born after about 1860; for most, from around 1905, excepting West End *cognoscenti*, the 'modern French school' meant selected works by Debussy and Ravel.

As with Gounod, audiences appear often to have been more sympathetic to Debussy than critics, who often denigrated his harmonic language and approach to form. Roger Nichols claims the earliest British press coverage of Debussy's music was probably the *Musical Times*'s brief review of *Nocturnes*, partially performed in Paris in January 1901;[52] the Paris premiere of *Pelléas* in 1902 drew the first detailed coverage (see above). A strong contender for the first public British performance is Percy Grainger's rendition of the Toccata from *Pour le piano* (**1903**-1) but it merited only passing comment, *The Times* deeming it a 'very interesting little example of the art of M Debussy, of which there has been much talk recently'.[53]

Wood's performance of *L'après-midi d'un faune* at the Proms (**1904**-4) reached a more broad-based audience and received wider coverage. *The Times* gingerly declared Debussy 'a modern of the moderns'; its reviewer (Maitland?) liked the work despite himself: 'it certainly is beautiful in a way, and exquisitely scored ... [It] was a work of purest atmosphere, depicted with the utmost sureness'.[54] Paul Seer deemed Debussy 'a man of the most exquisite sensibility and of sweetest fantasy'; of *L'après-midi*, Seer rhapsodised:

> the harmonic scheme was, of course, exceedingly plastic, but it seemed to be too ethereal to be the result of ingenuity or searching after effect: it would seem rather that the soft breezes gently impelled the harmonies hither and thither, and the composer followed with pen in hand. There was much subtlety in the polyphony, and the colouring was delicious.[55]

Sceptical reviews appeared in the *Graphic* and *Observer*; the latter, though allowing that *L'après-midi* was 'prettily orchestrated', found its themes 'so vague and their treatment so flimsy that the prelude made little impression'.[56] Brevity, a placid sound-world and relative practicality facilitated dissemination, with performances at Queen's Hall and the Philharmonic Society, and in Liverpool, Glasgow and Manchester before the end of 1906. In this case, 'ultra-modern' music did not induce fear amongst audiences.

Two months after *L'après-midi*, the String Quartet was introduced by Royal College of Music (RCM) students but attracted much less attention (**1904**-5).[57] *The Times*'s notice (Maitland again?) was positive, despite underlying puzzlement:

> Strange harmonies, decided rhythms, and elaborate polyphony arrest one's attention more than definiteness of melodic outline and construction ... At any rate, it is evident that the composer means what he says, and it is something to write with conviction. The writing for the instruments is extremely ingenious, picturesque, and highly effective.[58]

As chamber music was less high-profile than orchestral and theatre music, early performances of Debussy's solo piano works and songs often received only brief press coverage,[59] but two exceptions are *Estampes* (**1905**-1) and *Images (I)*. Following the first complete performance (according to *The Times*) of *Estampes*, its reviewer gave qualified praise to both 'Jardins sous la pluie' ('a most picturesque study') and 'La soirée dans Grenade': 'another perfectly successful picture in music, with suggestions of distant tinkling music and cathedral bells, with a sheep-bell here and there; such things really do serve a purpose, if not a very high one'.[60] When repeated by Richard Buhlig at Aeolian Hall, with 'Reflets dans l'eau', *The Times* was confident that Debussy's style had become sufficiently familiar 'that even the least instructed person in the audience would probably recognise the chord of the added sixth as suggesting this music at once'.[61] Louise Liebich, an ardent Francophile, praised Debussy unreservedly; of the two 'water' pieces, she wrote, 'anyone who has been fascinated by the wonderful effects of light seen upon river, lake or stream and the magic of double reflection sometimes noticed in a wayside pool will understand the genius of Debussy in mirroring these fantastic aspects of nature in his music'.[62]

Further evidence of acclimatisation, though tinged with some mystification, is found in reviews of the String Quartet, performed several times in 1906; the *Manchester Guardian*'s London correspondent stated,

> What we know of [Debussy] hardly prepares us to find a musician who has sympathy for chamber music ... He has a fondness for strange harmonies which have an exotic subacid flavour. Some will no doubt call them cacophony, but the composer has sufficient discretion to know when to stop ... [T]he total effect is one of great originality.[63]

The Leeds Bohemian Quartet's performance suggests that provincial critics and audiences were also engaging positively, despite lacking familiarity: the *Musical Times*'s Yorkshire correspondent (Herbert Thompson?) described the work as 'strange in idiom, but though some passages seem on a first hearing to affect strangeness, the general impression is one of power and genuine individuality'.[64] The Edith Robinson Quartet's performance in Manchester, though poor, elicited comments from the *Guardian*'s local reviewer (Samuel Langford?) more perceptive than those of his London colleague:

> We do not get much of the real Debussy – the Debussy who later revels in scales of six full tones, and chords ... of twelve semitones ... The quartet is quite a normal piece of music, written with much cleverness and a certain fineness pervading the whole, from the most beautiful to the most grotesque parts.[65]

Debussy's first public visit to London in February 1908 was a major step. Hitherto, *L'après-midi* had been the only orchestral work performed in Britain, but Wood's arrangement resulted in the introduction of *La mer* (**1908**-1).[66] Although privately sceptical of British regard for music,[67] Debussy was received enthusiastically; as with Saint-Saëns and Berlioz, his urbane conduct helped. *La mer* generated only mild enthusiasm; even writers who praised *L'après-midi* found it lacking in variety and formal coherence:

> Regarded as programme music – of the special Debussy kind – the three sections are all too much of the same tone. It is a wonderful score, and all the effects in tonal peculiarities come out clearly ... but the subjects

seem to call for at least a breath here and there, of real force, of elemental strength, and in this point the composer seems to have failed.[68]

The *Musical Times* concurred but counselled patience:

> Such atmospheric strains, so unlike what one is accustomed to, must be listened to in a passive frame of mind ... There can be no question as to the cleverness of the music or its poetic import; the only thing is to get one's ears educated, so to speak, in order to appreciate its strange idiom.[69]

Wood's networking also brought the much earlier *La demoiselle élue* (**1908**-2) to London, a work critics found easier; the *Athenaeum* perceived 'rich imagination and beautiful tone-colouring [and] characteristic thematic material which, deftly handled, gives a certain form yet no formality'.[70] Henry Caunt was more sceptical: 'something is left to the listener, whose attention cannot fail to be attracted by the wiliness of Debussy's characterisation – that it is inclined to make you see and feel more than the work actually possesses'.[71] Repeat performances, some enabled by personal connections, came quickly: the Norwich Festival, which Wood conducted, gave the work in October 1908, while Henry Coward, chorus-master of the Leeds Choral Union, which gave the Queen's Hall performance, may have facilitated *La demoiselle*'s inclusion at the Leeds Festival in 1910. *L'enfant prodigue* (**1908**-3) also benefitted, being premiered at the Sheffield Festival, where Wood was also conductor and Coward chorus-master; Debussy revised the orchestration for this performance.[72] The more familiar idiom again made this early work easier to appraise but many critics missed Debussy's mature individuality: 'The music makes no strain upon the attention. It is simple, and often beautiful, but it displays no genius'.[73]

Nichols correctly proposes that Debussy's reputation was substantially enhanced in 1908. Short biographies by Louise Liebich and William Daly appeared (see Bibliography) and, encouraged, Debussy revisited in February and May 1909 for the premieres of *Nocturnes* (**1909**-2) and *Pelléas*.[74] A summary of British perceptions came in the *Musical Times*:

> The Debussy cult is making great progress in this country. It has reached that interesting stage when many people, who are really desperately bewildered, affect to perceive beauties and wonderful meaning that have probably entirely escaped the attention of the composer. But there is no mistaking the depth and the width of the influence Debussy is exerting on the art. His music may be classed as nebulous, fragile, diaphanous, and so on, but one cannot resist the languor of the hazy atmosphere with which it envelops and mesmerises the listener.[75]

Contrasting with his ambivalent view of *Pelléas* (see above), Kalisch appreciated *Nocturnes* as Debussy had 'not so completely cut himself adrift from all tradition' and deemed 'Nuages' 'poetical and attractive, and [of] no little originality'.[76] John Baughan praised Debussy's orchestration and noted a key factor in his positive reception: 'his dissonances are peculiarly absent in all elements of harshness'.[77] Echoing earlier debates, though, Baughan took issue with what he perceived as Debussy's fundamental aesthetic:

> It made some of us almost believe that Debussy would write better music if he abandoned his so-called 'impressionism' and turned his attention to composition on normal lines, not ignoring the value of melody ... Music cannot paint pictures. It is an emotional art and it seems noblest when the impression it makes on us cannot be translated into words ... Of course, we enjoyed the *Nocturnes* well enough, but the music is so definitely understood at a first hearing that we doubt whether there is any beauty we have not grasped ... How different was the impression of the Elgar Symphony [No. 1 in A flat]. But, then, Elgar is a far greater composer than an experimenter and apparently non-emotional musician like Debussy.

Whatever Baughan's reservations, the work was acclaimed by the audience and 'Fêtes' encored.[78]

Between 1909 and 1914, Debussy's slow rate of composition inhibited reputational advance and he did not revisit Britain. Reception of new works mutated slightly: while still regarded as modern, a sense of his being a 'one trick pony' emerged; reviews, though positive, are often briefer. As with Saint-Saëns, British critics developed expectations and were inclined to pass over new works unless confounded by their quality or originality; from 1911, fashionable London was particularly entranced by Russian ballet and opera, distracting attention from Debussy and others. *Rondes de printemps*, the last of the *Images pour orchestre*, was heard at the London Musical Festival (**1911-3**) but overshadowed by Elgar's Second Symphony and disadvantageously placed at the end of a long programme; *The Times* sarcastically stated that the piece 'represents the vague stirring of life in early spring [and] takes an unusual amount of instruments and very little thematic material to do it'.[79] Baughan found it 'interesting in the usual Debussy way', but added, 'one cannot live on orchestral tricks alone'.[80] Conversely, though, Baughan appreciated the second book of *Préludes* (**1913-2**), despite stating that 'one does not say Debussy is a great composer: but he does very well within his particular sphere'.[81] The music of *Jeux* (**1913-4**) was overshadowed by interest in the ballet: in the *Spectator*'s words, 'With [Debussy and Bakst (designer)] we are all familiar and their share of the entertainment contained little that was unexpected ... but [Nijinsky's] choreography ... will come as a shock to all but the most hardened revolutionaries'.[82] *Ibéria* (**1913-6**) fared better; according to 'C N', 'The first and last movements are exceptionally brilliant ... Debussy has certainly given us something refreshing', and *The Times* concurred, stating that '[Debussy] has never written anything more fascinating in its scintillating colour than the first few pages of the dawn of the festival'.[83]

Knowledge of Ravel grew more slowly, being confined for several years to chamber music; *Jeux d'eau* appears to have been the work first performed publicly (**1904**-1).[84] The first known appearance of the *Sonatine* (**1906**-2) struggled for attention in a concert of modern works from France, Spain and Russia; *The Times* merely called it 'very odd'.[85] Performances then increased incrementally, with the London premiere of the String Quartet a significant landmark (**1907**-5). Given at the first of two concerts organised by Tony Guéritte (see below), it was thought noteworthy but puzzling;[86] the *Athenaeum*, though unenthusiastic, noted that 'Ravel, like Debussy, has something to say, and ... says it in his own way ... [T]he strangest effects ... struck one as not ugly but merely peculiar'.[87] The *Musical Times* criticised the Quartet's 'vagueness of significance, incoherence and weird harmonic eccentricities',[88] but *Violin and String World* thought it the 'most startling' of the pieces in Guéritte's concerts, which included works by Franck, Debussy, de Séverac, Schmitt, D'Indy and Roussel:

> The suggestion that the modern French school of composers is a band of lunatics has been hazarded by one or two critics ... Such a suggestion is preposterous and cannot possibly be taken seriously.
>
> The indisputable fact remains that Ravel is a master of his particular mode of expression. The opening of the first movement ... is a graceful and melodious theme ... of extreme sensitiveness but, nevertheless, as the music proceeds, we are made to feel that we only imperfectly grasp the contents. The whole conception is foreign to the traditions which have been sacred to us for generations ... [Even so,] the work expresses something – it is at present hard to know precisely what. The harmonies used throughout are of the most novel order, *but they are logical*, and that is much ...
>
> The second movement ... is strikingly rhythmical and full of new effects. The two remaining movements give a fitting finish to a remarkable work.[89]

Even baffled critics did not deny the Quartet's appeal, demonstrated by its rapid dissemination. While a positive review from ardent Francophile Louise Liebich is unsurprising,[90] more noteworthy is a *Times* review from 1911, which praised 'a composition of very considerable beauty, containing amongst its many eccentricities passages which have a truer and more lasting beauty than that which is solely derived from "atmosphere"', while Clutsam referred to 'fanciful material and fertile harmonies that characterise the work of one of the most ingenious disciples of the modern French school'.[91] The Quartet also reached provincial centres including Leeds (1909), Bournemouth, Newcastle and Edinburgh (1911); Ravel attended the last two performances.[92]

The first major orchestral work to be performed was *Rapsodie espagnole* (**1909**-10). Clutsam attributed the lukewarm audience response to a misconceived interpretation; comparing it with Debussy's 'La soirée dans

Grenade', he argued that 'the harmonic scheme runs on an entirely different plane, and is magnificently effective'.[93] John Baughan also praised Ravel's 'immense creative and technical cleverness', deeming him 'emphatically a composer with something to say'; the *Rapsodie* itself was a 'successful piece' written 'charmingly and newly'.[94] For *The Times*, though, the attempt to combine 'impressionistic' and 'realistic' approaches to illustrative composition was problematic: the first movement, 'decorated with quaintly suggestive fragments of melody, produces a vague and elusive atmosphere which is entirely successful', but, in the finale, 'dance music becomes so definite that the whole attention is occupied by it and the impressions of the earlier part are violently destroyed'.[95]

By 1912, Ravel's music featured regularly in London concerts; works introduced included several songs, the Introduction and Allegro for Harp (**1907**-3), part, at least, of *Gaspard de la nuit*, and *Pavane pour une infante défunte* (**1911**-2). The orchestral version of *Ma mère l'oye* (**1912**-1) was quite cordially reviewed, but a sense that virtuosic orchestration overrode substance generated mild criticism; the light and evocative music, though, proved popular with audiences.[96] *Valses nobles et sentimentales* (**1913**-7) was more positively received; *The Times* praised Ravel's manipulations of waltz rhythms and echoed John Baughan (see above) in suggesting that 'one of [Ravel's] most salient characteristics is of writing dissonances as if they were consonances, not laying any particular emphasis upon them ... but treating them as though they were quite ordinary figures of speech'.[97] The *Manchester Guardian* was still more explicit:

> Mr [Romain] Rolland ... hints that French musicians work with the chisel while the Germans work with the axe ... [I]n Ravel we have one who is above all others the master of the chisel. He is never harsh, even with the usual audacity of the modern ... Everything is dainty and finished to a degree – colour, proportion, volume of sound, number of bars to a semiquaver [*sic*]. Above everything stands his fascinating idiom, so simple, apparently, and yet so intensely original ... The one puzzling thing about him is that the public should take him as easily and unmistakably as it does.[98]

Daphnis et Chloë (**1914**-1) was the last major new French work to appear before the war, during Joseph Beecham's final season of opera and ballet at Drury Lane. Its significance was overshadowed by Beecham's ambition: within two weeks came the British premieres of Rimsky-Korsakov's *Le coq d'or* and *La nuit de mai*, Stravinsky's *Le rossignol*, and, the night before *Daphnis*, Borodin's *Prince Igor*. A public spat between Ravel and Diaghilev regarding excised chorus parts distracted further.[99] As with *Jeux*, more space was devoted to the visual; most critics thought *Daphnis* accomplished but as a large-scale work only partially successful. *The Times* viewed the dancers as primarily 'illustrations of the symphonic poem played by the orchestra' and singled out the 'Lever du jour' for particular praise.[100] Kalisch found *Daphnis* 'rich on imaginative charm' but lacking variety in its first part,[101] while the *Manchester Guardian* felt that, although engaging, *Daphnis* was neither fully coherent or especially original:

> [F]or the first time, [Ravel] came before us with a larger canvas and, on the whole, this very charming mosaic did not quite seem as convincing as, for instance, that quaint *Mother Goose ... Daphnis and Chloë* does not step much further than some of the Russian ballets we have already seen. It is not nearly as revolutionary or as stimulating as *Le sacre du printemps* for example.[102]

Ravel and Debussy were among many composers promoted by the *Société des Concerts Français* (SCF).[103] Despite its name, the SCF does not appear to have operated as a society and is perhaps better considered as a brand. Its primary organiser was Tony Guéritte, a French engineer based in Newcastle-upon-Tyne; his brother-in-law was Parisian music critic Georges Jean-Aubry.[104] Acting discreetly, Guéritte liaised between French composers and performers and British venues and promoters. While focused primarily on London, the SCF's brand was also used occasionally elsewhere, typically when artists appearing under its aegis in London performed outside the capital,[105] and also for part of a concert series in Manchester, managed by another French émigré, Lucie Barbier.[106]

Guéritte's first venture into professional concert organisation appears to have been in 1907 when the Parisian Quartet and pianist Ricardo Viñes appeared in Newcastle, Leeds and Sheffield (3, 4 and 5 December), before concerts at Leighton House and Bechstein Hall; in Sheffield and London, Ravel's String Quartet was introduced (see above).[107] Guéritte officially inaugurated the SCF on 26 February 1909 with a concert devoted to Debussy (see below); in total, there were 25 SCF concerts in London, mostly at Bechstein Hall, ending on 15 May 1914. The connection between Barbier and Guéritte is unclear but they certainly knew each other and co-ordinated some activities. Barbier's two Manchester seasons, initially promoted independently as 'French Concerts', also started in December 1907, and comprised eight events; the SCF label was used from 2 March 1909, a repeat of a London programme. Shortly afterwards, however, Barbier and her husband moved to Aberystwyth and a third season announced for autumn 1909 fell through.

Guéritte's agency is a classic example of its kind. The first performances of Ravel's Quartet were significant in promoting his music in Britain and arose from Guéritte's interest and his connection with Jean-Aubry, who knew Ravel. Debussy, well known by 1909, probably intended his presence at the SCF's inaugural concert as a convenient but supportive gesture, as it was followed the next day by the premiere of *Nocturnes*; this thesis is supported by the SCF programme as, other than *Danses sacrées et profanes* (**1909**-1), the works (including the String Quartet, *Estampes* and *L'isle joyeuse*) were familiar to regular concertgoers.[108]

SCF concerts included an eclectic selection of music and Guéritte's choices (or possibly Jean-Aubry's) appear sometimes indiscriminate. Some focused on one or two composers, but selection programmes were more common; the only consistent strategy seems to have been avoiding such familiar composers as Saint-Saëns, Gounod, Massenet and Berlioz. Personal appearances were encouraged: Ravel was present when his *Cinq mélodies populaires grecques* was introduced (**1909**-6), as was Florent Schmitt, whose music appeared particularly regularly. As well as Debussy, D'Indy, Franck, Chausson and Fauré, less familiar composers, including de Séverac, Roussel, Magnard, Caplet, Lekeu, Hüe, Duparc and Février were included; composers associated with D'Indy were especially well supported. Although solo piano, string chamber works and solo songs dominated, other genres were explored: on 29 November 1910, for example, music for wind ensemble was performed (D'Indy's *Chansons et danses* and Bernard's *Divertissement*), and several programmes included early music, including works by Couperin, Rameau, Blavet, André Campra and Jean-Féry Rebel. Performers varied likewise; the Parisian Quartet, Viñes and soprano Hélène Luquiens were regulars, but others included the *Société des concerts d'autrefois* and *Société moderne d'instruments à vent* (which both also gave independent London concerts).

Barbier's Manchester concerts were almost as varied, allowing for their much smaller number; music by Couperin, Rameau and Lully appeared as well as by Franck, Chausson and Duparc. Saint-Saëns, Géloso, Février, Hahn, D'Indy and Fauré all performed in person; Debussy, billed to appear at Manchester's first SCF-branded concert, unfortunately fell ill and cancelled engagements in Manchester and Edinburgh.

The impact of SCF concerts on London audiences is unclear, but they attracted regular and often extensive press attention. Despite some haphazard programming, in 1913 the *Academy* noted that

> The *Société des Concerts Français* has been thoroughly justifying its existence ... Last week its concert was memorable for a performance of one of the very finest productions of modern French music, Chausson's Concerto for Violin and Piano with String Quartette ... This richly sonorous music, with its lovely lyricism, its finely sustained and deeply felt emotion, shaped and guided with truly French sense of proportion, made a very marked impression.[109]

Schmitt's Piano Quintet was also well received, reservations about its duration notwithstanding: the *Musical Times* thought it 'an appealing work of great elaboration and length, and a corresponding wealth of ideas. Its harmonies are advanced without being uncouth, and the workmanship is masterly'.[110] Early music also proved popular,[111] but, unsurprisingly, given the range of repertory, some programmes backfired: a concert dominated by the Reuchsel brothers failed badly; the *Observer* complained that they were 'not representative of French music in any shape or form' and concluded that 'the *Société des Concerts Français* can do better than this'.[112]

Guéritte later wrote that he relied initially on French ex-patriots, estimating that they constituted 65% of early audiences; by 1914, though, he thought this proportion had fallen to 19%.[113] Barbier was well supported in Manchester but in Aberystwyth, an isolated and much smaller town, her ventures struggled.[114] Overall, the SCF's legacy is mixed: most of the new composers it promoted remained largely unknown, though the reputations of some, such as D'Indy, Chausson and Hahn, undoubtedly benefitted. Guéritte was a zealous enthusiast and the SCF a respected venture; while results were variable, its activities were appreciated, at least among *cognoscenti*, and awareness, if not profound knowledge, of new French music increased.

The broad range of music presented by the SCF both encouraged and reflected the increasingly catholic interests of London audiences, especially but not exclusively at their rarefied end. Considering the profiles of composers less prominent than Debussy and Ravel further extends understanding of audience and critical taste.

Reynaldo Hahn's modest renown was aided by willingness to visit and perform. Brief references in the musical press first appear in the late 1890s;[115] during his first traced visit in 1898 he accompanied Victor Maurel in a lecture-recital that included 'L'heure exquise', which became Hahn's best-known work in Britain,[116] and his songs featured subsequently in recitals by many singers, including Maurel, Calvé and Clara Butt.[117] Appraisals were typically brief; songs appearing as 'fillers' in orchestral programmes or in wide-ranging vocal recitals did not receive detailed discussion.

When Hahn performed at Bechstein Hall (16 May 1906), *The Times* declared that his best-known songs 'are so popular with our young singers that it was only to be expected that there would be a large audience'.[118] The prevalent critical view was that they were well-wrought and touching, though *The Times* referred to a 'lack of virility' and diversity:

> they produced the effect of a row of small impressionist landscapes, all of the same colour, and nearly all treating the same sort of subjects in the same sort of way ... [A] whole series of them produces of a rather cloying and not quite wholesome kind of sweetness.[119]

Hahn evidently thought visiting Britain worthwhile and appeared several times; aided by urbanity and networking, he enhanced his standing: in June 1907, he gave two lecture-recitals at the home of French-born Lady Aline Sassoon,[120] and in March 1908 appeared at the French Concerts in Manchester. The *Manchester Guardian* was generous:

> [H]is work presents an individuality of conception, an attractive personality, which compels attention ... There is less of the pioneer in him than

in Debussy, but it is decidedly good to see modern ideas and modern means so skilfully and effectively employed.[121]

Two more visits followed in 1909. In July, Hahn conducted the *Société moderne d'instruments à vent* in his chamber suite *Bal de Béatrice d'Este* at Bechstein Hall, viewed by the *Musical Standard* as 'flavoured with a delicate archaism ... [though] it is graceful, dainty music of but little consequence'.[122] In November, thanks to Guéritte, Hahn appeared in Edinburgh, Newcastle and London (note 105); *The Times* again noted the songs' popularity, referring to their 'delicate sense of atmosphere, the beauty of their melodies, and the exquisite declamation of the words'.[123]

Hahn's reputation rested on his songs, although some instrumental music (not only *Béatrice d'Este*) was heard and performances of his operas in Paris were mentioned in the press. The only large work to appear was the one-act ballet *Le dieu bleu*, given by the *Ballets Russes* (**1913**-1). Once again, production and choreography attracted most attention (the leading roles were played by Nijinsky and Tarsavina), and the mainly lukewarm comments on Hahn's score appear almost an afterthought, perhaps influenced by knowledge of its earlier failure in Paris. *The Times* tactfully noted that Cocteau's scenario 'does not give quite so many opportunities to M Reynaldo Hahn as to MM Bakst and Fokine' and concluded that 'Much of the music is lacking in character ... It is written with the beautifully clear technique to which M Hahn has accustomed us, but there is little driving force in it'.[124] Tellingly, the *Athenaeum* noted that it was 'certainly clever, but after the exciting music of Stravinsky it sounded tame', while the *Academy* suggested that Hahn was 'not strong enough to paint the passion, the fear, the ecstasy, or the horror of the rich Indian scenes'.[125] As with Ravel and Debussy, the intense excitement aroused by the experimental Russian works seen in London worked to Hahn's disadvantage.

In contrast to Hahn, Vincent D'Indy's reputation depended principally on orchestral music. Although only six years younger than Fauré, D'Indy was regularly presented by reviewers as a 'new composer', a construction seemingly based on his relatively recent appearance in Britain and his music's slow dissemination. A performance of the Trio, Op. 29 (**1894**-7), by the aptly named Society for the Cultivation of Modern Music gained attention but an equivocal reception: the *Musical News* described it as 'remarkable for its piquancy and richness of colouring, and like most of the modern French works, [it] appeals rather to the sense than to the intellect'.[126] The *Musical Standard* did not think greater familiarity would help; it recognised 'a measure of cleverness' but also 'an impression of triviality and something approaching a vulgar twist'.[127]

Thereafter, D'Indy's music appeared occasionally in London but without gaining significant traction: Lamoureux conducted the first part of *Wallenstein* (**1896**-3), *La forêt enchantée* (**1896**-9) and *Sauge fleurie* (**1897**-5) but, despite some positive comments, none made any immediate headway. 'Wallenstein's Camp' was praised by the *Musical Standard* as a 'remarkable composition, full of colour and picturesqueness and harmonic and instrumental ingenuity', while Shedlock opined that the work was 'programme music of the higher kind ... The thematic material is bright and varied, the working out clever and often humorous'.[128] It was another five years, however, until Parts II and III of *Wallenstein* were heard (**1902**-1), and a further seven before it was performed complete (see below). Ysaÿe also promoted D'Indy's music, introducing the 'Istar' Variations (**1900**-3) and Piano Quartet (**1901**-2), though neither generated much interest; Ysaÿe's metamorphosis from violinist to conductor dominated reviews of 'Istar', while D'Indy's music was thought by the *Musical Times* to be curious in form and too Wagnerian.[129]

Wood's premiere of *Symphonie sur un chant montagnard français* (**1907**-4) attracted positive notices; the *Manchester Guardian* thought it 'of a very high order' and the *Musical Standard* 'thoroughly enjoyable from start to finish'.[130] Despite finding the principal theme trivial, *The Times* stated that 'the whole work is full of bright colouring and piquant orchestral devices, and yet the character and simplicity which belong to the original theme is never lost'.[131] Positive comments notwithstanding, only one other pre-1914 performance, by Beecham in 1910, has been traced.

The previous year, Beecham introduced *Jour d'été à la montagne* (**1909**-3) which, despite superficial resemblance to the *Symphonie*, received some good press notices.[132] This coincided with D'Indy's first visit to England and was the highpoint for his pre-war reputation. He played the piano in his Trio at the Manchester SCF concert on 8 March,[133] and probably also attended Beecham's concert. Most important, though, was the first complete performance of *Wallenstein* (**1909**-4).[134] D'Indy may have been disappointed by some press notices; while his conducting and contribution to French musical culture were lauded, some equivocation is apparent. Richard Capell noted that, although *Wallenstein* was not a new work, 'It remains, however, noble and striking music, invigorating and uplifting to hear ... London must know more of this music that is as keen and untainted as the wind among arid, romantic mountains'.[135] The *Athenaeum* was less convinced: the second movement contained 'some clever and effective writing, though lacking in strong feeling', while the final movement, despite possessing 'many impressive moments ... is not entirely convincing'.[136] *The Times* was particularly disappointed:

> It seems just a little old-fashioned; for D'Indy stands midway between the iconoclastic young composers on the one hand and the ultra-conservative party on the other ... It is often open to the charge of excessive Wagnerian influence ... [We] do not mean to employ a euphemism for plagiarism, for of that there is none; it is only that the shape, so to speak, of many of the themes is such as they would not have had if Wagner had not lived.[137]

While D'Indy was greeted warmly, his visit's impact was limited; *Wallenstein* was heard complete in Edinburgh, Glasgow and Liverpool in late 1909 but there were no other significant performances before 1914.[138] A second visit, in

1911, during which D'Indy was engaged to conduct the Philharmonic Society, was cancelled due to illness.

D'Indy's relatively low profile arose for several reasons: he first visited Britain aged 58 (having already been to the United States) and had neither a single persistent advocate nor a wider group of supporters. Interest in his music was sporadic and only a few works attracted attention; his operas were entirely ignored. Despite often being presented as new, the works performed dated mostly from the 1880s or earlier, making D'Indy's style appear old-fashioned compared to Debussy, Ravel and other 'modern' composers. Perhaps most problematically, D'Indy did not conform to standard British ideas of Frenchness; while his advocacy of Franck was widely acknowledged, perceived Wagnerian tendencies proved puzzling: in 1900 the *Musical Times* commented that the Prelude to *Fervaal* and 'Istar' Variations 'deepen one's doubts whether any great good can come out of so strong an infusion of Wagnerian blood into French veins',[139] a point echoed by Capell:

> [D'Indy] stands almost alone in the loftiness of his outlook, the high ser-
> iousness of his aims. In his reserve, his aloofness, his austerity, he shows
> characteristics not conventionally ascribed to the French musician. In
> effect, if on the one hand his music is drenched in the pungent air of his
> native Cévennes, he is allied to the Teutonic spirit by his submission to the
> influences of Wagner, the German, [and] César Franck, the Fleming.[140]

Diverse as they were, Saint-Saëns, Debussy, Ravel and Hahn conformed more easily to stereotypes of French urbanity, luxuriance and wit accepted by many British commentators, while widely perceived French animosity to Wagner and contradictions between the French and German 'races', made D'Indy a conundrum.

Veterans revisited: Berlioz, Saint-Saëns and Fauré

While there was increasing interest in new music from across Europe during the Edwardian years, older French repertory was not discarded. In 1900 Berlioz had been dead just over 30 years, while Saint-Saëns and Fauré continued to engage directly with Britain: Saint-Saëns paid his last visit in 1913, aged 78, and Fauré appeared the following year, aged 69. Though individuated in British perceptions, their ongoing receptions share certain common characteristics.

The most comprehensive post-Victorian appraisals of Berlioz came during his centenary in 1903. Having made his final visit to Britain in 1855, Berlioz was cast as a historical figure, with assessments mainly coming from those who first encountered his music during its 1880s resurgence. He was the first French composer to be appraised in this manner, with substantial articles appearing in several journals.[141] Although there was disagreement about Berlioz's legacy (Runciman was especially critical), he was, from the British perspective, the only French composer approaching canonical status. Such views were hardly new, and echoed those of Henry Hadow and Dannreuther, in whose eyes Berlioz was a flawed iconoclast who rarely fulfilled his potential.[142]

Berlioz's standing was sufficient to inspire several commemorative performances. There was no 'official' event in London but three unconnected concerts in Queen's Hall in November and December, conducted (ironically, perhaps?) by Richter, Weingartner and Strauss, were widely billed as a 'Berlioz Festival'. Between them, these covered six overtures, *Symphonie fantastique*, *Harold en Italie*, *La mort de Cléopâtre*, and extracts from *Faust*, *Roméo et Juliette* and *Nuits d'été*; lack of co-ordination resulted in *Carnaval romain* appearing in all three programmes. Many reviewers noted poor attendance at the second and third concerts; the *Athenaeum* perceived a disjunction between aficionados and the wider public, arguing that Berlioz's role 'is for musicians interested in the evolution of their art one of singular importance; but the general public evidently cares little for his music'.[143] Devoting entire programmes to one composer only made the situation worse.[144] Competing events, some of which presented more unusual repertory, may also have had an impact: the RCM orchestra under Stanford performed *Roméo et Juliette* complete, while the amateur Dulwich Philharmonic and Stock Exchange Orchestral societies also gave commemorative concerts.[145] *Harold* was performed in Liverpool, Birmingham, Cheltenham and Newcastle, and *Faust* at Manchester, Newcastle and Crystal Palace, coinciding with the publication of two new English adaptations (by Novello, with words by Paul England, and Breitkopf & Härtel, by William Wallace), reflecting its established popularity with British choral societies.

The 'celebrations' changed few critical minds. Reviewing Richter's concert, the *Manchester Guardian* commented:

> The more one hears his music the more one wonders at the audacity which impressed [Berlioz] to revolutionise the orchestra, to teach it a new language which it still to all intents and purposes speaks today. But further familiarity shows us also his limitations. For all his critical and literary powers, he belongs, after all, to what one may call the unintellectual class of composers in the sense that he is deficient in emotional subtlety. His romanticism is almost childlike compared to that of the Germans who lived soon after him.[146]

Others were still more cutting: the *Monthly Musical Record* demanded:

> Why does the public not care about him? It is not enough to say that his music is insincere, artificial, claptrap. Berlioz was absolutely sincere, tremendously in earnest, and he had, besides, an unlimited belief in himself … The truth is that Berlioz had a second-rate mind, that his conceptions had no true nobility, and that the better they are expressed the more their inherent deficiencies are made plain.[147]

The *Musical Opinion* was succinct: 'To us of today, Berlioz's instrumental experiments sound theatrical and cheap. If there has been any real artistic descendant from Berlioz, John Philip Sousa is his name'.[148] Views of Berlioz remained ambivalent: while Dannreuther had given him the benefit of the doubt, perceptions later hardened; by 1903 many were prepared to argue that Berlioz was no misunderstood genius and that those who deprecated his music had been right all along.

Saint-Saëns remained the French composer who cultivated connections with Britain most assiduously. Perceptions had largely been set in the 1880s (see Chapter 4) and remained consistent, with a somewhat greater degree of respect after Saint-Saëns succeeded Gounod as France's 'senior' musician. Performances, though, were mainly restricted to a few favourite pieces, including the Second Piano Concerto, B minor Violin Concerto, shorter tone poems, selected chamber works and *Samson et Dalila* (extracted solo vocal items, as an 'oratorio' and, finally, on stage).[149] New works were occasionally introduced but met with mixed fortunes and rarely repeated. Through regular visits, however, during which he appeared as composer and pianist, Saint-Saëns maintained his profile; in addition to his own music he consistently promoted Mozart's piano concertos, few of which were then well known.

Saint-Saëns's appearances at the London Musical Festival in 1901 drew distinctly varied reactions: the *Manchester Guardian* acidly observed that 'Dr Saint-Saëns was sent into the world to show what cleverness, brilliance, and versatility may accomplish in music without greatness or genius', a mild criticism compared to Runciman's diatribe in the *Saturday Review*.[150] Edward Baughan was more charitable, despite starting from a negative position:

> Saint-Saëns is not a strong composer, and a concert entirely composed of his music promised rather a monotonous evening. But it fell out otherwise. For one thing ... [he] is one of those men to whom an audience feels as a friend. He is modest and self-contained, and yet smiles genially as if he were really enjoying the concert. And then his music is never heavy and pedantic, however clever it may be. It is always music, and though one can trace in it the composer's studies – it is individual.[151]

Saint-Saëns's 'veteran' status undoubtedly helped, as did his stamina: in 1910 he played in a concert of his chamber music on 7 June, saw *Samson* at Covent Garden two days later, and, in recitals on 8, 15 and 22 June, was the soloist in twelve Mozart piano concertos;[152] in the Edwardian years he also appeared in Birmingham, Oxford (to receive an honorary doctorate), Edinburgh and Manchester.[153]

Saint-Saëns's final public appearance in Britain was at the premiere of *The Promised Land* at Gloucester (**1913**-5) (see Figure 5.5). It was received poorly; with a libretto by Hermann Klein, the work was thought old-fashioned and

DR. C. H. LLOYD.   DR. A. H. BREWER.   SIR EDWARD ELGAR.

DR. CAMILLE SAINT-SAËNS.
Photograph by H. E. Jones, Gloucester.)

Fig 5.5 Saint-Saëns, with Charles Lloyd, Edward Elgar and Herbert Brewer at the
Gloucester Festival (*Musical Times*, 1 October 1913, p. 665) (by kind permis-
sion of the University of Birmingham)

lacking in power. Though it was originally conceived 25 years earlier, Klein
apparently made no revisions to accommodate developments wrought in the
interim by composers such as Elgar.[154] Gloucester, which prioritised British
works, took a significant and unfortunate gamble, encouraged, it seems, by
Klein and perhaps also Novello, publishers of the vocal score.[155] The good-
will engendered by Saint-Saëns conducting (and playing a Mozart concerto
the previous evening) was insufficient. Few reviewers seemed to have been
aware of Klein's account (note 154) and were inclined to blame the composer: Herbert Antcliffe regretted that Saint-Saëns had been

> so sadly misled as to English tastes ... He had a Biblical libretto compiled
> in a style ... which went out of fashion a quarter of a century or more
> ago. The music to which it is set is equally old-fashioned, and entirely

lacking in originality … Whatever the cause, his latest work can only be written down a failure.[156]

The *Musical Times* attempted a salvage operation but could barely hide its disappointment: acknowledging the work's anachronistic style, it stated:

[W]e think there will be a considerable number of concert-goers who will not grieve on this account. The choruses especially are likely to please performers. They are numerous, well-developed, broad, and comparatively simple, and occasionally contrapuntal in the style beloved by most choralists.[157]

A London performance by the Royal Choral Society on 27 November did not change the prevalent view.[158]

A happier occasion, earlier in the year, was a celebration of 75 years of Saint-Saëns's professional career (initiated by Klein and based on the dubious starting point of his first piano lesson), comprising a concert at Queen's Hall (2 June), and gala performance of *Samson* at Covent Garden the next day. In the circumstances, reviewers inclined to be complimentary. Although dominated by the 'Organ' Symphony, *The Times* found Saint-Saëns's piano playing (in the K. 450 concerto once more) more impressive than his music, adding that, 'one would hesitate, because of the greatness of others, to speak of him as a composer of the first rank'.[159] The *Academy* was respectfully effusive and drew on familiar stereotypes:

Most of the gifts which we look upon as essentially French are his in abundant measure. Wide learning, yet exact polished style, melodious invention, incisive eloquence, bright geniality, urbanity, moderation, his music shows him to have possessed all these precious qualities.[160]

At the concert, Alexander Mackenzie addressed Saint-Saëns directly, highlighting his Anglophilia and stating that he had 'helped not a little to strengthen the musical "entente" between your great land and our own', explicitly linking British interest in French music with closer political association.

Fauré's reputation, by contrast, continued to develop only slowly; despite his elevated status in France, his pre-war renown in Britain remained modest. In part this was due to his focus on chamber music and song which, although esteemed in Britain, were not accorded status or publicity as great as for orchestral and choral music; like Massenet and others, Fauré promoted his music in person only sporadically. A third aspect was accessibility and performability: while many of Fauré's songs, like those of Chaminade and Hahn, had an appeal that reached the amateur market, the language and technical demands of his instrumental chamber music were closer to Franck and Chausson, restricting performances to professionals and highly skilled amateurs.

After his London visits in the 1890s, Fauré does not appear to have returned to Britain in a professional capacity until 1908. Reviews in the interim were typically brief and low-profile, rendering him a secondary figure for most British concertgoers; a rare performance of an orchestral work was that of *Pelléas et Mélisande* in 1902 but it attracted only glancing attention.[161] It is unclear why, after a long absence, Fauré chose to visit London twice in 1908; Jones and Orledge suggest that he enjoyed the first visit when he met members of the royal family[162] and played at Bechstein Hall. Although this recital gained moderately good reviews, it fell foul of critical distaste for single-composer programmes; *The Times* and *Manchester Guardian* both argued that not even Jeanne Raunay's praiseworthy singing could sustain interest through 21 songs by one man.[163] Barbier facilitated the second visit, during which Fauré appeared at the Manchester SCF concert on 30 November. The programme, comprising the C minor Piano Quartet, A major Violin Sonata, songs and solo items for flute and harp, was better balanced, and the *Guardian*'s Samuel Langford more fulsome.[164] A vocal recital in London on 5 December by Elizabeth Swinton, accompanied by Fauré, was largely overlooked.[165]

In the light of such patchy interest, it is curious that Fauré returned to London in 1914, to participate in a 'Fauré Festival' organised by his former student Robert Lortat; over three concerts (16, 19 and 22 June) all his solo piano music and several chamber works were performed.[166] Positive comments came from a conservative commentator in the *Musical Standard*, who remarked that, 'After the fearful and wonderful innovations of the ultra-moderns, it is refreshing indeed to listen to music so limpid, sincere and melodious'.[167] The *Observer*, though, felt that Fauré's piano pieces lacked a convenient niche:

> [O]nly a few years ago [they] would have been recognised as extremely modern examples of salon music, cultured, artistic and refined in style and rather exclusive in their pianistic appeal. Without being strong enough for the strenuous programme of the average piano recital, they scarcely filled the demand of the amateur pianist, whose abilities the works tested rather severely. The result was that these interesting works have never attained their popularity their merits deserve, and now, one would fear, it is almost too late to expect a proper recognition.[168]

Others were less convinced: *The Times* wondered whether a 'Fauré Festival' was 'the most politic way of pleading his cause', while Runciman, in an article entitled 'Frivolous Music', declared that 'Each concert was enjoyable enough by itself; but two I found monotonous and a third would have been intolerable', before adding the barb: 'The audiences ... were wildly enthusiastic and demonstrative. The many ladies and few gentlemen who attended wanted music of an agreeable and harmless sort, making no demands on the intellect or the emotions, and they got it'.[169] As was common during London's social season, more spectacular occasions claimed greater attention: Richard

Strauss was conducting and two opera seasons were in full swing, with the British premiere of Stravinsky's *Le rossignol* coming the evening before Fauré's second recital. His visit did, though, inadvertently earn Fauré the distinction of being the last significant French composer to appear in Britain before the outbreak of war seven weeks later.

Conclusions

The stylistic breadth of French repertory presented between 1901 and 1914 was unprecedented, reflecting both its own diversity and the interest, especially in London, of concert promoters and audiences in new music from across Europe. Social function and obligation were as significant as passionate enthusiasm but the practical effect in terms of music disseminated remains. The positive symbolism of the *Entente Cordiale* created a supportive atmosphere that shrewder cultural agents exploited effectively.

As French art music diversified, it became less common for British critics to deploy standard tropes of Frenchness. For newer works these were sometimes adapted: qualities long associated with the French – delicacy, 'polish', ornament, wit and grace – continued in use, acting as a convenient shorthand to communicate a sense of style, especially in brief or hastily conceived reviews, and were applied to elements of music by Debussy, Ravel and others.

Reactions to younger composers, although inconsistent, were rarely overtly hostile, especially after 1905. Critics who started working in the 1890s mostly aimed to be more 'objective' than their predecessors[170] and rarely found new French music disagreeable, although they expressed reservations regarding perceived formlessness, absence of developed melody or tonal ambiguity. Audiences also reacted variably; in relation to Debussy, if repeat performances indicate acceptance, *L'après-midi* and the String Quartet were embraced as, to a lesser extent, were *La demoiselle élue* and *Pelléas*, but *La mer* and *Jeux* provoked boredom or confusion more than enthusiasm. One aspect that drew critical and audience approval was a perceived tendency to treat 'dissonances as if they were consonances, not laying any particular emphasis upon them';[171] this largely removed the abrasive sounds often identified in such composers as Strauss, while subtle orchestration contrasted with the spectacular but percussive style of the Russians whose music was sweeping into London. In a substantial article on Ravel, *The Times*'s critic wrote:

> It is no figure of speech to speak of the pleasure of his music, for its salient characteristic is that it pleases. There are few modern composers of whom one could say that with such certainty … Ravel neither bullies nor bewilders his audience. He neither impresses nor oppresses us with things hard to understand. All his work … comes, as it were, to meet the hearer half-way. It adopts what one can only call the attitude of courtesy, and that in itself is bound to charm.[172]

Observers apprehended two limitations. Firstly, that new French composers, peculiarly attentive to detail and nuance, were more suited to small-scale, intimate works than symphonies or epic tone poems, and lacked the grand gesture of a broad emotional sweep. *The Times* article above countered this point by asserting that 'there are other things well worth having besides bigness of outlook and design, and it is the appreciation of that fact which has given French composers such importance in modern European music'. The second limitation, exemplified in reviews of Ravel, Hahn and Fauré, was a perceived lack of forthright expression, often expressed via implicitly gendered phraseology reminiscent of the eighteenth century, when French culture was commonly thought effeminate: pleasing and attractive but lacking virility and boldness. *The Times*'s sympathetic article insinuates this by references to 'charm', 'courtesy' and to Ravel meeting 'the hearer half-way'.

Leading academics tended to be less sympathetic; in part this reflects attachment to the Austro-German canon, but also, if sometimes obliquely, aesthetics of technique and generational difference, their professional careers having mainly started in the 1870s. Stanford, who reacted to new music with increasing bewilderment and antagonism, made Debussy (specifically the whole-tone scale) and Strauss the primary targets in his satirical *Ode to Discord*;[173] he also disliked *Pelléas*, judging by his joke proposal of a 'modernist' programme for the 1910 Leeds Festival.[174] Conversely, though, he conducted *La demoiselle élue* at the RCM (1909) and Leeds (1910), calling it 'fascinating stuff' in a letter to Leeds Festival committee member W S Hannam.[175] Frederick Corder, meanwhile, widely regarded as more liberal, 'could see nothing in Debussy'; after perusing *L'après-midi*, Corder allegedly 'rose with that familiar volcanic sigh of his, and exclaimed, almost tearfully: "I've tried, *honestly* I have, but I *cannot* understand it!"'.[176]

Parry, the most prolific essayist of the composer-teachers, reiterated the traditional view of French music in *Style in Musical Art*. While acknowledging France as one of the great nations of Western Europe, he viewed its music overall (like Burney, 140 years previously) as insular, superficial and theatrical:

> The idea of purely abstract art, of the development of large works upon copious artistic principles, has seemed as alien to French disposition as the expression of deep feeling … [T]he French have always seemed to regard music as the minister of gaiety. Its two essential requirements with them are rhythm and dexterity of presentation … They seem disposed to regard manner as of almost more consequence than matter … Their dexterity in dealing with the orchestra is part of that same exaggerated estimate of style.[177]

For Parry, French preference for style over substance sat below German profundity and English unaffectedness; only music from Eastern Europe – inherently primitive in Parry's Spencerian view – was treated more harshly.

Outside the academy, observers were often more open-minded; Arthur Hervey, Louise Liebich and Edwin Evans all praised French music, the latter asserting in 1909 that, amongst recent attempts to forge distinctive national styles, 'it is in France that the greatest degree of independence has been attained'.[178] So strong was this voice, Evans thought, that 'it threatens in its turn to become a danger to weaker musical organisms in other countries'.[179] Evans too, though, employed generalisations: the French were inherently 'quick-witted', disliked long-winded explanations and identified logical developments before they were elucidated, so that 'it is the unexpected which fascinates [them], and which has become characteristic of French music'. Similarly, while the English and Germans were 'sentimental', the French were sceptical and valued subtlety above all. A crucial difference arose in consequence: 'It is in France that the battle has opened between music which is rhetoric[al] in form and music which is purely aesthetic', a trend Evans associated especially with Debussy.[180]

This belief that new French music was 'aesthetic' and unstructured, rather than focused on motivic development within an almost didactic use of form, also contributed to the application of 'impressionist' to selected composers. The term was well known in Britain in relation to painting so transposition to music was not difficult; Ronald Byrnside has suggested that its earliest use was Liebich's in her 1908 biography of Debussy,[181] but she had already used it, though imprecisely, four years earlier,[182] and was herself preceded by Hervey, who, in 1903, referred to Debussy as 'a coming man, a composer of individual talent, an impressionist ... who wanders dreamily through a maze of ever-changing harmonies'.[183] Hervey, an ardent Francophile and moderately well-known composer, probably heard the term while training in Paris; his application may be the first in English.

'Impressionism' was used only intermittently by pre-war critics: for some it became code for aspects of Debussy's style but others ignored it; examples include the *Graphic*'s review of *L'après-midi*, the *Daily Telegraph*'s of the Paris premiere of *La mer* and the *Manchester Guardian* reverse-applying it to the String Quartet.[184] Evans's earliest known usage was in 1908, when juxtaposing 'isolated composers, of whom Debussy is the archetype' with the Schola Cantorum: '[they] endeavour to recreate in their listeners, by the means of sensuous impressions, the emotional sensations stimulated in them by other sensuous impressions. This explains the tacit consent by which they are dubbed impressionists'.[185]

The label was more rarely applied to Ravel; in August 1906 the *Musical Standard* stated:

Those who are tired of the more orthodox harmonic progressions and of the usual rhythmic procedures, should examine *Miroirs* ... The pieces belong to the impressionistic school and contain many original and clever ideas. The piano is used in an effective and characteristic manner and indefinite chords and mists of harmony are produced in an easy profusion. The pieces are difficult.[186]

In *The Times*'s 1913 article, however, the 'impressionist' label was carefully applied only to pictorial pieces such as *Rapsodie espagnole* and *Gaspard de la nuit*, with 'abstract' works considered a different group:

> The delights of unfolding the intricacies of a purely musical design some-times supply him with the impulse which imagery outside music brings at other times. One finds examples of it in the [*Sonatine*, String Quartet and *Valse nobles et sentimentales*]. Here he shows how different are his aims from those of the 'impressionist' musicians, of whom France has produced more than any other nation.[187]

Upon the outbreak of the Great War, French music, while not in the position of almost obsessive popularity witnessed during the 1870s and '80s operetta craze, occupied a prominent place in British cultural life. In London, a catholic range of stylistically diverse music from Berlioz to Ravel was presented in concert halls. In theatres and provincial Britain this range was less evident, although music from the same temporal frame drawn from a smaller pool of works, was available. While German music remained the backbone of instrumental repertory, and Italian and German works in combination dominated the output of Britain's opera troupes, French music nevertheless occupied a significant place; the only major gap – though a very significant one – was in choral music, where German and British works were overwhelmingly dominant. Regardless of dependence on well-worn tropes and clichés, the perception that French music was distinctive undoubtedly helped maintain interest, giving a profitable outlet for the substantial and entrenched network of agents facilitating cultural transfers from Paris to London. The Franco-British alliance in the Great War served only to enhance that partiality.

Notes

1 See Philip Bell, *France and Britain 1900–1940: Entente and Estrangement* (London and New York, 2013), and Alan Sharp and Glyn Stone (eds), *Anglo-French Relations in the Twentieth Century* (London and New York, 2000).
2 For the origins of the phrase, see Chapter 3, note 16.
3 Aided, in Frank McDonagh's view, by a largely non-partisan approach to British foreign policy; see Sharp and Stone, pp. 36–49.
4 Bell, p. 48.
5 *Times*, 25 May 1908, p. 9.
6 *Times*, 21 April 1914, p. 9.
7 *MG*, 22 April 1914, p. 9; see also *Times*, same date, p. 10.
8 *MG*, 24 April 1914, p. 8.
9 The initial idea came from Imre Kiralfy, a Hungarian-Jewish impresario and former owner of the Earl's Court showground, which displayed selections from the Paris Expositions in 1890 and 1902; see Alexander Geppert, *Fleeting Cities: Imperial Expositions in* Fin-de-Siècle *Europe* (Basingstoke, 2010) pp. 102–31; and Martyn Cornick, ' "Putting the Seal on the *Entente*": The Franco-British Exhibition, London, May-October 1908', *Franco-British Studies*, **35** (2004), pp. 133–44.

10 Cornick, pp. 137–8.

11 *Penny Illustrated Paper*, 30 May 1908, p. 339.

12 *France-British Exhibition: London (Shepherd's Bush) 1908 Official Guide* (London, 1908), p. 2 (and in French, p. 66).

13 Colonies were also allocated space; non-white communities, especially from Ceylon and Senegal, were represented by standard imperialist tropes.

14 Allegedly due to Queen Alexandra's intervention; see *Observer*, 25 April 1909, p. 9. Hitherto works had been temporally or geographically reset (*Hérodiade* and Strauss's *Salome*) or given as oratorios (*Samson* and Gounod's *La reine de Saba*).

15 *Times*, 27 April 1909, p. 8; see also *Athenaeum*, 1 May, p. 537; *MS*, same date, p. 275.

16 *MS*, 26 June 1909, p. 409; *Times*, 19 June, p. 12.

17 *MG*, 19 June 1909, p. 9.

18 *MT*, 1 July 1909, p. 466; see also *Observer*, 20 June, p. 7; *Athenaeum*, 26 June, p. 766.

19 *MMR*, 1 June 1902, p. 107; see also *Times*, 3 May, p. 8; *Athenaeum*, 31 May, p. 699.

20 Debussy visited London to superintend rehearsals; due to stage manager Fernand Almanz's unhelpfulness ('I've rarely had such a strong desire to kill anybody') Debussy complained that 'I have to act as electrician [and] machine operator' (letter to Jacques Durand, 18 May 1909). Debussy did not attend the performance but welcomed its success: see François Lesure and Roger Nichols, *Debussy Letters* (London, 1987), pp. 199–201.

21 *MT*, 1 June 1909, p. 386.

22 *MG*, 22 May 1909, p. 8.

23 As note 21.

24 *Observer*, 23 May 1909, p. 7; see also *Athenaeum*, 29 May, p. 655.

25 *Times*, 22 May 1909, p. 13.

26 *Times*, 28 May 1909, p. 11.

27 Denhof's company collapsed and was rescued by Thomas Beecham; see Paul Rodmell, *Opera in the British Isles 1875–1918* (Aldershot, 2013), pp. 162–5.

28 Hammerstein viewed Massenet as a substitute for Puccini, for whom he possessed no performing rights (see Rodmell, pp. 105–8). His seasons floundered so badly that he revived Planquette's *Les cloches de Corneville* in an attempt to attract audiences.

29 For representative reviews of *La muguette* see *Times*, 26 May 1910, p. 10; *MG*, same date, p. 8; *MS*, 4 June, p. 360; and of *Le chemineau*, *Observer*, 16 October 1910, p. 7; *MT*, 1 November, p. 732. A revival of *Werther* also failed; see John Lucas, *Thomas Beecham: An Obsession with Music* (Woodbridge, 2008), p. 62.

30 Although a 'suburban' theatre, the Coronet was lavishly furnished and occasionally produced French drama and operetta; *Chilpéric* was revived in 1903 and a Parisian company followed *Véronique*, giving *La dame aux camélias* and (in French) Pinero's *The second Mrs Tanqueray* (see www.arthurlloyd.co.uk/ CoronetTheatreNottingHillGate.htm, accessed 9 March 2019).

31 *Country Life*, 16 May 1903, p. lxiv.

32 Quoted in *MS*, 30 May 1903, p. 335; see also *Times*, 6 May, p. 12; *MG*, 7 May, p. 7.

33 Edwardes took over the Gaiety from Hollingshead in 1885, introduced Cellier's *Dorothy*, and effectively inaugurated musical comedy with *In Town* and *A Gaiety Girl* in the early 1890s; he also introduced *The Merry Widow* to London.

34 J P Wearing, *The London Stage 1900–1909* (2nd ed, Lanham, 2014), p. 185.

35 *MS*, 28 May 1904, p. 343; see also *MG*, 19 May 1904, p. 12.
36 *Country Life*, 29 May 1904, p. lxii.
37 Wearing, *London Stage 1900–09*, p. 230. For reviews see *Observer*, 30 April 1905, p. 5; *MG*, 2 May, p. 12; and 'Another Blow to Musical Comedy', *MS*, 6 May, p. 271.
38 *MS*, 27 April 1907, p. 268; see also *Times*, 9 April, p. 5; 13 April, p. 14; and 17 April, p. 7.
39 *Observer*, 21 April 1907, p. 4; see also *Times*, 18 April, p. 12; *MS*, 27 April, p. 267; *MT*, 1 May, p. 318.
40 Rodmell, pp. 119 and 123.
41 Wearing, *London Stage 1900–09*, pp. 414 and 416.
42 Translated libretto, quoted in *Times*, 21 December 1911, p. 10.
43 *Academy*, 30 December 1911, p. 816.
44 As note 42; see also *MG*, 21 December 1911, p. 7; *Observer*, 24 December, p. 10; *Observer*, 14 January 1912, p. 7.
45 *Times*, 23 December 1911, p. 9.
46 Lucas, pp. 33–6, 41 and 43. Beecham's performances included the first of Berlioz's *Te Deum* for over twenty years and a revival of Franck's *Les Djinns* (22 February and 23 March 1909 respectively).
47 Berlioz and Saint-Saëns were best represented, the former most strongly and the latter mainly by concertos; visiting soloists' preferences may also explain occasional performances of Franck's *Symphonic Variations*. *L'après-midi d'un faune* was the only work by Debussy Richter conducted (twice in both 1908 and 1910); for complete programmes, see Christopher Fifield, *Hans Richter* (Suffolk, 2016)). *MG* implicitly criticised Richter's approach (Editorial, 9 November 1907, p. 8); Lucie Barbier (see p. 174 and note 106 below), did likewise for the post-Richter period (*MG*, 1 June 1911, p. 9).
48 Leanne Langley, 'Building an Orchestra, Creating an Audience', in Jennifer Doctor and David Wright (eds), *The Proms: A New History* (London, 2006), pp. 32–73.
49 The analysis does not scale for length of work: most composers' tallies would be dominated by short vocal items.
50 In Leeds, D'Indy's *Wallenstein's Camp*, Saint-Saëns's C minor Piano Concerto and *Le rouet d'Omphale*, a lecture recital on *Pelléas*, excerpts from Berlioz's *Faust* and Franck's D minor Quartet; an unnamed suite by Bizet and *Carnaval romain* (Bradford); Berlioz's *Faust* (Scarborough); *L'après-midi*, Bizet's *Jeux d'enfants* and Saint-Saëns's *Suite Algérienne* (Hull); his G minor Piano Concerto and part of the D minor Violin Concerto (York) and *Afrique* (Ossett).
51 The earliest traced public performance of Debussy's first series of *Préludes* is Franz Liebich's at Bechstein Hall (**1910**–4). Two reviews state that four *Préludes* were given, but only *The Times* names them all (3 June, p. 7; *MS*, 11 June, p. 367); a third states five (*MT*, 1 July, p. 459), and *MG* merely 'some' (3 June, p. 7); Liebich later claimed eight (letter to *MS*, 5 April 1913, p. 294); none claims the performance a premiere.
52 See Roger Nichols, 'The Reception of Debussy's Music in England up to 1914', in Richard Langham-Smith (ed.), *Debussy Studies* (Cambridge, 1997), p. 139.
53 *Times*, 21 February 1903, p. 9. The Sarabande also received only superficial attention (*Times*, 3 May 1904, p. 10, and *MS*, 7 May, p. 295).
54 *Times*, 24 August 1904, p. 9; see also *Athenaeum*, 27 August, p. 282; *MG*, 28 November, p. 6 (of Queen's Hall performance on 26 November). *L'après-midi* was

followed by a rare performance of Guilmant's First Symphony, throwing it into even sharper relief.

55 *MS*, 27 August 1904, p. 128.
56 *Graphic*, 27 August 1904, p. 280; *Observer*, 21 August, p. 6.
57 Frank Bridge was the violist; the performance seems all the more remarkable given the RCM's reputation of favouring of the Austro-German tradition.
58 *Times*, 20 October 1904, p. 4; see also *MMR*, 1 December, p. 234.
59 For examples see *Athenaeum*, 18 February 1905, p. 218 ('Chevaux de bois' and 'Mandoline'); *Athenaeum*, 3 March 1906, p. 275 (six unspecified songs).
60 *Times*, 26 February 1906, p. 12.
61 *Times*, 24 May 1906, p. 7.
62 *MS*, 2 June 1906, p. 344.
63 *MG*, 6 February 1906, p. 6 (Nora Clench Quartet, Bechstein Hall); see also *MS*, 31 March, p. 195.
64 *MT*, 1 March 1906, p. 197.
65 *MG*, 3 November 1906, p. 6.
66 For his own account, see Henry Wood, *My Life in Music* (London, 1938), pp. 207–9 and 297–9; see also Lesure and Nichols, pp. 179–80.
67 Debussy wrote to Georges Jean-Aubry in October 1907 that 'the sympathies of the English for music are only of the official variety, and so far Handel and Sullivan have met their needs perfectly well' (Lesure and Nichols, p. 185).
68 *Observer*, 2 February 1908, p. 5.
69 *MT*, 1 March 1908, p. 172; see also *Athenaeum*, 8 February, p. 170; *MG*, 3 February, p. 14. Most reviews noted Debussy's warm reception; *La mer*'s distinctiveness was emphasised as it was sandwiched between the 'Egmont' overture and Schubert's 'Unfinished' symphony. Debussy's completing *La mer* in Eastbourne was not, seemingly, public knowledge.
70 *Athenaeum*, 7 March 1908, p. 298; see also *MT*, 1 April 1908, p. 244; *Times*, 2 March, p. 8.
71 *MS*, 7 March 1908, p. 149; see also *Observer*, 1 March, p. 5.
72 Lesure and Nichols, pp. 179 and 182.
73 *MT*, 1 November 1908, p. 727; see also *MG*, 9 October, p. 8; *Athenaeum*, 17 October, p. 482.
74 The Society of English Composers hosted a reception for Debussy in February 1909; to Durand he wrote, 'It seems I can't get out of it because of the *Entente Cordiale* and other sentimental notions, invented to hasten the death of one's neighbour, probably' (Lesure and Nichols, pp. 197–8).
75 *MT*, 1 April 1909, p. 258.
76 *MG*, 1 March 1909, p. 9.
77 *MS*, 6 March 1909, p. 147.
78 Possibly as much due to a visible hesitation by Debussy and shaky start by the orchestra, as enthusiasm for the music; see *MT* (note 75) and Wood (note 66).
79 *Times*, 24 May 1911, p. 12.
80 *MS*, 27 May 1911, p. 320; see also *Athenaeum*, same date, p. 610; *Observer*, 28 May, p. 9.
81 *MS*, 21 June 1913, p. 541 (Walter Rummel, Aeolian Hall, 19 June).
82 *Spectator*, 28 June 1913, p. 1115.
83 *MS*, 27 September 1913, p. 303; *Times*, 19 September 1913, p. 8.
84 *MS*, 7 May 1904, p. 295.

85   *Times*, 27 October 1906, p. 4; this article covered six further recitals. When Ravel played the *Sonatine* at a salon promoted by the *Société des Concerts Français*, *VSW* described it as 'a charming little composition, delicate and ingenious' (27 January 1911, p. 7), though *MT*'s writer remained unimpressed: Ravel was a 'modern amongst moderns ... [whose] compositions probably provoked more mystification than admiration' (1 February, p. 116).

86   Preceded by a 'dry run' in Sheffield (*MS*, 14 December 1907, p. 376).

87   *Athenaeum*, 14 December 1907, p. 777.

88   *MT*, 1 January 1908, p. 40; see also *Times*, 9 December 1907, p. 3.

89   *VSW*, 4 January 1908, pp. 1–2. This recital also included *Alborada del gracioso*; a review quoted in *VSW* described it as the 'nearest approach to musical dementia capable of being committed to paper by means of the accepted notation'.

90   *MS*, 4 December 1909, p. 363 (Solly Quartet, Bechstein Hall, 29 November).

91   *Times*, 10 February 1911, p. 11; *Observer*, 12 February, p. 7 (Brussels Quartet, Bechstein Hall, 9 February); see also *Academy*, 18 February, p. 202.

92   See *MT*, 1 January 1910, p. 43 (Leeds); *MS*, 4 February 1911, p. 76 (Bournemouth); Arbie Orenstein, *Ravel: Man and Musician* (New York & London, 1975), p. 64 (Newcastle and Edinburgh).

93   *Observer*, 24 October 1909, p. 6.

94   *MS*, 30 October 1909, p. 275.

95   *Times*, 22 October 1909, p. 11.

96   See *MG*, 6 May 1911, p. 7; *Athenaeum*, 11 May, p. 943; *VSW*, 25 May, p. 21.

97   *Times*, 26 September 1913, p. 7; for score reviews see *Times*, 23 March 1912, p. 11 (piano); 4 January 1913, p. 10 (orchestra).

98   *MG*, 26 September 1913, p. 8.

99   See Orenstein, p. 69; *Times*, 9 June 1914, p. 9, and 10 June, p. 11; *MG*, 26 June, p. 8.

100 *Times*, 10 June 1914, p. 11.

101 *MT*, 1 July 1914, p. 470.

102 *MG*, 10 June 1914, p. 10; see also *Academy*, 20 June, p. 796.

103 Apart from press reviews, the primary source of information on the SCF remains Martha Stonequist's PhD thesis, 'The Musical Entente Cordiale 1905–16' (University of Colorado, 1972).

104 Jean-Aubry later wrote two books on French music for anglophone readers, published in the late 1910s (see Bibliography).

105 Guéritte was particularly active in Newcastle: Reynaldo Hahn, Ravel and Florent Schmitt performed there in 1909, 1911 and 1914 respectively; all three went on to Edinburgh (Stonequist, pp. 180 and 186).

106 A graduate of Paris Conservatoire, Barbier (*née* Hirsch) gave vocal recitals in London in 1902 before marrying and moving to Manchester in 1903 (Stonequist, p. 32). A collection of her papers is at NLW (see Bibliography).

107 In Newcastle and Leeds, Debussy's Quartet and Chausson's Piano Quartet were given (*MT*, 1 January 1908, pp. 46 and 49).

108 The programme was also given in Leeds the previous day (*MT*, 1 April 1909, p. 268).

109 *Academy*, 22 February 1913, p. 244.

110 *MT*, 1 February 1911, p. 116; see also *Athenaeum*, 28 February 1914, p. 323, reviewing a repeat performance. In 1911, Ravel played his *Sonatine* (see note 85).

111 See *Athenaeum*, 20 January 1912; p. 75 (performance by the *Société des concerts d'autrefois*); *MT*, 1 March 1913, 176.

112 *Observer*, 3 December 1911, p. 11; see also *MS* (supplement), 6 January 1912, p. 2.

113 Guéritte to *MT*, 1 July 1918, p. 308.

114 These included a concert focused on Franck (25 February 1911) and a selection programme performed with Viñes (6 November 1912) (see NLW, Ms 22694D, ff 80 and 111).

115 Hahn is first mentioned in *MT* on 1 December 1897 (p. 838), in a notice of his *Nuit d'amour bergamasque* given at a Colonne Concert in Paris.

116 *Times*, 14 July 1898, p. 14; see also *MN*, 16 July, p. 54.

117 See *MS*, 12 November 1904, p. 310 (Butt, Albert Hall); *Times*, 21 February 1906, p. 12 (Maurel, Bechstein Hall); *MS*, 26 June 1909, p. 411 (Calvé, Queen's Hall).

118 *Times*, 17 June 1906, p. 8.

119 See also *MG*, 17 May 1906, p. 6; *Athenaeum*, 19 May, p. 619; *Violin Times*, 1 June, p. 86.

120 *Observer*, 30 June 1907, p. 3.

121 *MG*, 18 March 1908, p. 6.

122 *MS*, 10 July 1909, p. 26. When repeated at the Proms, the *Observer* called it 'light and very graceful' (14 September 1913, p. 7), but *MT* reported that it was 'listened to without great interest' (1 October, p. 672).

123 *Times*, 16 November 1909, p. 14; see also *MT*, 1 December, pp. 805 (Edinburgh) and 807 (Newcastle).

124 *Times*, 28 February 1913 p. 9; see also *Observer*, 2 March, p. 8.

125 *Athenaeum*, 8 March 1913, p. 292; *Academy*, same date, p. 305.

126 *MN*, 1 December 1894, p. 457; see also *Academy*, same date, p. 454

127 *MS*, 1 December 1894, p. 427.

128 *MS*, 25 April 1896, p. 261; *Academy*, same date, p. 351; see also *Athenaeum*, same date, p. 553. For *La forêt enchantée*, which Manns also gave at Crystal Palace, see *MS*, 21 November 1896, pp. 321 and 323; *Academy*, same date, p. 434; *Athenaeum*, same date, p. 722; *MMR*, 1 December, p. 280. For *Sauge fleurie* see *Times*, 11 November 1897, p. 4; *MS*, 13 November, p. 307; *MT*, 1 December, p. 817; *Lute*, same date, p. 658.

129 *MT*, 1 December 1900, p. 817; see also *MS*, 17 November, p. 305, and *Athenaeum*, same date, p. 654. For the Quartet see *MS*, 2 March 1901, p. 138; *MT*, 1 April, p. 246.

130 *MG*, 24 October 1907, p. 4; *MS*, 2 November, p. 278.

131 *Times*, 24 October 1907, p. 10.

132 See *MG*, 16 March 1909, p. 7; *Times*, same date, p. 12.

133 See *MS*, 20 March 1909, p. 181. Debussy appeared in Manchester the week before (see above).

134 Followed by an evening reception, at which Myra Hess gave D'Indy's Piano Sonata (**1909**-5; see *Times*, 29 March 1909, p. 5). D'Indy's antisemitism apparently led him to doubt Hess's ability but he was won over; see Andrew Thomson, *Vincent D'Indy and His World* (Oxford, 1996), p. 170.

135 *MS*, 3 April 1909, p. 212.

136 *Athenaeum*, 3 April 1909, p. 419.

137 As note 134.

138 See *MT*, 1 January 1910, pp. 32, 39 and 40.

139 *MT*, 1 December 1900, p. 817.

140 As note 135.

141 See *MOMTR*, 1 May 1903, pp. 610–2 (by Tom Wotton); *MMR*, 1 December, pp. 221–2 (Shedlock); *FR*, same date, pp. 928–40 (A E Keeton); *SR*, 21 November, pp. 638–9, 28 November, pp. 667–8, and 12 December, pp. 729–31 (Runciman); *MT*, 1 July, pp. 441–9, 1 August, pp. 520–3, 1 October, pp. 654–6, and 1 November, pp. 714–7 (F G Edwards).

142 Henry Hadow, *Studies in Modern Music* (London, 1893), pp. 124–46; for Dannreuther, see Chapter 4. Maitland replaced Dannreuther's article on Berlioz in *Grove's Dictionary* with one by Hadow, who largely affirmed Dannreuther's position on Berlioz's music, but omitted earlier judgements on its moral effect; see J A Fuller Maitland (ed.), *Grove's Dictionary of Music and Musicians* (2nd ed, 5 vols, London, 1906), vol. 1, pp. 310–5.

143 *Athenaeum*, 19 December 1903, p. 835; see also *MS*, same date, p. 384; *Academy*, same date, pp. 702–3; *MT*, 1 December, p. 808.

144 London critics regularly complained about such concerts, Beethoven and Wagner nights excepted; composer-performers were the usual targets.

145 *MS*, 19 December 1903, pp. 392–3.

146 *MG*, 4 November 1903, p. 5.

147 *MMR*, 1 January 1904, p. 15.

148 *MOMTR*, 1 January 1904, p. 277.

149 Indicative of *Samson*'s continuing popularity are Festival performances at Birmingham (1901), Cardiff (1902 and 1904), Brighton (1910) and Bristol (1912).

150 *MG*, 2 May 1901, p. 9; *SR*, 4 May, pp. 567–8.

151 *MS*, 4 May 1901, p. 275. In addition to Saint-Saëns's own music, the programme included Mozart's B flat Concerto, K. 450.

152 *Times*, 8 June 1910, p. 13; 16 June, p. 13; 23 June, p. 12.

153 See *MT*, 1 December 1902, p. 821 (Birmingham); *Scotsman*, 20 May 1907, p. 6 (Edinburgh); *MT*, 1 August 1907, p. 527 (Oxford); *MG*, 13 May 1908, p. 10 (Manchester).

154 For Klein's own recollections, see his *Thirty Years of Musical Life in London* (London, 1903), pp. 174–6.

155 In advance, *MT* issued a substantial analysis by Herbert Thompson to generate publicity (1 August 1913, pp. 508–12).

156 *Academy*, 20 September 1913, p. 371; see also *Times*, 12 September, p. 4; *Athenaeum*, 20 September, p. 291.

157 *MT*, 1 October 1913 p. 666.

158 See *Observer*, 30 November 1913, p. 8.

159 *Times*, 3 June 1913, p. 11; see also *Athenaeum*, 7 June, p. 631. A new work, *Ouverture d'un opéra comique inachevé*, was also performed (**1913**-3).

160 *Academy*, 7 June 1913, p. 722; see also *MT*, 1 July, p. 467.

161 See *Times*, 22 September 1902, p. 9; *Athenaeum*, 27 September, p. 422.

162 See Robert Orledge, *Gabriel Fauré* (London, 1979), p. 24, and J Barrie Jones, *Gabriel Fauré: A Life in Letters* (London, 1989), p. 129.

163 *Times*, 20 March 1908, p. 19; *MG*, same date, p. 7. Fauré estimated recital profits of between 950 and 1,000 francs (£38–£40), which were greater than expected (letter to his wife, quoted in Jones, p. 130).

164 *MG*, 1 December 1908, p. 7. Somewhat incongruously, Ethel Smyth also appeared, directing some of her songs.

165 The only substantive traced review is Filson Young's in *SR*, 19 December 1908, pp. 756–7.

166 In the interim, the only significant performances were a brief revival of *Pelléas* in July 1911, starring Mrs Patrick Campbell, and a Proms performance of the Ballade, Op. 19, on 23 October 1913.

167 *MS*, 27 June 1914, p. 617.

168 *Observer*, 21 June 1914, p. 4.

169 *Times*, 17 June 1914, p. 5; *SR*, 18 July, p. 75.

170 See Paul Watt, *The Regulation and Reform of Musical Criticism in Nineteenth-Century England* (Abingdon, 2018).

171 See note 97.

172 *Times*, 20 December 1913, p. 11.

173 Premiered at Queen's Hall, 9 June 1909. Stanford also criticised the whole-tone scale in his treatise *Musical Composition* (London, 1911) (pp. 17–18); that Debussy was not the first to employ it does not need highlighting.

174 Stanford to Herbert Thompson, 7 August 1910, quoted in Paul Rodmell, *Charles Villiers Stanford* (Aldershot, 2002), pp. 265–6.

175 Stanford to Hannam, 21 October 1909, quoted in Harry Plunket Greene, *Charles Villiers Stanford* (London, 1935), p. 143.

176 Arnold Bax, *Farewell My Youth* (London, 1943), p. 21. Corder mocked 'modern' music in a short article, 'How Can I Be Ugly?', in which he reharmonised 'Home, sweet home' entirely with augmented eleventh chords (*MT*, 1 December 1909, pp. 782–3).

177 Hubert Parry, *Style in Musical Art* (London, 1911), pp. 162–3.

178 Edwin Evans, 'French Music of Today', *Proceedings of the Musical Association*, **36** (1909–10), p. 48.

179 Evans, p. 50.

180 Evans, p. 52.

181 Ronald Byrnside, 'Musical Impressionism: The Early History of the Term', *Musical Quarterly*, **66** (1980), pp. 522–37.

182 In 'An Impressionist Composer: Claude Debussy' (*MS*, 20 February 1904, p. 119), Liebich stated that 'the orchestration [of *Pelléas*] redounds with impressionism' and translated *Estampes* as 'Impressions'. See also 'Symbolism and Impressionism: Stephane Mallarmé and Claude Debussy', *MS*, 3 December 1904, p. 357; while only used in the title, Liebich argued that *L'après-midi* 'preserves the feeling of elusiveness, of mirage'.

183 Arthur Hervey, *French Music in the XIXth century* (London, 1903), p. 252.

184 *Graphic*, 27 August 1904, p. 280 ('an attempt at modern impressionism in music'); *Daily Telegraph*, quoted in *MS*, 28 October 1905, p. 275 ('a series of orchestral impressions, and the effect of picturesqueness is gained, not by a characteristic theme, but by the combinations of instruments employed'); *MG*, 3 November 1906, p. 6 ('For this impressionist, Whistleresque Debussy, the varied orchestra or the piano with one or both pedals down is the favourite medium, and with the dry lines of the string quartet his atmospheric effects are impossible to get').

185 Edwin Evans, 'Some aspects of modern French music', *MS*, 25 January 1908, pp. 52–3; this is a preliminary version of the paper cited in note 178.

186 *MS*, 11 August 1906, p. 87 (signed 'P S', possibly Percy Scholes).

187 As note 174.

6   Conclusions

The position of French music in British culture was transformed between 1830 and 1914. Starting from virtual non-existence and widespread disparagement, by the Edwardian decade French music occupied a major place in British concert halls and theatres. It did not dislodge German orchestral or chamber music from its pre-eminence, nor Italian opera, although the latter's dominance was reduced, but its growth was a highly impressive development, hitherto largely neglected, in Victorian Britain. Given long-standing British engagement with wider French culture, it could be suggested that the nineteenth century witnessed the delayed establishment of French music after the aberrant years of the long eighteenth century.

Theoretical frameworks of Cultural Exchange and Reception enable an informed consideration of the empirical evidence in this study. Cultural exchanges – or, more specifically here, cultural transfers – demonstrate the importance of networks of agents in facilitating inter-communal relocations of commodities and services; in music's case, agents were strikingly diverse, from leading composers to casual travellers. The extent to which individual agency was exercised and distinctive (that is, whether it was pioneering or duplicated by others) varied greatly; certain individuals showed especial autonomy and were prime movers in bringing new French music to Britain.

Anticipated by occasional productions of Boïeldieu's works in London from 1810, the first significant successful transfers of theatre music were Auber's operas in the 1830s, followed by those of Meyerbeer. Theatre music then effectively subdivided into two branches: one perceived as highbrow, following a line from Gounod to Debussy, and the other middlebrow (lowbrow in some eyes), initially dominated by Offenbach. Largely unencumbered by the concept of the masterpiece or monument that was increasingly important in orchestral and chamber music, theatre repertory retained a certain amount of 'churn' which, despite a much more limited volume of performance opportunities when compared to concerts, resulted in an environment in which new music could potentially prosper; the realignment William Weber has identified in nineteenth-century concert programmes towards the music of dead composers was nowhere near as marked in opera. The social and commercial realities of West End theatre life required impresarios to take significant risks in order to satisfy a demand for novelty, while experiencing disappointment much more frequently than success. Auber, Meyerbeer, Gounod and Offenbach all benefitted, with their most successful works holding the stage sometimes for years and occasionally decades before being displaced by other, still more recent, music. Outside the West End, commercial pressures operated in a different manner. The touring regimes of companies playing 'grand opera', which typically involved moving to a new theatre every Sunday, with all but the largest cities experiencing no more than two or three weeks of opera each year, meant that repertories were smaller and relatively static. Only if new works were 'hits' in the West End or built up a sustained reputation over at least five years, were they taken up by provincial touring companies; a few works that fell out of fashion in the West End, such as Auber's *Fra Diavolo*, survived longer elsewhere. The dissemination of *opéra bouffe* in theatres was different again: a troupe dedicated to performing the latest West End 'hit' might well bring it to any British town of a reasonable size but, normally, within three or four years the company would dissolve and another, performing a newer work, would take its place.

Partly due, up to the mid-nineteenth century, to French composers focusing primarily on stage works, and partly to the ongoing process of canon formation, growth in the performance of concert music (excluding opera extracts) was much slower; excepting the interest in Berlioz in London around 1850, orchestral and chamber music appeared regularly only from the 1870s, led by Saint-Saëns and Gounod. The consistent, if incremental increase in the overall number of concerts meant that, even though French music still formed a small, though growing, proportion of the overall repertory performed, in terms of absolute numbers of appearances the expansion was impressive. This afforded enthusiastic, affluent concertgoers in London and large provincial cities opportunities to hear unfamiliar works by a broad range of composers, while more casual listeners were also exposed to a steadily expanding repertory, though opera extracts remained at its heart. Only in choral music did French composers remain almost invisible; the particularities of British taste and practice render this unsurprising but still a major gap. Gounod's success was a rare exception, as, to a much lesser extent, was that of Berlioz, but the failures of Saint-Saëns and Fauré at British festivals and the avoidance of Massenet is indicative of largely insurmountable differences in aesthetics and taste.

All these developments should be seen within the context of the overall diversification of theatre and especially concert hall repertory, particularly after 1880, as, in addition to French works, new pieces by British, German, Eastern European and Russian composers were introduced, all of which had to compete with the music of such established pillars as Beethoven, Mendelssohn, Wagner and Handel. In parallel, audiences for French music inevitably also changed, from a small, affluent group in 1830 to a much larger and more socially diverse field by 1914, reflecting trends arising from urbanisation and technological change. In one respect, French music was unusual in that its reach to new middle- and working-class audiences was achieved primarily via theatres (excepting, possibly, organ recitals); less affluent consumers were most likely to encounter French music in the forms of *opéra comique* or *opéra bouffe* than in concert halls.

Networks of cultural transfer also evolved. Compared to Germany and Italy, relatively few French musicians visited Britain; the impact of high-profile visitors (for example, Saint-Saëns, Berlioz, Gounod and Lamoureux), though important, was dwarfed by Germans such as Joachim and Clara Schumann and the consistent flow of jobbing instrumentalists and conductors working at all levels. Few French émigrés settled permanently (Prosper Sainton and Jules Rivière were rare exceptions) and they were again outnumbered by the likes of Benedict, Dannreuther, Manns and Richter.[1] The majority of agents were British; strong cultural and economic connections attracted British visitors to Paris consistently and these Francophiles exploited the increasing interest in London for new music that came with some form of recognised imprimatur. French music's agents of cultural transfer were typically impresarios and managers, such as Lumley, Mitchell, Hollingshead and Harris in theatres, and Guéritte in concerts. London theatres' heavy reliance on Paris for repertory and inspiration enabled the transfer of French works relatively easily once initial resistance had dissipated. Agents of concert music were fewer, but conductors played a significant role, including Hallé, Manns and Wood, though their agency was different as they introduced music from across Europe. Additionally, it is important to acknowledge the role of audiences; as Paris became ever easier to visit, the ability of *beau monde*, and later bourgeois and middle-class citizens, to access and then promote French music among friends and neighbours increased.

Aspects of Reception Theory are crucial aids in interpreting the significance of this music in its new context, taking into account not only what was presented and how, but also with what impact. The diversity of critical views and audience bases makes summarising the British reception of French music challenging. No composer gained the 'great' or 'genius' status accorded to Beethoven, or (with different trajectories) Mendelssohn and Wagner; a sustained debate regarding Berlioz was inconclusive, many commentators being anxious not to be on the wrong side of a future 'judgement of history'. Views of some composers formed quickly and remained stable: the reception of Saint-Saëns especially is remarkable for its consistency and has, arguably, continued similarly in anglophone thought ever since, though individual works' reputations have changed.[2] Views of Auber were also consistent, as were those regarding Meyerbeer once initial resistance was overcome, though both later declined in popularity. It is notable how quickly the 'modern French school' was accepted: selected works at least by Debussy and Ravel were embraced soon after initial appearance. Berlioz's was the most mercurial historic reception examined in this study but, for diverse reasons, other reputations were also equivocal or variable: Gounod's popularity with audiences was far greater than with critics, and not only because of his conduct and personal associations being well known to the latter group; perceptions of sentimentalism became a negative connotation via the implicit accusation of effeminacy, contributing to his twentieth-century marginalisation. Notably, this concerned arbiters of taste far more than 'ordinary' concertgoers. For different reasons, Offenbach was in a similar position: accusations that his works were immoral were reiterated regularly but exercised virtually no influence on wider attitudes, judged by *opéra bouffe*'s popularity with audiences of all classes (see below). Few composers experienced outright hostility, although the sexist comments aimed at Chaminade after her initial success are notable, but even works initially found puzzling, unpleasant or crude had supporters, and acculturation resulted typically in initial criticisms being toned down.

Reputations were often enhanced by willingness to engage in self-promotion: Gounod and Saint-Saëns best exemplify the value of direct engagement, but Debussy and Berlioz also benefitted. Those less interested or able often found progress difficult, such as Massenet, D'Indy and Fauré. Strong advocacy helped but was rarely a comprehensive substitute; only Auber and Offenbach, whose reputations in Britain were almost entirely founded on their popularity in Paris, achieved renown with little or no direct engagement.

The 'academy' (here, music professionals whose primary role was teaching at senior levels) also tried to influence wider views. Although usually in step with critics (ascetics such as Parry worried about music's ability to seduce or demoralise those less educated than themselves), there were differences. 'Academy' musicians, especially those born before about 1860, had greater doubts about Gounod, the 'modern French school' and Berlioz among others, due to these composers' ignorance or flouting of technical conventions and aesthetics, especially regarding form, harmony, treatment of dissonance and 'colour'. Their direct connections and attachment to Germany were strong, leading them to believe that music from other nations (except Britain) was mainly of lesser value; many had been educated partly in Germany.[3] Of all arbiters of taste, 'academy' musicians proved the most resistant to French music; critics and audiences, in general, exercised an unconscious cosmopolitanism, caring little about a work's national origins if they enjoyed it.

As music was transferred and received in its new guise (in terms of Reception Theory, its *Wirkung*) it was redefined, becoming something foreign and implicitly exotic or Othered. It remained a constant in the process of cultural transfer to promote the 'Frenchness' of material imported. Consumers' 'horizons of expectations' consistently associated France with quality, so emphasising national provenance was an act of assurance and implied desirability. Regarding music, critics typically used references to Frenchness as shorthand for certain attributes, exploiting other aspects of the horizon. The paradigm was largely self-perpetuating: when presented with French (or, more accurately, Parisian) music, critics looked for French traits and promulgated aspects that concorded with their assumptions. Earlier chapters have illustrated how strongly this impacted upon perceptions of certain composers (Auber, Offenbach, Massenet and Hahn), but was rather less effective for others (Berlioz and D'Indy). Established tropes of Frenchness remained strong, evolving to the extent that, as eighteenth-century Francophobia receded, unflattering aspects were modified to become more palatable: effeminacy became femininity, sarcasm became wit, and immorality became flirtation. Even the last of these, which buffeted hardest against (cliched) Victorian prudery, became more acceptable, especially as, in English adaptations of operettas, 'naughtiness' was toned down.

It is especially important to remember that many of these cultural transfers – mainly in theatres – were not only Othered but also amended to be 'de-Othered' in order to accord with assumed consumer preferences and values. In the earliest cases this meant significant revisions to libretti and music, exemplified by productions of Auber and Meyerbeer's operas in the 1830s; from the 1840s, an emphasis on musical fidelity led to more active adherence to 'authorised' musical sources in the cases of *opéra comique* and 'grand' opera.[4] *Opéras bouffes* were subjected to greater alteration; although the primary focus was on dramatic and literary aspects, it could extend on occasion to replacing some or even most of the original score and *opéra bouffe* remains a particularly complex activity to examine.

These tropes' durability meant that British perceptions of the French altered only slightly – indeed, *opéra bouffe* only reinforced them – but 'chalk and cheese' British and French characteristics were increasingly thought complementary rather than antagonistic; as French music gained ground in Britain, it played a significant role in developing that relationship, an aspect of Franco-British cultural relations that has been hitherto largely unappreciated.

British interest in French culture remained largely impervious to fluctuations in Franco-British political relations. French culture and produce were consumed and valued in Britain to such an extent that the contrary would be surprising: even during the eighteenth century, fashionable British consumers looked primarily to Paris for inspiration and music was unusual in being marginalised. The post-*Entente Cordiale* period was exceptional; closer diplomatic relations enabled cultural agents, with the tacit support of politicians and wealth-creators (industrialists, financiers, merchants etc.), to promote still closer relations with France, further reinforcing political and cultural ties and augmenting economic activity.

In writing the first overview of this subject, the aim has been to provide a 'wide sweep', to show how circumstances and perceptions developed over an extended period. Many aspects would repay deeper investigation: as noted in the Introduction, popular musics and amateur music-making were excluded to maintain manageability, but deserve further examination, as do the roles of military bands, organ recitals, arrangements and transcriptions. Placing French art music in London between 1900 and 1914 in the broader context of the immense diversity of aesthetics and styles provided from across Europe would further contextualise and develop understanding of its reception. Due to long-standing prejudice against his music, the impact of Gounod on British musical culture remains substantially ignored and misunderstood, yet his music infiltrated a greater range of British practice than any other French composer in this period and was almost unique in influencing the way in which British composers themselves worked. British musical culture between 1830 and 1914 may have been primarily orientated towards Germany, but opening up to France broadened repertory, expanded perspectives on taste, and helped strengthen cultural links between the two nations such that, in 1914, Franco-British relations were the strongest they had ever been.

Notes

1 The role of the émigré French community (that is, a cultural enclave) played a far smaller role than the cross-Channel traffic of agents; apart from a brief flurry in 1870–71, there was no substantial French migration to Britain in the nineteenth century and the ex-patriot community remained small.
2 Despite some initial hostility, *Danse macabre* and the 'Organ' Symphony have endured better than *Samson et Dalila*, while the Second Piano Concerto was popular with soloists and audiences from the outset.
3 Sterndale Bennett, Stanford, Cowen, Corder and Mackenzie all studied in Germany with varying degrees of formality, while Parry was taught by Dannreuther; even Sullivan who, owed much to French music for his own style and regularly visited Paris for leisure, was educated in Leipzig. Goring Thomas and Hervey were atypical instances of British musicians educated in Paris, but neither held a conservatoire teaching post.
4 Certain aspects of adaptation remained common, including, for example, translation to English or Italian and the inclusion of sung recitative.

Appendix

Selected first performances of French works in Britain, 1830–1914

Abbreviations specific to this Appendix; for journal title abbreviations see pp. x–xi.

a-	music and/or text arranged/adapted/translated by
AH	Aeolian Hall
AP	Alexandra Palace
BH	Bechstein Hall
c-	Conducted by
CG	Covent Garden Theatre (Royal Opera House)
CP	Crystal Palace
DL	Theatre Royal, Drury Lane
EOH	English Opera House (Lyceum Theatre)
ENG	Performed in English
ExH	Exeter Hall
FRE	Performed in French
GER	Performed in German
HM	His/Her Majesty's Theatre, Haymarket
HSR	Hanover Square Concert Rooms
IT	Performed in Italian
KT	King's Theatre
L	Alfred Loewenberg, *Annals of Opera 1597–1940* (London, 1978) (followed by column number).
LOH	London Opera House, Kingsway
NPS	New Philharmonic Society
OC	Opéra Comique Theatre
PhilS	Philharmonic Society, London
PhilT	Philharmonic Theatre, Islington, North London
PoW	Prince of Wales's Theatre
QH	Queen's Hall
RAH	Royal Albert Hall
RCM	Royal College of Music
RCT	Royal Court Theatre
REO	Royal English Opera House
s-	Soloist(s)

SCF	Société des Concerts Français
SH	Steinway Hall
SJH	St James's Hall
SJT	St James's Theatre
SMH	St Martin's Hall
TH	Town Hall
TR	Theatre Royal

Dates in the Notes and Sources column are in date.month.year format.

Year & ref	Date	Composer	Work	Venue (London unless otherwise stated)	Notes and sources (where not cited in main text)
1829-1	4-May	Auber	La muette de Portici	DL	ENG as Masaniello; previously KT ENG as ballet with two sung choruses as Masaniello 29.3.1829 (Observer, 29.3.1829, p. 3)); Edinburgh 30.7.1829; Dublin TR 2.12.1829; CG FRE 23.6.1845 and IT 15.3.1849
1829-2	17-Nov	Boïeldieu	Les deux nuits	CG	ENG, a-Fitzball & Bishop as The Night before the Wedding (L719)
1830-1	4-Feb	Auber	La fiancée	DL	ENG, a-Planché as The National Guard; Edinburgh 22.12.1830 (L717)
1830-2	24-Nov	Auber	Fra Diavolo	Queen's	Olympic 13.1.1831; DL ENG, a-Lee as The Devil's Brother 1.2.1831; CG a-Lacy, 3.11.1831; SJT FRE 20.4.1849; Lyceum IT 4.7.1857; Dublin TR 6.8.1857 (L723)
1831-1	27-Oct	Auber	Le philtre	Olympic	ENG as The Love Spell; DL a-Planché & Bishop as The Love Charm 3.11.1831; DL FRE 10.8.1846 (L734)
1832-1	20-Feb	Meyerbeer	Robert le diable	DL	ENG, a-Bishop as The Daemon; CG ENG as The Fiend-Father 21.2.1832; Adelphi ENG, a-Fitzball & Buckstone 23.1.1832; KT FRE 11.6.1832; Dublin TR ENG 26.11.1832 and IT 25.9.1869; DL GE 18.6.1841 (L736)
1833-1	16-Mar	Auber	Le dieu et la bayadère	DL	ENG, a-Bishop as The Maid of Cashmere (L727)
1833-2	23-Mar	Auber	Le serment	CG	ENG, a-Lacy as The Coiners (L745)
1833-3	19-Apr	Hérold	Zampa	HM	GER; Olympic ENG 10.6.1833 a-Oxenford as The Bridal Promise; DL ENG 21.3.1836; SJT FRE 16.1.1850; CG IT 5.8.1858 (L732)
1833-4	9-Sep	Hérold	Le pré aux clercs	Adelphi	ENG a-Planché & Hawes as The Court Masque; CG ENG, a-Cooke as The Promise 1.4.1834; SJT FRE 2.5.1849; CG IT 26.6.1880 (L746)

1833-5	13-Nov	Auber	*Gustave III*	CG	*ENG*, a-Planché & Cooke; Edinburgh 7.2.1835; HM *IT* 29.3.1851 (L749)
1835-1	21-Feb	Auber	*Lestocq*	CG	*ENG*, a-Macfarren & Cooke (L759)
1835-2	14-Dec	Auber	*Le cheval de bronze*	CG	*ENG*, a-Fitzball & Rodwell; DL *ENG* 5.1.1836 (L769)
1837-1	13-Mar	Adam	*Le postillon de Lonjumeau*	SJT	*ENG*, a-A'Beckett & Stanbury as *Postilion!*; DL *FRE* 9.7.1845; SJT *FRE* 20.2.1850 (L782)
1838-1	16-Feb	Auber	*Le domino noir*	CG	*ENG*, a-Kenney & Morton; condensed versions Olympic *ENG* 18.1.1838, Adelphi *ENG* 22.1.1838 and SJT *ENG* 29.1.1838; DL *FRE* 10.8.1846; SJT *FRE* 15.1.1849 (L790)
1838-2	5-Mar	Auber	*L'ambassadrice*	SJT	*ENG*, a-A'Beckett; Princess's *ENG* 2.12.1847; SJT *FRE* 27.1.1849 (L786)
1839-1	13-May	Auber	*Le lac des fées*	Strand	*ENG*, a-Selby, with music also by Marschner, Hérold and Mercadante; DL *ENG* 26.10.1839 (L801)
1840-1	29-Jan	Boïeldieu	*Le nouveau seigneur de village*	DL	*ENG* a-Dance as *My Lord is not my Lord*; SJT *FRE* 22.1.1849 (L634–5)
1840-2	30-Mar	Berlioz	*Les francs-juges*	Opera Concert Room	Societa Armonica, c-Forbes (*MW*, 2.4.1840, pp. 211–2)
1840-3	1-Jun	Berlioz	*Waverley*	Opera Concert Room	Societa Armonica, c-Forbes (*MW*, 4.6.1840, pp. 354–5)
1841-1	15-Mar	Berlioz	*Benvenuto Cellini* (Overture)	HSR	PhilS
1841-2	25-Mar	Thomas	*La double échelle*	Lyceum	*ENG*, a-Macfarren as *The Matrimonial Ladder* (L789)
1841-3	14-Jun	Adam	*La reine d'un jour*	Surrey	*ENG* a-Haines (L803)
1842-1	20-Jun	Meyerbeer	*Les Huguenots*	CG	GE; CG *FRE* 30.6.1845; CG *IT* 20.7.1848; Surrey *ENG* 16.8.1849; Dublin TR *IT* 1.10.1857
1844-1	2-May	Auber	*Les diamants de la couronne*	Princess's	*ENG*; CG *FRE* 11.6.1845; DL *ENG* 16.4.1846; CG *IT* 8.7.1873

Year & ref	Date	Composer	Work	Venue (London unless otherwise stated)	Notes and sources (where not cited in main text)
1844-2	2-Oct	Thomas	Le panier fleuri	Adelphi	ENG, a-Webster & Boucicault as *The Fox and the Goose*; DL *FRE* 23.7.1845 (L801)
1844-3	14-Oct	Auber	La sirène	Princess's	ENG a-Soane; DL ENG a-Bunn 17.10.1844; SJT *FRE* 8.7.1854 (L839)
1845-1	27-Mar	David	Le désert	HM	c-Costa
1845-2	14-Apr	Auber	Le duc d'Olonne	Princess's	ENG a-Reynoldson (L818)
1845-3	6-Jun	Adam	Le chalet	CG	FRE (L761)
1845-4	13-Jun	Paer	Le maître de chapelle	CG	FRE; SJT *FRE* 15.1.1849 (L673)
1845-5	13-Jun	Auber	La part du diable	CG	FRE; Grecian ENG a-Horncastle 13.2.1849 (L830)
1845-6	7-Jul	Halévy	La reine de Chypre	DL	FRE
1846-1	18-Jul	Lebrun	Le rossignol	DL	FRE (L647)
1846-2	29-Jul	Halévy	La juive	DL	FRE; CG *IT* 25.7.1850; Surrey *ENG* 21.6.1854 (L767)
1846-3	3-Aug	Halévy	Les mousquetaires de la reine	DL	FRE (L853)
1847-1	5-Apr	Auber	La barcarolle	Princess's	ENG (L847)
1848-1	7-Feb	Berlioz	Harold en Italie	DL	c-Berlioz
1848-2	7-Feb	Berlioz	Le carnaval romain	DL	c-Berlioz
1848-3	7-Feb	Berlioz	La damnation de Faust	DL	c-Berlioz (Parts 1 and 2) (see **1880**-1)
1848-4	7-Feb	Berlioz	Grand messe des morts	DL	c-Berlioz (Offertory) (see **1883**-1)
1848-5	7-Feb	Berlioz	Symphonie funèbre et triomphale	DL	c-Berlioz (finale) (see **1882**-4)
1848-6	3-Apr	Auber	Haydée	Strand	ENG, a-Soane; CG ENG a-Chorley & Lavenu 4.11.1848 (L867)
1849-1	18-Jan	Hérold	Marie	Princess's	ENG, a-Loder (L705)
1849-2	26-Feb	Auber	Le concert à la cour	SJT	FRE (L693)
1849-3	18-Apr	Carafa	La prison d'Édimbourg	Princess's	ENG, additional music by Loder as *The Heart of Midlothian* (L752)

1849-4	24-Jul	Meyerbeer	Le prophète	CG	IT; Surrey ENG 7.8.1854; Dublin TR IT 6.9.1855; CG FRE 23.6.1890 (L873–4)
1849-5	22-Jan	Gaveaux	Le bouffe et le tailleur	SJT	FRE (Times, 23.1.1849, p. 5)
1849-6	22-Jan	Montfort	Polichinelle	SJT	FRE; as **1849**-5
1849-7	12-Feb	Auber	Zanetta	SJT	FRE (Times, 13.2.1849, p. 8)
1849-8	26-Jan	Girard	Les deux voleurs	SJT	FRE (Observer, 28.1.1849, p. 3)
1849-9	12-Mar	Auber	Actéon	SJT	FRE (L775)
1849-10	21-May	Boisselot	Ne touchez pas à la reine	SJT	FRE (L859-60)
1850-1	7-Jan	Halévy	Le val d'Andorre	SJT	FRE; Princess's ENG 28.1.1850
1850-2	13-Mar	Auber	Le maçon	SJT	FRE (L696)
1850-3	8-Jun	Halévy	La tempesta	HM	IT
1850-4	28-Jan	Thomas	Le caïd	SJT	FRE; Little Haymarket ENG 18.6.1851 (L870)
1850-5	11-Feb	Adam	Le roi d'Yvetot	SJT	FRE (Observer, 17.2.1850, p. 6)
1851-1	19-Feb	Auber	L'enfant prodigue	DL	ENG, a-Fitzball & Laurent as *Azael, the Prodigal*; HM IT 12.6.1851 (L888)
1851-2	29-May	Grisar	Bonsoir, M Pantalon	Adelphi	ENG (L889)
1851-3	22-Jul	Auber	Zerline	HM	IT (L894)
1851-4	9-Aug	Gounod	Sapho	CG	IT, c-Costa (L894)
1852-1	24-Mar	Berlioz	Roméo et Juliette	ExH	NPS, c-Berlioz (Part 1)
1853-1	25-Jun	Berlioz	Benvenuto Cellini	CG	IT
1853-2	1-Dec	Gounod	Ave Maria	SMH	Original version for violin, piano and organ (*MW*, 3.12.1853, p. 763)
1854-1	7-Jun	Adam	Le bijou perdu	SJT	FRE (L910)
1854-2	12-Jun	Clapisson	La promise	SJT	FRE (L913)
1855-1	19-Jul	Meyerbeer	L'étoile du nord	CG	IT; DL ENG 17.4.1890 (L912)
1856-1	23-Apr	Gounod	Symphony No. 2 in E flat	HSR	NPS, c-Benedict
1857-1	20-May	Offenbach	Les deux aveugles	SJT	FRE; previously semi-staged HSR, 27.6.1856; Gaiety ENG a-Farnie, 15.4.1871 (L919; Times, 30.6.1856, p. 6)
1857-2	22-May	Adam	Les pantins de Violette	SJT	FRE (L921)
1857-3	24-Jun	Offenbach	Pepito	SJT	FRE (L910)
1857-4	7-Nov	Gounod	Symphony No. 1 in D	CP	c-Manns; PhilS, c-Gounod 8.3.1871

Year & ref	Date	Composer	Work	Venue (London unless otherwise stated)	Notes and sources (where not cited in main text)
1859-1	18-Feb	Adam	Le toréador	SJT	FRE (L875)
1859-2	26-Jul	Meyerbeer	Le pardon de Ploërmel	CG	IT as Dinorah; CG ENG 3.10.1859; Dublin TR IT 14.9.1869
1860-1	15-Feb	Gounod	Messe solennelle à Sainte-Cécile	SMH	Original version, c-Hullah (MP, 16.2.1860, p. 5)
1860-2	11-May	Offenbach	Le mariage aux lanternes	Lyceum	FRE; New Royalty ENG 18.1.1862 (L928)
1860-3	26-Nov	Massé	Les noces de Jeannette	CG	ENG a-Harris; OC FRE 16.5.1872 (L905)
1860-4	26-Dec	Adam	La poupée de Nuremberg	Cork	ENG as Dolly; CG ENG with additional music by Linley as The Toy-Maker, 19.11.1861 (L897)
1860-5	26-Dec	Massé	La reine Topaze	HM	ENG a-Oxenford & Linley (L925)
1861-1	5-Dec	Vieuxtemps	Violin Concerto No. 5 in A minor	Manchester FTH	Beale, Charles Hallé, p. 248
1862-1	8-Mar	Méhul	Symphony in G minor	CP	c-Manns (Standard, 10.3.1862, p. 3)
1863-1	11-Jun	Gounod	Faust	HM	IT; CG IT 2.7.1863; HM ENG 23.1.1864
1864-1	5-Jul	Gounod	Mireille	HM	IT; Dublin TR IT 17.11.1864; CG FRE 10.6.1891 (L967)
1865-1	31-Jan	Maillart	Lara	HM	ENG a-Oxenford (L968)
1865-2	27-Feb	Gounod	Le médecin malgré lui	CG	ENG a-Kenney as The Mock Doctor (L930)
1865-3	22-Jul	Meyerbeer	L'Africaine	CG	IT; CG ENG a-Kenney 21.10.1865 (L971)
1865-4	12-Aug	Gounod	La reine de Saba	CP	ENG, concert performance c-Manns a-Farnie as Irene
1865-5	26-Dec	Offenbach	Orphée aux enfers	HM	ENG a-Planché; SJT FRE 12.7.1869
1866-1	2-Jun	Offenbach	Barbe-bleue	Olympic	ENG; SJT FRE 28.6.1869; Gaiety ENG 29.8.1870
1866-2	30-Jun	Offenbach	La belle Hélène	Adelphi	ENG a-Burnand as Helen, or Taken from the Greek; SJT FRE 13.7.1868
1867-1	11-Jul	Gounod	Roméo et Juliette	CG	IT; CG FRE 15.6.1889; DL ENG 5.4.1890
1867-2	18-Nov	Offenbach	La Grande-Duchesse de Gérolstein	CG	ENG a-Kenney; SJT FRE 22.6.1868; Dublin TR ENG 10.5.1869

1868-1	13-Apr	Hervé	*L'oeil crevé*	Olympic	*ENG* a-Burnard as *Hit or Miss; OC ENG* arr Farnie 21.10.1872 (L993)
1869-1	19-Jun	Thomas	*Hamlet*	CG	*IT; CG FRE* CG 22.6.1898 (1998)
1870-1	22-Jan	Hervé	*Chilpéric*	Lyceum	*ENG* a-Reece
1870-2	16-Apr	Offenbach	*La princesse de Trébizonde*	Gaiety	*ENG* (L1008)
1870-3	18-Apr	Hervé	*Le petit Faust*	Lyceum	*ENG* a-Farnie
1870-4	2-May	Offenbach	*Le violoneux*	Gaiety	*ENG* as *Breaking the Spell* (*Graphic*, 7.5.1870, p. 546)
1870-5	27-Jun	Offenbach	*La Périchole*	Princess's	*FRE*; Royalty *ENG* 30.1.1875 (L1003-04)
1870-6	5-Jul	Thomas	*Mignon*	DL	*IT*; Dublin TR *ENG* 18.8.1879; Edinburgh *ENG* 1.9.1879; HM *ENG* 13.1.1880 (all *ENG* productions by Carl Rosa) (L986)
1870-7	22-Aug	Offenbach	*Trombalcazar*	Gaiety	*ENG* (*Era*, 28.8.1870, p. 11)
1870-8	20-Sep	Gounod	*La colombe*	CP	*ENG* a-Farnie as *The Pet Dove* (L948)
1870-9	22-Dec	Hervé	*Aladin II*	Gaiety	*ENG* (pantomime) (*Observer*, 25.12.1870, p. 3)
1871-1	22-Apr	Offenbach	*Les brigands*	Globe	*ENG* a-Leigh as *Falsacappa*; Lyceum *FRE* 1.7.1871 (L1011)
1871-2	1-May	Gounod	*Gallia*	RAH	c-Gounod; Manchester c-Hallé 11.1.1872; London SJH c-Gounod, 31.5.1873
1871-3	1-Jul	Offenbach	*La chanson de Fortunio*	Gaiety	*FRE* (L950)
1871-4	11-Nov	Offenbach	*Geneviève de Brabant*	PhilT	*ENG* a-Farnie (L944)
1872-1	30-Mar	Offenbach	*La vie parisienne*	Holborn	*ENG* a-Burnand (L985)
1872-2	8-May	Gounod	*Te Deum*	RAH	c-Gounod
1872-3	23-May	Massé	*Galatée*	OC	*FRE* (L898)
1873-2	18-Nov	Offenbach	*Le pont des soupirs*	SJT	*ENG* a-Leigh (L951)
1873-1	29-Jan	Poise	*Bonsoir, Voisin*	Royalty	*FRE* (L909)
1873-2	8-Feb	Gounod	*Messe brève pour les morts*	SJH	c-Gounod (first complete performance) (*MS*, 15.2.1873, p. 103)
1873-3	13-Feb	Bazin	*Le voyage en Chine*	Royalty	*FRE*; Garrick *ENG* 5.6.1879 (L979)

Year & ref	Date	Composer	Work	Venue (London unless otherwise stated)	Notes and sources (where not cited in main text)
1873-4	17-May	Lecocq	La fille de Madame Angot	SJT	FRE (Brussels, Fantaisies-Parisiennes); PhilT ENG a-Byron 4.10.1873; Edinburgh ENG 22.6.1874 (L1025)
1873-5	31-May	Gounod	Funeral March of a Marionette	SJH	c-Gounod (MS, 7.6.1873, p.359)
1873-6	21-Jun	Lecocq	Les cent vierges	SJT	FRE; Gaiety ENG a-Reece as The Island of Bachelors 14.8.1874 (L1022)
1873-7	12-Jul	Offenbach	L'île de Tulipatan	OC	ENG à-Burnand (L1003)
1873-8	21-Jul	Offenbach	Les braconniers	SJT	FRE (Illustrated Review 24.7.1873, p. 114)
1873-9	6-Dec	Saint-Saëns	Cello Sonata in C minor, Op. 32	SJH	Saturday Popular Concert, s-Bülow & Piatti (MS, 13.12.1873, p. 370)
1874-1	2-May	Offenbach	Vert-vert	SJT	ENG a-Herman & Mansell
1874-2	4-Mar	Saint-Saëns	Suite for Cello and Piano, Op. 16	HSR	Coenen Chamber Concert
1874-3	18-May	Offenbach	La jolie parfumeuse	Alhambra	ENG a-Herman & Mansell (L1006)
1874-4	6-Jun	Lecocq	Giroflé-Girofla	OC	FRE (Brussels, Fantaisies-Parisiennes); PhilT ENG a-O'Neil & Clarke 3.10.1874 (L1035)
1874-5	28-Nov	Lecocq	Les prés Saint-Gervais	Criterion	ENG a-Reece (Athenaeum, 5.12.1874, p. 759)
1874-6	26-Dec	Offenbach	Dick Whittington	Alhambra	ENG (pantomime) a-Farnie
1875-1	24-Jun	Maillart	Les dragons de Villars	Gaiety	FRE; Folly ENG a-Hersee as The Dragoons 14.4.1879 (L923)
1875-2	29-Jun	Saint-Saëns	Variations on a Theme of Beethoven, Op. 35	SJH	Ella's Musical Union (Athenaeum, 3.7.1875, p. 29)
1875-3	13-Nov	Saint-Saëns	Introduction et rondo capriccioso	AP	c-Weist Hill; s-Sainton (MS, 20.11.1875, p. 335)
1875-4	20-Nov	Massenet	Scènes pittoresques	AP	c-Weist Hill (MMR, 1.12.1875, p. 177)
1876-1	13-Jan	Offenbach	Madame l'Archiduc	OC	ENG a-Farnie (L1040)
1876-2	26-Feb	Saint-Saëns	Cello Concerto in A minor, Op. 33	AP	c-Weist Hill (MS, 4.3.1876, p. 143)

1876-3	16-Mar	Saint-Saëns	Piano Trio in F, Op. 18	St George's Hall	Coenen Chamber Concert (*Observer*, 19.3.1876, p. 6)
1876-4	6-May	Lecocq	*La petite Mariée*	OC	*FRE* (L1048); Gaiety 4.7.1881 (*Era*, 9.7.1881, p. 8); Shaftesbury *ENG* 17.11.1897 as *The Scarlet Feather* (L1049)
1876-5	4-Jul	Saint-Saëns	Piano Quartet in B flat, Op. 41	SJH	Ella's Musical Union (*Athenaeum*, 8.7.1876, p. 59)
1876-6	6-Jul	Saint-Saëns	*Marche héroïque*, Op. 34	SJH	Arranged for piano duet; s-Saint-Saëns & Marlois
1876-7	21-Sep	Adam	*Giralda*	Lyceum	*ENG* a-Baildon (L884)
1877-1	15-Sep	Offenbach	*La créole*	Folly	*ENG* a-Reece & Farnie; preceded by try-outs at Brighton from 3.9.1877
1877-2	20-Oct	Saint-Saëns	*La jeunesse d'Hercule*	CP	c-Manns (*Athenaeum*, 27.10.1877, p. 541)
1878-1	23-Feb	Planquette	*Les cloches de Corneville*	Folly	*ENG* a-Farnie as *The Chimes of Normandy*; Edinburgh *ENG* 17.6.1878
1878-2	30-Mar	Lalo	*Symphonie espagnole*	CP	c-Manns, s-Sarasate (*MS*, 6.4.1878, p. 209)
1878-3	27-Apr	Lecocq	*Le petit duc*	PhilT	*ENG* a-Rowe (L1069); Gaiety *FRE* 27.6.1881 (*ISDN* 2.7.1878, p. 370)
1878-4	30-Apr	Massenet	*Scènes dramatiques*	SJH	Mme Viard-Louis's concert, c-Massenet (extracts) c-Massenet; see **1879-7**
1878-5	4-May	Massenet	*Le roi de Lahore*	CP	c-Massenet
1878-6	4-May	Massenet	*Les Errinyes*	CP	*IT* (L1060)
1878-7	1-Jun	Massé	*Paul et Virginie*	CG	NPS, c-Ganz, s-Saint-Saëns (*Athenaeum*, 22.6.1878, p. 807)
1878-8	15-Jun	Saint-Saëns	Piano Concerto No. 2 in G minor, Op. 22	SJH	*IT*; Dublin TR *ENG* 9.9.1878; HM *ENG* a-Hersee 5.2.1879 (Carl Rosa); HM *FRE* 8.11.1886
1878-9	22-Jun	Bizet	*Carmen*	HM	c-Sullivan (*MW*, 31 August 1878, p. 557; *Orchestra*, 1.9.1878, p. 76, which refers to earlier untraced performance at AP); CP c-Manns, see **1879-9**
1878-10	19-Aug	Saint-Saëns	*Le rouet d'Omphale*	CG	(ballet music) c-Manns (*MS*, 23.11.1878, p. 319); see **1893-4**
1878-11	16-Nov	Saint-Saëns	*Samson et Dalila*	CP	

Year & ref	Date	Composer	Work	Venue (London unless otherwise stated)	Notes and sources (where not cited in main text)
1879-1	9-Jan	Berlioz	*Symphonie fantastique*	Manchester	c-Hallé; SJH c-Ganz 30.4.1881 and 14.5.1881
1879-2	29-Mar	Hervé	*La belle poule*	Gaiety	*ENG* as *Poulet and Poulette* (*Observer*, 30.3.1879, p. 3)
1879-3	12-Apr	Offenbach	*Madame Favart*	Strand	*ENG* a-Farnie (L1075)
1879-4	24-May	Saint-Saëns	Symphony in A minor (1859)	SJH	NPS, c-Saint-Saëns
1879-5	24-May	D'Ivry	*Les amants de Vérone*	CG	*IT* (L1074)
1879-6	29-May	Saint-Saëns	*Danse macabre*	SJH	Mme Viard-Louis's concert, c-Saint-Saëns
1879-7	28-Jun	Massenet	*Le roi de Lahore*	CG	*IT* (L1065)
1879-8	28-Aug	Saint-Saëns	*La lyre et la harpe*	Birmingham TH	c-Saint-Saëns
1879-9	6-Dec	Saint-Saëns	Piano Concerto No. 3 in E flat, Op. 29	CP	c-Manns, s-Saint-Saëns (*MS*, 13.12.1879, p. 367)
1880-1	5-Feb	Berlioz	*La damnation de Faust*	Manchester	c-Hallé (complete); Liverpool RCT *ENG* a-Friend (staged Carl Rosa) 3.2.1894
1880-2	4-Mar	Massenet	*Phèdre* (overture)	SJH	PhilS (*MMR*, 1.4.1880, p. 56)
1880-3	19-Apr	Offenbach	*La fille du tambour-major*	Alhambra	*ENG* a-Farnie; Shaftesbury *FRE* 1.6.1908 (L1080–1)
1880-4	1-May	Saint-Saëns	Piano Concerto No. 1 in D minor	SJH	c-Ganz, s-Saint-Saëns (*MS*, 8.5.1880, p. 290)
1880-5	1-Jun	Fauré	Violin Sonata in A, Op. 13	SH	s-Musin & Saint-Saens (*MT*, 1.7.1880, p 344)
1880-6	26-Jun	Saint-Saëns	Prelude to *Le déluge*	SJH	c-Ganz (*MS*, 3.7.1880, p. 3)
1880-7	31-Jul	Cohen	*Les bleuets*	CG	*IT* (L994)
1880-8	18-Sep	Audran	*Les noces d'Olivette*	Strand	*ENG* a-Farnie
1880-9	31-Oct	Varney	*Les mousquetaires au couvent*	Globe	*ENG* a-Farnie; Coronet *FRE* 10.4.1907 (L1084–5)
1880-10	30-Oct	Massenet	*La Vierge*	CP	c-Manns (Danse galiléenne; Dernier sommeil de la Vierge) (*MS*, 6.11.1880, p. 288)
1880-11	6-Nov	Saint-Saëns	*La princesse jaune*	CP	c-Manns (overture) (*MS*, 13.11.1880, p. 302)

1880-12	30-Dec	Berlioz	*L'enfance du Christ*	Manchester	c-Hallé
1881-1	15-Mar	Gouvy	Symphony No. 2 in F	SJH	c-Lamoureux (*MS*, 19.3.1881, p. 181)
1881-2	15-Mar	Godard	*Aurore*, for contralto and orchestra	SJH	c-Lamoureux; as **1881**-1
1881-3	28-Mar	Lacome	*Jeanne, Jeanette, et Jeanneton*	Alhambra	*ENG* a-Reece (L1058)
1881-4	22-Mar	Massenet	*Suite d'orchestre (Scènes de féerie)*	SJH	c-Lamoureux (Intermezzo omitted) (*MS*, 26.3.1881, p. 195)
1881-5	22-Mar	Widor	Piano Concerto in F minor	SJH	c-Lamoureux; as **1881**-4
1881-6	22-Mar	Reyer	*Sigurd*	SJH	(Prelude) c-Lamoureux; as **1881**-4; see **1884**-2
1881-7	6-Jul	Offenbach	*La belle Lurette*	Gaiety	*FRE* (*MP*, 11.7.1881, p. 3)
1881-8	23-Jul	Planquette	*Les voltigeurs du 32ème*	Gaiety	*FRE* (*Standard*, 25.7.1881, p. 2)
1881-9	15-Oct	Audran	*La mascotte*	Comedy	*ENG* a-Farnie & Reece; preceded by try-outs at Brighton from 19.9.1881; Royalty *FRE* 23.1.1888 (L1087)
1881-10	24-Oct	Berlioz	*Nuits d'été*	SJH	c-Richter
1881-11	29-Oct	Berlioz	*Lélio*	CP	c-Manns (*MT*, 1.12.1881, p. 630)
1882-1	4-Jul	Lenepveu	*Velléda*	CG	*IT* (L1097)
1882-2	30-Aug	Gounod	*The Redemption*	Birmingham TH	c-Gounod
1882-3	14-Oct	Planquette	*Rip van Winkle*	Comedy	*ENG* a-Farnie
1882-4	3-Jun	Berlioz	*Symphonie funèbre et triomphale*	CP	c-Manns (*Era*, 10.6.1882, p. 7)
1883-1	26-Mar	Berlioz	*Grand messe des morts*	CP	c-Manns
1883-2	29-Oct	Chassaigne	*Le droit d'aînesse*	Comedy	*ENG*, a-Farnie as *Falka* (*Observer*, 4.11.1883, p. 6)
1883-3	19-Nov	Audran	*Gillette de Narbonne*	Royalty	*ENG*, a-Clarke (L1101)
1883-4	15-Dec	Dupont	Piano Concerto	CP	c-Manns, s-Frickenhaus (*Athenaeum*, 22.12.1883, p. 823)
1884-1	7-Feb	Planquette	*Nell Gwynne*	Avenue	*ENG* (original) (Gänzl, *British Musical Theatre*, p. 248)
1884-2	15-Jul	Reyer	*Sigurd*	CG	*IT* (L1107)

Year & ref	Date	Composer	Work	Venue (London unless otherwise stated)	Notes and sources (where not cited in main text)
1884-3	23-Oct	Massenet	L'invocation d'Apollon	Norwich	ENG a-Farnie (L1062)
1884-4	17-Nov	Audran	Le grand mogol	Comedy	c-Manns (Graphic, 23.3.1884, p. 179)
1884-5	16-Feb	Saint-Saëns	Henri VIII (ballet 'Fêtes populaires')	CP	
1885-1	17-Jan	Massenet	Manon	Liverpool RCT	ENG; DL ENG 7.5.1885; CG FRE 19.5.1891
1885-2	6-Jun	Delibes	Lakmé	Gaiety	FRE (L1104)
1885-3	18-Apr	Berlioz	Te Deum	CP	c-Manns
1885-4	20-Nov	Saint-Saëns	Psalm 18	SJH	Sacred Harmonic Society, c-Cummings (MT, 1.12.1885, p. 718)
1885-5	26-Aug	Gounod	Mors et vita	Birmingham TH	c-Richter
1886-1	19-May	Saint-Saëns	Symphony No. 3 in C minor ('Organ'), Op. 78	SJH	PhilS, c-Saint-Saëns
1886-2	4-Oct	Messager	La Béarnaise	PoW	ENG; try-outs in Birmingham from 27.9.1886
1886-3	11-Oct	Audran	Indiana	Avenue	ENG a-Farnie; preceded by try-outs at Manchester Comedy from 4.10.1886 (Gänzl, British Musical Theatre p. 311; Era, 9.10.1886, p. 14)
1886-4	20-Feb	Delibes	Le roi s'amuse	CP	c-Manns (Scène de ballet) (Athenaeum, 27.2.1886, p. 304)
1887-1	22-Apr	Bizet	Les pêcheurs de perles	CG	IT as Leila (L964)
1888-1	7-Nov	Chassaigne	Les noces improvisées	Avenue	ENG a-Murray as Nadgy (Theatre, 1.12.1886, p. 311–2)
1890-1	19-Apr	Chassaigne	The Brazilian	Newcastle TR	ENG a-Pemberton & Lestocq (Era, 10.5.1890, p. 10)
1890-2	25-Aug	Planquette	Captain Thérèse	PoW	ENG a-A'Beckett & Burnand (Wearing, London Stage 1890–99, p.34)
1890-3	9-Oct	Audran	La cigale	Lyric	ENG a-A'Beckett & Burnand; additional music by Caryll and Lila Clay (Wearing, London Stage 1890–99, p. 38; ISDN, 18.10.1890, p. 178)

1891-1	23-Jul	Audran	*Miss Helyett*	Criterion	*ENG* a-Burnand as *Miss Decima* (*MP*, 24.7.1891. p. 3); PoW *ENG* 26.11.1891 (Wearing, *London Stage 1890–99*, p. 81)
1891-2	10-Oct	Gounod	*Philémon et Baucis*	CG	*FRE*; preceded by amateur performance *ENG*, College Hall, Liverpool 9.2.1888 (*Liverpool Mercury*, 10.2.1888, p. 5); DL *ENG* 26.4.1894
1891-3	29-Oct	Bruneau	*Le rêve*	CG	*FRE* (L1149)
1891-4	3-Nov	Messager	*La Basoche*	REO	*ENG* a-Harris (Wearing, *London Stage 1890–99*, p. 91)
1891-5	9-Nov	Fauré	Piano Quartet in G minor, Op. 45	SJH	Monday Popular Concert (Ysaÿe, Staus, Whitehouse, Schönberger)
1891-6	18-May	Messager	*Fauvette*	Edinburgh Lyceum	*ENG* a-Rae (*Edinburgh Evening News*, 19.5.1891 p. 2); Royalty 16.11.1891 (17.11.1891, p. 5)
1892-1	2-Aug	Offenbach	*Pomme d'Api*	Criterion	*ENG* a-Reeve & Schade as *Poor Mignonette* (Wearing, *London Stage 1890–99*, p. 133)
1892-2	10-Sep	Bizet	*Djamileh*	Dublin Gaiety	*ENG* a-Bennett (Carl Rosa); CG *FRE* 13.6.1893 (L1024)
1892-3	6-Oct	Lecocq	*Le coeur et la main*	Lyric	*ENG* a-Burnand as *Incognita* (Wearing, *London Stage 1890–99*, p. 137)
1893-1	20-Feb	Adam	*Si j'étais roi*	Newcastle	*ENG* a-Smith; Parkhurst Theatre *ENG* 23.5.1893 (L901)
1893-2	19-Apr	Franck	Violin Sonata in A	SJH	s-Frickenhaus & Ortmans
1893-3	6-May	Hervé	*Mam'zelle Nitouche*	Trafalgar	*ENG* (Wearing, *London Stage 1890–99*, p 164)
1893-4	12-Jun	Saint-Saëns	*Afrique*, Op. 89	Cambridge	c-Stanford, s-Saint-Saëns
1893-5	25-Sep	Saint-Saëns	*Samson et Dalila*	CG	*ENG*, c-Cowen (concert perf); CG *FRE* 26.4.1909 (staged)
1894-1	13-Jan	Messager	*Fanchette*	Liverpool RCT	*ENG* (Carl Rosa) (*MT*, 1.2.1894, p. 103)
1894-2	11-Jun	Massenet	*Werther*	CG	*FRE*: HM *ENG* 27.5.1910 (L1153)
1894-3	20-Jun	Massenet	*La Navarraise*	CG	*FRE* (L1177)
1894-4	4-Jul	Bruneau	*L'attaque du moulin*	CG	*FRE* (L1170)
1894-5	13-Jul	Messager	*Mirette*	Savoy	*ENG* (*MG*, 4.7.1894, p. 5)

Year & ref	Date	Composer	Work	Venue (London unless otherwise stated)	Notes and sources (where not cited in main text)
1894-6	22-Nov	Fauré	Piano Quartet in C minor, Op. 15	SJH	s-Fauré, Wolff, van Waefelghem & Stern
1894-7	28-Nov	D'Indy	Trio, Op. 29	Brinsmead's Rooms	s-Ernest, Draper, & van der Straeten
1894-8	13-Dec	Delibes	Le roi l'a dit	PoW	ENG a-Temple, c-Stanford, RCM students (L1030)
1895-1	25-Apr	Audran	L'Oncle Célestin	Trafalgar	ENG as Baron Golosh, additional music by Lutz; preceded by try-outs at Swansea from 15.4.1895 (Wearing, London Stage 1890–99, p. 249)
1895-2	13-Jun	Chaminade	Concertstück for Piano and Orchestra	SJH	PhilS, c-Mackenzie
1896-1	10-Mar	Godard	La vivandière	Liverpool RCT	ENG a-Whyte (Carl Rosa) (MS, 14.3.1896, p. 191)
1896-2	13-Apr	Chabrier	Gwendolen	QH	c-Lamoureux (Overture) (MS, 26.3.1881, p. 195) (Part 1); as 1896-2; see 1902-1 and 1909-3
1896-3	16-Apr	D'Indy	Wallenstein, Op. 12	QH	Version for piano duet and female chorus
1896-4	29-Apr	Fauré	Caligula, Op. 52	(Private)	c-Wood; CP, 7.11.1896 c-Manns
1896-5	3-Sep	Chaminade	Callirrhoë	QH	c-Colonne (2nd movement: 'Psyche enlevée par les zephirs') (MS, 17.10.1896, p. 238)
1896-6	14-Oct	Franck	Psyche	QH	(part); as 1896-6
1896-7	14-Oct	Massenet	Scènes alsaciennes	QH	as 1896-6
1896-8	16-Oct	Bizet	Suite 'Roma'	QH	c-Manns; QH c-Lamoureux 17.11.1896
1896-9	14-Nov	D'Indy	La forêt enchantée, Op. 8	CP	c-Lamoureux (Prelude to Part 2) (MG, 17.11.1896, p. 7)
1896-10	16-Nov	Franck	Rédemption	QH	
1896-11	15-Nov	Dubois	Overture 'Frithiof'	QH	c-Lamoureux (MT, 1.12.1896, p. 807)
1896-12	19-Nov	Franck	Symphony in D minor	QH	as 1896-11
1896-13	19-Nov	Chevillard	Ballade symphonique	QH	as 1896-11
1897-1	24-Feb	Audran	La poupée	PoW	ENG a-Sturgess (Wearing, London Stage 1890–99, p. 331)
1897-2	22-Mar	Boëllmann	Fantaisie dialoguée	QH	c-Lamoureux (MS, 27.3.1897, p. 205)

1897-3	26-Mar	Saint-Saëns	Piano Concert No. 5 in F	QH	c-Lamoureux (*Athenaeum*, 3.4.97, p. 452)
1897-4	30-Mar	Berlioz	*Les Troyens*	Liverpool	Liverpool Philharmonic Society, concert performance, c-Cowen (*Athenaeum*, 3.4.1897, pp. 452–3)
1897-5	11-Nov	D'Indy	*Sauge fleurie*, Op. 21	QH	c-Lamoureux (*MMR*, 1.12.1897, p. 277)
1897-6	24-Nov	Franck	*Le chasseur maudit*	QH	c-Lamoureux (*MT*, 1.1.1898, p. 26)
1898-1	2-Feb	Franck	*Les Djinns*	QH	c-Lamoureux (*Athenaeum*, 5.2.1898, p. 191)
1898-2	18-Feb	Thomas	*Le songe d'une nuit d'été*	Glasgow	*ENG* a-Kingston as *A poet's dream* (L881)
1898-3	20-Apr	Dubois	Piano Concerto in F minor	QH	c-Lamoureux (*MT*, 1.5.1898, p. 316)
1898-4	21-Jun	Fauré	*Pelléas et Mélisande*	PoW	*FRE* (L1103)
1898-5	14-Jul	Saint-Saëns	*Henri VIII*	CG	c-Fauré
1898-6	8-Oct	Fauré	*La naissance de Vénus*	Leeds TH	
1899-1	7-Jan	Chabrier	*L'etoile*	Savoy	*ENG* a-Goodwin & Morse as *The Lucky Star*; most of Chabrier's score was discarded (L1067)
1899-2	21-Sep	Rabaud	*Eglogue*, Op. 7	QH	c-Wood (*MN*, 7.10.1899, p. 304)
1899-3	23-Sep	D'Indy	*Chansons et danses*	QH	As **1899-2**
1900-1	6-Feb	Franck	*Les béatitudes*	Glasgow	Glasgow Choral Union, c-Bradley
1900-2	26-Oct	Gounod	*Cinq Mars*	Leeds	*ENG* a-Van Noorden & Fitzgerald; Coronet *ENG* 17.11.1900 (both with Carl Rosa) (L1063)
1900-3	14-Nov	D'Indy	'Istar' Variations	QH	c-Ysaÿe
1900-4	24-Feb	Berlioz	Overture 'Rob Roy'	CP	c-Manns (*Observer*, 25.2.1900, p. 6)
1901-1	12-Jan	Saint-Saëns	String Quartet in E minor, Op. 112	SJH	Saturday Popular Concert (Ysaÿe Quartet) (*MT*, 1.2.1901, p. 118)
1901-2	25-Feb	D'Indy	Piano Quartet	SJH	Monday Popular Concert (Ysaÿe Quartet)
1901-3	17-Jul	Lalo	*Le roi d'Ys*	CG	*FRE* (L1132)
1902-1	20-Sep	D'Indy	*Wallenstein*, Op. 12	QH	c-Wood (parts 2 and 3) (*Athenaeum*, 27.9.1902, p 423); see **1909-3**
1903-1	19-Feb	Debussy	*Pour le piano*	BH	Toccata, s-Grainger; Toccata, s-Suart SJH 19.11.1903 (*MS*, 28.11.1903, p. 343); Sarabande, s-Suart BH 2.5.1904

Year & ref	Date	Composer	Work	Venue (London unless otherwise stated)	Notes and sources (where not cited in main text)
1903-2	11-Apr	Audran	L'enlèvement de la Toledad	Windsor	ENG a-Moore & Wood as *La Toledad*; Kennington ENG 20.4.1903 (L1179; *MG*, 21.4.1903, p. 6)
1903-2	5-May	Messager	Véronique	Coronet	FRE; Apollo ENG a-Hamilton 18.5.1904 (Gänzl, *British Musical Theatre*, p. 865)
1903-3	8-Jun	Serpette	Amorelle	Kennington	ENG a-White & Boyd-Jones; Comedy ENG 18.2.1904 (Wearing, *London Stage 1900–09*, pp. 174–5)
1903-4	20-Jul	Missa	Maguelone	CG	FRE (L1248)
1903-5	12-Nov	Berlioz	La mort de Cléopâtre	QH	c-Weingartner (*Times*, 13.11.1903, p. 8)
1904-1	2-May	Ravel	Jeux d'eau	BH	s-Suart (*VT*, 1.6.1904, p. 83)
1904-2	20-Jun	Saint-Saëns	Hélène	CG	FRE (L1257)
1904-3	6-Jul	Massenet	Hérodiade	CG	FRE as *Salomé*; LOH FRE as *Hérodiade* 15.12.1911 (L1094)
1904-4	20-Aug	Debussy	L'après-midi d'un faune	QH	c-Wood
1904-5	19-Oct	Debussy	String Quartet	RCM	s-Warwick-Evans, Kinze, Bridge & James
1905-1	24-Feb	Debussy	Estampes	BH	('Pagodes') s-Grainger (*MS*, 25.11.1905, p. 343); AH (complete) s-Cracroft 24.2.1906 (*Times*, 26.2.1906, p. 12)
1905-2	29-Apr	Messager	Les p'tites Michus	Daly's	ENG a-Hamilton (L1205)
1906-1	15-Jun	Massenet	Le jongleur de Notre-Dame	CG	FRE (L1239)
1906-2	26-Oct	Ravel	Sonatine	BH	s-Navas (*Times*, 27.10.1906, p. 4)
1907-1	17-Apr	Offenbach	Les contes d'Hoffmann	Adelphi	GER; HM ENG 12.5.1910; CG ENG 5.10.1910
1907-2	2-Jul	Saint-Saëns	Fantaisie for Harp and Violin, Op. 124	AH	s-Clara & Marianne Eissler (*Times*, 4.7.1907, p. 4)
1907-3	5-Sep	Ravel	Introduction and Allegro for Harp	QH	(*Times*, 6.9.1907, p. 8)
1907-4	23-Oct	D'Indy	Symphonie sur un chant montagnard français	QH	c-Wood; QH PhilS c-Beecham 7.12.1910 (*Times*, 8.12.1910, p. 12)

				Sheffield Montgomery Hall	Parisian Quartet (*MS*, 14.12.1907, p. 376)
1907-5	5-Dec	Ravel	String Quartet	Sheffield Montgomery Hall	
1908-1	1-Feb	Debussy	*La mer*	QH	c-Debussy
1908-2	29-Feb	Debussy	*La demoiselle élue*	QH	c-Wood
1908-3	8-Oct	Debussy	*L'enfant prodigue*	Sheffield	*FRE* c-Wood; CG *FRE* c-Beecham (staged) 28.2.1910 (L1297)
1909-1	26-Feb	Debussy	*Danses sacrées et profanes*	BH	SCF (*Observer*, 28.2.1909, p. 5)
1909-2	27-Feb	Debussy	*Nocturnes*	QH	c-Debussy
1909-3	15-Mar	D'Indy	*Jour d'été à la montagne*	QH	c-Beecham
1909-4	27-Mar	D'Indy	*Wallenstein*, Op. 12	QH	c-D'Indy (complete)
1909-5	27-Mar	D'Indy	Piano Sonata	Novello's Hall	s-Hess
1909-6	26-Apr	Ravel	*Cinq mélodies populaires grecques*	BH	SCF (*Times*, 27.4.1909, p. 8)
1909-7	21-May	Debussy	*Pelléas et Mélisande*	CG	*FRE* (L1241)
1909-8	18-Jun	Charpentier	*Louise*	CG	*FRE* (L1225)
1909-9	14-Sep	Saint-Saëns	*La foi*	HM	Incidental music to Brieux's play (*Times*, 15.9.1909, pp. 10 and 11)
1909-10	21-Oct	Ravel	*Rapsodie espagnole*	QH	c-Wood
1910-1	7-Jun	Saint-Saëns	*La muse et le poète*, Op. 132	QH	Version for violin, cello and piano (*MT*, 1.7.1910 pp. 457–8)
1910-2	13-Nov	Nouguès	*Quo vadis?*	LOH	*FRE* (L1289)
1910-3	25-May	Missa	*La muguette*	HM	*ENG* a-Wallace, c-Beecham (L1247)
1910-4	2-Jun	Debussy	*Préludes* (Book 1)	BH	s-Liebich (Nos 3, 5, 9 and 10) (*Times*, 3 June, p. 11); Liebich claimed first complete performance at 'Matinée Intime' at his home in Kensington 30.11.1912 (*MS*, 7.12.1912, p. 360)
1910-5	18-Jul	Laparra	*La habanera*	CG	*FRE* (L1284)
1910-6	12-Oct	Leroux	*Le chemineau*	CG	*ENG*, a-Wallace, c-Beecham (L1282)
1911-1	19-Jan	Schmitt	Piano Quintet	(Private)	SCF 'salon', The Limes, Holland Park

Year & ref	Date	Composer	Work	Venue (London unless otherwise stated)	Notes and sources (where not cited in main text)
1911-2	27-Feb	Ravel	Pavane pour une infante défunte (orchestral version)	Manchester	'Gentlemen's Concert', c-Wood (*MG*, 28.2.1911, p. 6); QH c-Wood 16.8.1911; publicly performed in its piano version since at least 1908 (*Times*, 10.11.1908, p. 13)
1911-3	23-May	Debussy	Rondes de printemps	QH	c-Wood
1911-4	18-Jul	Massenet	Thaïs	CG	FRE (L1174)
1912-1	4-May	Ravel	Ma mère l'oye	QH	c-Wood
1912-2	17-May	Massenet	Don Quichotte	LOH	FRE (L1297)
1913-1	27-Feb	Hahn	Le dieu bleu	CG	c-Monteux
1913-2	29-May	Debussy	Préludes (Book 2)	AH	Selection, s-Walker (*MT*, 1.7.1913, p. 469); complete s-Rummel BH 12.6.1913 (*Athenaeum*, 21.6.1913, p. 678)
1913-3	2-Jun	Saint-Saëns	Ouverture d'un opéra comique inachevé, Op. 140	QH	c-Beecham
1913-4	25-Jun	Debussy	Jeux	CG	c-Monteux
1913-5	11-Sep	Saint-Saëns	La terre promise	Gloucester	ENG as *The Promised Land*, c-Saint-Saëns
1913-6	18-Sep	Debussy	Ibéria	QH	c-Wood
1913-7	25-Sep	Ravel	Valses nobles et sentimentales	QH	c-Wood
1914-1	9-Jun	Ravel	Daphnis et Chloë	DL	c-Monteux

Bibliography

Primary sources (books only; articles from newspapers, journals and serials are referenced in the main text)

Lucie Barbier Papers, National Library of Wales, NLW MSS 22692–98 (papers relating to Société des Concerts Français)

—, *Euterpe; or, Remarks on the Use and Abuse of Music as a Part of Modern Education* (London: J Dodsley,? 1778)

—, *Etiquette for Gentlemen: With Hints on the Art of Conversation* (London: Charles Tilt, 1838)

—, *Advice to a Young Gentleman, on Entering Society* (2nd ed, London: A H Baily, 1839)

—, *Record of the Musical Union* [annually 1845–80]

—, *All About Etiquette: or, The Manners of Polite Society* (London: Ward, Lock & Co., 1875)

—, *Franco-British Exhibition, London, 1908: Official Guide* (4th ed, Derby: Bemrose, 1908)

—, *Baedeker's Guide to Paris and Environs with Routes from London to Paris* (Leipzig: Karl Baedeker, 1910)

Andrews, John, *A Comparative View of the French and English Nations, and their Manners, Politics and Literature* (London: Longman & Robinson, 1785)

Batley, Thomas (ed.), *Sir Charles Hallé's Concerts in Manchester* (Manchester: Charles Sever, 1896)

Bax, Arnold, *Farewell My Youth* (London: Longmans, Green & Co, 1943)

Berry, Mary, *Extracts of the Journals and Correspondence of Miss Berry* (3 vols, London: Longmans, 1865–66)

Betham-Edwards, M, *Anglo-French Reminiscences 1875–1899* (Leipzig: Bernhard Tauchnitz, 1900)

Bingham, Denis, *Journal of the Siege of Paris* (London: Smith, Elder & Co., 1871)

Brown, John, *An Estimate of the Manners and Principles of the Times* (London: L Davis & C Reymers, 1757)

Bunn, Alfred, *The Stage: Both Before and Behind the Curtain* (3 vols, London: Richard Bentley, 1840)

Burgh, Allatson, *Anecdotes of Music, Historical and Biographical; in a Series of Letters from a Gentleman to his Daughter* (3 vols, London: Longman & Co., 1814)

Burney, Charles, *The Present State of Music in France and Italy* (London: T Becket & Co., 1771)

Burney, Charles, *A General History of Music from the Earliest Ages to the Present Day* (4 vols, London: Payne & Son, 1776–89)

Butler, Samuel, *The Poetical Works of Samuel Butler* (2 vols, London: William Pickering, 1835)

Chorley, Henry Fothergill, *Thirty Years' Musical Recollections* (2 vols, London: Hurst & Blackett, 1862)

Chorley, Henry Fothergill, *The National Music of the World* (London: Sampson Lown, 1880)

Cowen, Frederic, *My Art and my Friends* (London: Edward Arnold, 1913)

Daly, William H, *Debussy: A Study in Modern Music* (Edinburgh: Methven Simpson, 1908)

Diehl, Alice Mangold, *Musical Memories* (London: Richard Bentley, 1897)

Disraeli, Benjamin, *Coningsby* (2nd ed, 3 vols, London: Henry Colburn, 1844)

Dryden, John, *The Complete Works of John Dryden* (18 vols, London: William Miller, 1808)

Dumas, F G (ed.), *The Franco-British Exhibition, Illustrated Review, 1908* (London: Chatto & Windus, 1908)

Edgcumbe, Richard [2nd Earl of Mount Edgcumbe], *Musical Reminiscences of an Old Amateur, Chiefly Respecting the Italian Opera in England* (2nd ed, London: W Clarke, 1827)

Engel, Carl, *An Introduction to the Study of National Music* (London: Longman, 1866)

Engel, Carl, *The Literature of National Music* (London: Novello, Ewer & Co., 1879)

Evans, Edwin, 'French Music of Today', *Proceedings of the Musical Association*, **36** (1909–10), pp. 47–74

Fitzball, Edward, *Thirty-Five Years of a Dramatic Author's Life* (2 vols, London: T C Newby, 1859)

Garrick, David (ed. R C Alexander), *The Diary of David Garrick, Being a Record of his Memorable Trip to Paris in 1751* (Oxford: Oxford University Press, 1928)

Gaskell, Elizabeth, *Cranford* (London: J M Dent, 1904)

Grove, George (ed.), *A Dictionary of Music and Musicians* (1st ed, 4 vols, London: Macmillan, 1878–89)

Gruneisen, Charles, *Memoir of Meyerbeer* (London: T Brettell, 1848)

Hadow, Henry, *Studies in Modern Music* (London: Macmillan, 1893)

Hauk, Minnie [Baroness de Wartegg], *Memories of a Singer* (London: A M Philpot, 1925)

Haweis, H R, *Music and Morals* (London: Longman, Green & Co., 1900 [1870])

Hawkins, John, *A General History of the Science and Practice of Music* (2 vols, London: Novello, Ewer & Co., 1875)

Hervey, Arthur, *Masters of French Music etc.* ([no place]: [no publisher], 1894)

Hervey, Arthur, *French Music in the XIXth Century* (London: Grant Richards, 1903)

Hervey, Arthur, *Alfred Bruneau* (London: John Lane, 1907)

Hervey, Arthur, *Saint-Saëns* (London: Bodley Head, 1921)

Hollingshead, John, *Gaiety Chronicles* (London: A Constable, 1898)

Jean-Aubry, Georges (trans. Percy Scholes), *An Introduction to French Music* (London: C Palmer & Hayward, 1917)

Jean-Aubry, Georges (trans. Edwin Evans), *French Music of Today* (London, Keegan Paul & Co., 1919)

Klein, Herman, *Thirty Years of Musical Life in London* (London: William Heinemann, 1903)

Levey, R C, *Annals of the Theatre Royal, Dublin* (Dublin: Joseph Dollard, 1880)
Liebich, [Mrs Franz] Louise, *Claude-Achille Debussy* (London: John Lane, The Bodley Head, 1908)
Locke, Arthur Ware, *Music and the Romantic Movement in France* (London: [no publisher], 1920)
Lumley, Benjamin, *Reminiscences of the Opera* (London: Hurst & Blackett, 1864)
Lunn, Henry, *Musings of a Musician* (London: [no publisher], 1847)
Mapleson, James, *The Mapleson Memoirs* (2 vols, Chicago, New York and San Francisco: Belford, Clarke & Co., 1888)
Martyn, Thomas, *The Gentleman's Guide in his Tour through France* (London: G Kearsley, 1787)
Moore, John, *A View of Society and Manners in France, Switzerland and Germany* (Dublin: [no publisher], 1780)
Morgan, [Lady] Sydney, *France in 1829–30* (London: Saunders & Otley, 1831)
Parry, Hubert, *Style in Musical Art* (London: Macmillan & Co., 1911)
Pauer, Ernst, *The Elements of the Beautiful in Music* (London: Novello & Co., 1877)
Piatigorsky, Anna, 'The Campaign for French Music: The Société des Concerts Français and the Critical Reception of French Music in Britain 1907–1915', unpublished MMus thesis, University of Melbourne, 2018
Potter, John, *Observations on the Present State of Music and Musicians* (London: C Henderson, 1762)
Rivière, Jules, *My Musical Life and Recollections* (London: Sampson, 1893)
Shaw, Joseph, *Letters to a Nobleman* (London: Daniel Midwinter, 1709)
Smart, George (ed. H Bertrand Cox and C L E Cox), *Leaves from the Journal of Sir George Smart* (London: Longman, 1907)
Stainer, John, 'On the Progressive Character of Church Music', in *Authorised Report of the Church Congress* (London: William Gardner, 1874), pp. 530–8
Stanford, Charles, *Musical Composition* (London: Macmillan, 1911)
Stonequist, Martha, 'The Musical Entente Cordiale 1905–16', unpublished PhD thesis, University of Colorado, 1972
Thackeray, William, *Vanity Fair* (Harmondsworth: Penguin, 1968)
Wood, Henry, *My Life in Music* (London: Victor Gollancz, 1938)

Secondary Literature

Bashford, Christina, *The Pursuit of High Culture: John Ella and Chamber Music in Victorian London* (Woodbridge: Boydell & Brewer, 2007)
Beale, Robert, *Charles Hallé: A Musical Life* (Aldershot: Ashgate, 2007)
Bell, Philip M H, 'The *Entente Cordiale* and the Sea Serpent', *Diplomacy and Statecraft*, **17** (2006), pp. 635–45
Bell, Philip M H, *France and Britain 1900–1940: Entente and Estrangement* (London and New York: Routledge, 2013)
Black, Jeremy, *Natural and Necessary Enemies: Anglo-French Relations in the Eighteenth Century* (Georgia: University of Georgia Press, 1989)
Black, Jeremy, *The British Abroad: The Grand Tour in the Eighteenth-Century* (Stroud: Alan Sutton, 1992)
Bledsoe, Robert, *Henry Fothergill Chorley, Victorian Journalist* (Aldershot: Ashgate, 1998)

Bray, William (ed.), *The Diary of John Evelyn* (London & New York: Walter Dunne, 1901)

Brewer, John, *The Pleasures of the Imagination: English Culture in the Eighteenth Century* (London: HarperCollins, 1997)

Byrnside, Ronald, 'Musical Impressionism: The Early History of the Term', *Musical Quarterly*, **66** (1980), pp. 522–37

Cairns, David, *Berlioz* (2 vols, London: Allen Lane The Penguin Press, 1999)

Campos, Christophe, *The View of France: From Arnold to Bloomsbury* (London: Oxford University Press, 1965)

Carnelley, John, *George Smart and Nineteenth-Century London Concert Life* (Woodbridge: Boydell Press, 2015)

Carpenter, Kirsty, *Refugees of the French Revolution: Emigrés in London 1789–1802* (Basingstoke: Macmillan, 1999)

Carse, Adam, *The Life of Jullien* (Cambridge: W Heffer, 1951)

Carter, Philip, *Men and the Emergence of Polite Society: Britain 1660–1800* (Harlow: Longman, 2001)

Chamberlain, Muriel, *'Pax Britannica'? British Foreign Policy 1789–1914* (London: Longman, 1988)

Chassaigne, Philippe and Dockerill, Michael (eds), *Anglo-French Relations 1898–1998* (Basingstoke: Palgrave Macmillan, 2002)

Christensen, Thomas, 'Public Music in Private Spheres: Piano-Vocal Scores and the Domestication of Opera', in Orden, Kate van (ed.), *Music and the Cultures of Print* (New York: Garland Publishing, 2000), pp. 67–93

Clark, Roger, 'Threading the Mae: Nineteenth-Century Guides for British Travellers to Paris', in Sheringham, Michael (ed.), *Parisian Fields* (London: Reaktion Books, 1996), pp. 8–29

Cohen, Michèle, *Fashioning Masculinity: National Identity and Language in the Eighteenth Century* (London: Routledge, 1996)

Colley, Linda, *Britons: Forging the Nation 1707–1837* (London: Yale University Press, 2005)

Cormac, Joanne, 'From Satirical Piece to Commercial Product: The Mid-Victorian Opera Burlesque and its Bourgeois Audience', *Journal of the Royal Musical Association*, **142** (2017), pp. 69–108

Cornick, Martyn, '"Putting the Seal on the *Entente*": The Franco-British Exhibition, London, May-October 1908', *Franco-British Studies*, **35** (2004), pp. 133–44

Crewe, Frances (ed. Allen, Michael), *An English Lady in France: The Diary of Frances Anne Crewe, 1786* (St Leonard's: Oxford-Stockley Publications, 2006)

Crossley, Ceri and Small, Ian (eds), *Studies in Anglo-French Cultural Relations* (London & Basingstoke: Macmillan, 1988)

Crouzet, François, *Britain Ascendant: Comparative Studies in Franco-British Economic History* (Cambridge: Cambridge University Press, 1990)

Dames, Nicholas, 'Britain and Europe', in Flint, Kate (ed.), *The Cambridge History of Victorian Literature* (Cambridge: Cambridge University Press, 2012), pp. 622–40

Davis, Jim and Emeljanow, Victor, *Reflecting the Audience: London Theatregoing 1840–1880* (Hatfield: University of Hertfordshire Press, 2001)

Deruchie, Andrew, *The French Symphony at the Fin-de-Siècle* (Woodbridge: Boydell & Brewer, 2013)

Dibble, Jeremy, *John Stainer: A Life in Music* (Woodbridge: Boydell & Brewer, 2007)

Doctor, Jennifer and Wright, David (eds), *The Proms: A New History* (London: Thames and Hudson, 2006)

Duncan, Barry, *The St James's Theatre: Its Strange and Complete History 1835–1957* (London: Barrie & Rockliff, 1964)

Eagles, Robin, *Francophilia in English Society 1748–1815* (Basingstoke: Macmillan, 2000)

Eatock, Colin, 'The Crystal Palace: Canon Formation and the English Musical Renaissance', *Nineteenth-Century Music*, **34** (2010), pp. 87–105

Ehrlich, Cyril, *The Music Profession in Britain since the Eighteenth Century: A Social History* (Oxford: Clarendon Press, 1985)

Ehrlich, Cyril, *The Piano: A Social History* (Oxford: Clarendon Press, 1990)

Ehrlich, Cyril, *First Philharmonic: A History of Royal Philharmonic Society* (Oxford: Clarendon Press, 1995)

Faris, Alexander, *Jacques Offenbach* (London: Faber & Faber, 1980)

Fauser, Annegret, *Musical Encounters at the 1889 Paris World's Fair* (Woodbridge: Boydell & Brewer, 2005)

Fenner, Theodore, *Opera in London: Views of the Press 1785–1830* (Carbondale IL: Southern Illinois University Press, 1994)

Fifield, Christopher, *Hans Richter* (Suffolk: Boydell & Brewer, 2016)

Foreman, Lewis, *Music in England 1885–1920: As Recounted in Hazell's Annual* (London: Thames Publishing, 1994)

Fuhrmann, Christina, *Foreign Opera at the London Playhouses: From Mozart to Bellini* (Cambridge: Cambridge University Press, 2015)

Ganz, A W, *Berlioz in London* (London: Quality Press, 1950)

Gänzl, Kurt, *The British Musical Theatre, Volume 1: 1865–1914* (Basingstoke: Macmillan Press, 1986)

Gänzl, Kurt, *Emily Soldene: In Search of a Singer* (2 vols, Wellington (NZ): Steele Roberts, 2007)

Gatens, William, *Victorian Cathedral Music in Theory and Practice* (Cambridge: Cambridge University Press, 1986)

Geppert, Alexander, *Fleeting Cities: Imperial Expositions in* Fin-de-Siècle *Europe* (Basingstoke: Palgrave Macmillan, 2010)

Giroud, Vincent, *French Opera: A Short History* (New Haven CT & London: Yale University Press, 2010)

Greene, Harry Plunket, *Charles Villiers Stanford* (London: Edward Arnold, 1935)

Gwynn, Robin, *The Huguenots of London* (Brighton: Alpha Press, 1998)

Hayasaka, Makiko, 'Organ Recitals as Popular Culture: The Secularisation of the Instrument and its Repertoire in Britain, 1834–1950', unpublished PhD thesis, University of Bristol, 2016.

Hitchcock, Tim and Cohen, Michèle (eds), *English Masculinities 1660–1800* (Essex: Longman, 1999)

Hogarth, George, *Memoirs of the Musical Drama* (2 vols, London: Richard Bentley, 1838)

Holman, Peter, *Four and Twenty Fiddlers: The Violin at the English Court 1540–1690* (Oxford: Clarendon Press, 1993)

Huebner, Steven, *The Operas of Charles Gounod* (Oxford: Clarendon Press, 1990)

Hughes, Gervase, *Composers of Operetta* (London: Macmillan & Co., 1962)

Hughes, Meirion, *The English Musical Renaissance and the Press 1850–1914: Watchmen of Music* (Aldershot: Ashgate, 2002)

Irvine, Demar, *Massenet: A Chronicle of His Life and Times* (Portland OR: Amadeus Press, 1994)

Jones, Colin, McDonagh, Josephine, and Mee, Jon (eds), *A Tale of Two Cities and the French Revolution* (Basingstoke: Palgrave Macmillan, 2009)

Jones, J Barrie, *Gabriel Fauré: A Life in Letters* (London: B T Batsford, 1989)

Kelly, Barbara (ed), *French Music, Culture and National Identity 1870–1939* (Woodbridge: Boydell & Brewer, 2008)

Kelly, Debra and Cornick, Martyn (eds), *A History of the French in London: Liberty, Equality, Opportunity* (London: Institute of Historical Research, 2013)

Kumar, Krishan, *The Making of English National Identity* (Cambridge: Cambridge University Press, 2003)

Lacombe, Hervé, *The Keys to French Opera in the Nineteenth Century* (Berkeley CA, Los Angeles & London: University of California Press, 2001)

Lamb, Andrew, 'Offenbach in London', in Franke, Rainer (ed.), *Offenbach und die Schauplätze seines Musiktheaters* (Laaber: Laaber, 1999)

Langford, Paul, *Englishness Identified: Manner and Character 1650–1850* (Oxford: Oxford University Press, 2000)

Langham-Smith, Richard and Potter, Caroline, *French Music since Berlioz* (Aldershot: Ashgate, 2006)

Langley, Leanne, 'Building an Orchestra, Creating an Audience', in Doctor, Jennifer and Wright, David (eds), *The Proms: A New History* (London: Thames and Hudson, 2006), pp. 32–73

Langley, Leanne, 'Agency and Change: Berlioz in Britain 1870–1920', *Journal of the Royal Musical Association*, **132** (2007), pp. 306–48

Laurence, Dan H (ed.), *Shaw's Music: The Complete Musical Criticism of Bernard Shaw* (3 vols, London: Bodley Head, 1981)

Lesure, François and Nichols, Roger (eds and trans), *Debussy Letters* (London: Faber & Faber, 1987)

Loewenberg, Alfred, *Annals of Opera 1597–1940* (3rd ed, London, John Calder, 1978)

Long, Kenneth, *The Music of the English Church* (London: Hodder & Stoughton, 1972)

Lowe, John, *The Great Powers, Imperialism, and the German Problem 1865–1925* (London & New York: Routledge, 1994)

Lowerson, John, *Amateur Operatics: A Social and Cultural History* (Manchester & New York: Manchester University Press, 2005)

Lucas, John, *Thomas Beecham: An Obsession with Music* (Woodbridge: Boydell Press, 2008)

Maitland, John A Fuller (ed.), *Grove's Dictionary of Music and Musicians* (2nd ed, 5 vols, London: Macmillan, 1906)

Marshall, Gail (ed.), *The Cambridge Companion to the Fin-de-Siècle* (Cambridge: Cambridge University Press, 2007)

Mayne, Richard, Johnson, Douglas and Tombs, Robert (eds), *Cross Channel Currents: 100 Years of the Entente Cordiale* (London & New York: Routledge, 2004)

McGirr, Elaine, *Eighteenth Century Characters: A Guide to the Literature of the Age* (Basingstoke: Palgrave Macmillan, 2007)

McVeigh, Simon, *Concert Life in London from Mozart to Haydn* (Cambridge: Cambridge University Press, 1993)

Mero, Alison, 'The Climate for Opera in London 1834–1865', in Temperley, Nicholas (ed.), *Musicians of Bath and Beyond: Edward Loder and His Family* (Woodbridge: Boydell & Brewer, 2016), pp. 58–75

Moores, John Richard, *Representations of France in English Satirical Prints 1740–1832* (Basingstoke: Palgrave Macmillan, 2015)

Morris, Edward, *French Art in Nineteenth Century Britain* (New Haven CT & London: Yale University Press, 2005)

Murray, Venetia, *High Society: A Social History of the Regency Period 1788–1830* (London: Viking, 1988)

Musgrave, Michael, *The Musical Life of the Crystal Palace* (Cambridge: Cambridge University Press, 1995)

Nectoux, Jean-Michel (trans. Underwood, J A), *Gabriel Fauré: His Life through Letters* (London & New York: Marion Boyers, 1984)

Newman, Gerald, *The Rise of English Nationalism: A Cultural History 1740–1830* (London: Weidenfeld & Nicholson, 1987)

Newsome, David, *The Victorian World Picture: Perceptions and Introspections in an Age of Change* (London: Fontana, 1998)

Nichols, Roger, 'The Reception of Debussy's Music in England up to 1914', in Langham-Smith, Richard (ed.), *Debussy Studies* (Cambridge: Cambridge University Press, 1997), pp. 139–53

Norris, Gerald, *Stanford, the Cambridge Jubilee and Tchaikovsky* (Newton Abbot: David and Charles, 1980)

Northcott, Richard, *Gounod's Operas in London* (London: The Press Printers, 1918)

Orenstein, Arbie, *Ravel: Man and Musician* (New York & London: Columbia University Press, 1975)

Orledge, Robert, *Gabriel Fauré* (London: Eulenberg Books, 1979)

Otte, T G, 'From "War-in-Sight" to Nearly War: Anglo–French Relations in the Age of High Imperialism, 1875–1898', *Diplomacy and Statecraft*, **17** (2006), pp. 693–714

Pasler, Jann (ed.), *Camille Saint-Saëns and his World* (Princeton NJ & Oxford: Princeton University Press, 2012)

Rearick, Charles, *Paris Dreams, Paris Memories: The City and its Mystique* (Stanford CA: Stanford University Press, 2011)

Riley, Matthew and Smith, Anthony D, *Nation and Classical Music* (Woodbridge: Boydell & Brewer, 2016)

Rodmell, Graham, 'An Englishman's Impressions of France in 1775', *Durham University Journal*, **61** (1968/69), pp. 75–93

Rodmell, Paul, *Charles Villiers Stanford* (Aldershot: Ashgate, 2002)

Rodmell, Paul, ' "The Italians are Coming": Opera in mid-Victorian Dublin', in Cowgill, Rachel and Rushton, Julian (eds), *Europe, Empire and Spectacle in Nineteenth Century British Music* (Aldershot: Ashgate, 2006), pp. 97–112

Rodmell, Paul (ed.), *Music and Institutions in Nineteenth-Century Britain* (Abingdon: Ashgate, 2012).

Rodmell, Paul, *Opera in the British Isles 1875–1918* (Aldershot: Ashgate, 2013)

Rodmell, Paul, '*Carmen* – As Seen and Heard in Victorian Britain', in Langham-Smith, Richard, and Rowden, Clair (eds), *Carmen Abroad* (Cambridge: Cambridge University Press, 2020), pp. 186–99

Rosenthal, Harold, *Two Centuries of Opera at Covent Garden* (London: Putnam, 1958)

Rudorff, Raymond, *Belle Epoque: Paris in the Nineties* (London: Hamish Hamilton, 1972)

Rutherford, Susan, *The Prima Donna and Opera 1815–1930* (Cambridge: Cambridge University Press, 2006)

Scott, Derek, *Sounds of the Metropolis: The Nineteenth-Century Popular Music Revolution in London, New York, Paris, and Vienna* (Oxford & New York: Oxford University Press, 2008)

Sellar, W C and Yeatman, R, *1066 and All That* (London: Methuen, 1930)

Senelick, Laurence, *Jacques Offenbach and the Making of Modern Culture* (Cambridge: Cambridge University Press, 2017)

Shapiro, Susan C, '"Yon Plumed Dandebrat": Male "Effeminacy" in English Satire and Criticism', *The Review of English Studies*, **39** (New Series) (1988), pp. 400–12

Sharp, Alan and Stone, Glyn (eds), *Anglo-French Relations in the Twentieth Century* (London & New York: Routledge, 2000)

Smith, William, *Italian Opera and Contemporary Ballet in London 1789–1820* (London: Society for Theatre Research, 1955)

Spink, Ian (ed.), *Music in Britain: The Seventeenth Century* (Oxford: Blackwell, 1992)

Spitzer, John and Zaslaw, Neal, *The Birth of the Orchestra: History of an Institution 1650–1815* (Oxford: Oxford University Press, 2004)

Stedman, Gesa, *Cultural Exchange in Seventeenth Century France and England* (Aldershot: Ashgate, 2013)

Stradling, Robert and Hughes, Merion, *The English Musical Renaissance: Constructing a National Music* (2nd ed, Manchester: Manchester University Press, 2001)

Studd, Stephen, *Saint-Saëns: A Critical Biography* (London: Cygnus Arts, 1999)

Taylor, Ian, *Music in London and the Myth of Decline: From Haydn to the Philharmonic* (Cambridge: Cambridge University Press, 2010)

Temperley, Nicholas (ed.), *Music in Britain: The Romantic Age 1800–1914* (London: Athlone Press, 1981)

Thomson, Andrew, *Vincent D'Indy and his World* (Oxford: Clarendon Press, 1996)

Thomson, Ann, Burrows, Simon and Dziembowski, Edmond (eds), *Cultural Transfers: France and Britain in the Long 18th Century* (Oxford: Voltaire Foundation, 2011)

Thorold, Peter, *The British in France: Visitors and Residents since the Revolution* (London: Continuum, 2008)

Tombs, Robert and Isabelle, *That Sweet Enemy* (London: William Heinemann, 2006)

Tyre, Jess, 'Music in Paris during the Franco-Prussian War and the Commune', *Journal of Musicology*, **22** (2005), pp. 173–202

Varouxakis, Georgios, *Victorian Political Thought on France and the French* (London: Palgrave, 2002)

Walton, Whitney, *France at the Crystal Palace: Bourgeois Taste and Artisan Manufacture in the Nineteenth Century* (Berkeley CA: University of California Press, 1992)

Watt, Paul, *The Regulation and Reform of Musical Criticism in Nineteenth-Century England* (Abingdon: Routledge, 2018)

Wearing, J P, *The London Stage 1890–1899* (2nd ed, Lanham MD: Rowman & Littlefield, 2014)

Wearing, J P, *The London Stage 1900–1909* (2nd ed, Lanham MD: Rowman & Littlefield, 2014)

Wearing, J P, *The London Stage 1910–1919* (2nd ed, Lanham MD: Rowman & Littlefield, 2014)

Weber, William, *The Rise of Musical Classics in Eighteenth-Century England* (Oxford: Clarendon Press, 1992)

Weber, William, *Music and the Middle Class: The Social Structure of Concert Life in London, Paris and Vienna between 1830 and 1848* (2nd ed, Aldershot: Ashgate, 2004)

Weber, William, *The Great Transformation of Musical Taste: Concert Programming from Haydn to Brahms* (Cambridge: Cambridge University Press, 2008)

Wood, Gillen D'Arcy, *Romanticism and Music Culture in Britain 1770–1840* (Cambridge: Cambridge University Press, 2010)

Index

Note: Musical works, composers, adaptors, translators and conductors only mentioned in the Appendix are not included in this index.